American Medical Association
Physicians dedicated to the health of America

HIPAA
A Short- and Long-Term Perspective for Health Care

Michael Doscher, MS

Michael Doscher is Western Director, HIPAA Services, Healthink, Inc.
The content was reviewed and validated by Leon B. Barrett,
senior vice-president, HIPAA and e-Commerce

HIPAA: A Short- and Long-Term Perspective for Health Care

Internet address: www.ama-assn.org

Additional copies of this book may be ordered by calling 800 621-8335.
Mention product number OP319402

ISBN 1-57947-268-0

BP02:03-P-037:2/03

To my soul partner and toughest critic, ma mignonne, Jane.

ACKNOWLEDGMENTS

Ms Jane Van Stedum edited all of the text, excluding the appendices. Educated in English literature and social work, she ensured clarity and brevity and provided much-needed support. During many of our determined editing sessions, I found it hard to believe she was actually a licensed social worker. She was uncannily able to compartmentalize in order to keenly focus on the task at hand.

As my former employer, Mr Lee Barrett (often referred to as "Mr EDI"), former executive director of the Workgroup for Electronic Data Interchange (WEDI) and executive director of the Electronic Healthcare Network Accreditation Commission, provided the support needed to build the content for the book. He was conscientious in ensuring the validity of the conclusions regarding the meaning and intent of Health Insurance Portability and Accountability Act of 1996 (HIPAA). For the book's introduction, Lee also provided his informed perspective of the genesis of HIPAA and the roles of the standards bodies. Lee is now senior vice president, SAIC, HIPAA and e-Commerce.

Thanks to both Lee and Tom Gillem, chief editor of Healthleaders.com. I probably would never have pursued such an extensive documentation of HIPAA without them. They both encouraged me to pursue my possibly unique synthesis of HIPAA afforded by my background in health care information technology management, operations, consulting, and planning.

I also thank the law firm of Davis Wright Tremaine for their permission to include several of the appendices and for the occasional legal interpretation of various aspects of HIPAA.

I would also like to thank the following members of AMA press for shepherding this book through the editorial and production process: Marsha Mildred, Jean Roberts, Anne Serrano, Katharine Dvorak, Rosalyn Carlton, Ronnie Summers, and Shelley Benson.

CONTENTS

chapter 1

Introduction

The Health Insurance Portability and Accountability Act of 1996 (HIPAA), Public Law 104–191, has stimulated considerable attention and controversy within the health care industry. The act is consistently referred to by its acronym, HIPAA. The general goals of HIPAA are to improve portability and continuity of health insurance coverage and combat waste, fraud, and abuse in health insurance and health care delivery. The Centers for Medicare & Medicaid Services (CMS), formerly Health Care Financing Administration (HCFA), in the Department of Health and Human Services (DHHS) has been responsible for implementing the Administrative Simplification provisions of HIPAA. The Office of Civil Rights will have responsibility for enforcement.

Title II, Section F, of HIPAA, Administrative Simplification, is the actual driver of all the current scrutiny and activity surrounding the act. In response to the provisions of Administrative Simplification, the health care industry is in the frenetic midst of retooling its administrative and financial systems. At the same time, the entities covered by HIPAA must enhance the security of their business areas and computer systems in order to ensure the confidentiality and privacy of protected health care information (PHI).

This HIPAA guide provides a comprehensive review of Administrative Simplification. The intent is to be objective about the pros and cons of this major legislation while demonstrating that the provisions can be a net positive value to the industry. The general goal is to enhance understanding of HIPAA regarding the following topics:

- The original act and its genesis
- The value propositions behind implementation of electronic data interchange (EDI) and other standards
- The impacts of the security and privacy provisions
- The controversy surrounding the final privacy rule
- The key compliance issues
- The enforcement and certification of compliance
- The covered entity's readiness and risk assessment
- The opportunities and a blueprint for training staff

- The emerging tools and templates available on the Internet and from trade groups and professional associations
- The forums, regional alliances, and initiatives promoting collaboration of the affected stakeholders
- The relationships with software vendors
- The future of HIPAA and the electronic medical record
- The value in aligning HIPAA mandates with Internet and other business strategies.

HIPAA covers the following entities:

- Health plans
- Clearinghouses
- Providers who electronically process billing information.

WHAT IS HIPAA?

The Health Insurance Portability and Accountability Act of 1996 (HIPAA), Public Law 104–191 (known previously as the Kennedy–Kassebaum Bill), passed on August 2, 1996, and was signed into law on August 21. HIPAA was enacted primarily to provide improved portability of health benefits and greater accountability in the area of health care fraud.

The Intent of HIPAA

The act amends the Internal Revenue Code of 1986 and contains four sections referred to by their titles. They include:

- Title I—Health care access, portability, and renewability
- Title II—Preventing health care fraud and abuse, administrative simplification, medical liability reform
- Title III—Tax-related health provisions
- Title IV—Application and enforcement of group health plan requirements.

Administrative Simplification

The act states that the purpose of Title II, subtitle F, Administrative Simplification, is to improve the Medicare and Medicaid programs and "the efficiency and effectiveness of the health care system by encouraging the development of a health information system through the establishment of standards and requirements for the electronic transmission of certain health information." The current focus on HIPAA revolves around the Administrative Simplification provisions.

In this guide, all references to HIPAA pertain to the provisions of Administrative Simplification.

The Administrative Simplification regulations are designed to reduce administrative costs by standardizing the format of electronic data interchange (EDI) of certain types of health care administrative and financial transactions. The Administrative Simplification provisions also set forth far-reaching provisions for safeguarding the security, confidentiality, and privacy of health care information.

As a result of the HIPAA mandates, the health care industry has a clear set of EDI standards that will allow it to aggressively tackle the challenge of automating typical claims, eligibility and referral processes, and Internet-based e-Business.

In general, the original Administrative Simplification provisions called for:

- EDI standards for nine types of transactions
- Standard code sets for diagnosis and procedures
- Unique health identifiers for individuals, employers, health plans, and providers
- Privacy and security standards
- Civil penalties for failure to comply with requirements and standards
- Criminal penalties for the wrongful disclosure of individually identifiable health information.

To formulate the standards, as required by HIPAA, the secretary of DHHS consulted with the following standards bodies (See history and description of these standards bodies at the end of this chapter.):

- National Uniform Claim Committee (NUCC)
- National Uniform Billing Committee (NUBC)
- American Dental Association (ADA)
- Health Level 7 (HL7)
- National Council on Prescription Drug Programs (NCPDP)
- Workgroup for Electronic Data Interchange (WEDI).

The final rule defining transaction standards was released and published in August 2000. The transaction rule covered eight standard transactions and code sets, with compliance required by October 2002. H.R. 3323, passed in December 2001, permits covered entities to apply for a year's delay. The final privacy rule was released and published in December 2000, with compliance by April 2003. In March 2002, DHHS published a proposed rule for modifications to the final privacy rule. The proposed changes altered several key components. The remaining final rules covering security, unique identifiers, enforcement, and, possibly, the claims attachment transaction are expected to be released and published in late 2002 and early 2003. EDI standards, standard codes, and unique identifiers are included in the requirements because they will facilitate the electronic exchange of information between the various health care trading partners. The privacy and security components were added to decrease the risk of unauthorized or inappropriate access to sensitive health information.

Covered Entities

HIPAA covers the following general entities:

- All health plans, including Medicare and state Medicaid programs
- All health care clearinghouses
- Any health care providers that choose to submit transactions electronically.

For customers sending electronic transactions, a clearinghouse may accept nonstandard transactions for the sole purpose of translating them into standard transactions. Then, for customers receiving electronic transactions, they may accept standard transactions and translate them into nonstandard transactions (see Figure 1-1). Health plans and clearinghouses must be able to send or receive the designated transactions in standard electronic form no later than 26 months after the standard is adopted by and published by the secretary of DHHS—38 months for small plans.

All health care providers who elect to conduct these specific transactions electronically must conduct them according to the standards. To do so, health care providers will need to upgrade their information systems to produce the compliant transactions. They will also need to modify their business practices to ensure that the systems are used in a compliant manner. Health care providers may also contract with a

FIGURE 1-1

Sample Claim Data Flows

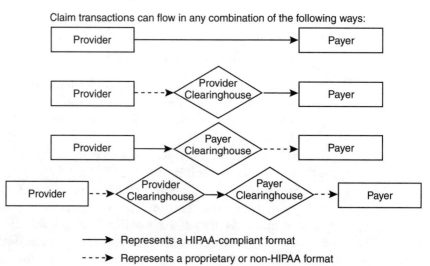

Claim transactions can flow in any combination of the following ways:

Provider → Payer

Provider ⇢ Provider Clearinghouse → Payer

Provider → Payer Clearinghouse ⇢ Payer

Provider ⇢ Provider Clearinghouse → Payer Clearinghouse ⇢ Payer

⟶ Represents a HIPAA-compliant format

⇢ Represents a proprietary or non-HIPAA format

clearinghouse to conduct standard transactions for them. When employers act in the role of a health plan or a health care provider, they must also comply with the standards. They may contract with a clearinghouse or third-party administrator (TPA) to conduct the standard transactions for them.

Health plans may not refuse to accept standard transactions submitted electronically on their own or through clearinghouses. Furthermore, health plans may not delay payment because the transactions are submitted electronically in compliance with the standards. There are a few exceptions:

Small Health Plans: HIPAA gives small health plans 36 months from the date of adoption of a standard to come into compliance. HIPAA defines a small plan as one with less than $5 million in receipts.

Workers' Compensation: The HIPAA definition of a health plan does not specifically include workers' compensation programs or carriers. However, the list of designated transactions for which the secretary must adopt standards for electronic transmission includes "First Report of Injury," which is the primary transaction used to initiate workers' compensation actions. For this reason, the secretary will propose a standard for First Report of Injury and will consider different ways of achieving compliance with this standard.

Health Plan Sponsors: Health plan sponsors, including employers when they act in the role of a sponsor, are not covered explicitly by the law but may benefit from the adoption of standards and electronic transactions. Sponsors may elect to use standard enrollment, disenrollment, and premium payment transactions, which must be accepted by all health plans when submitted electronically. Market forces may move health plans to require sponsors to use the standards for electronic transactions, although the law does not mandate this.

Administrative Simplification Rule-Making Process

HIPAA directed Congress to publish rules mandating the privacy standards. The process for promulgating the rules is initiated by the Notice for Proposed Rule-Making (NPRM.)

The NPRM describes, explains, and proposes changes to the Code of Federal Regulations (CFR) that the federal government proposes to adopt at some future date. In the case of HIPAA, DHHS invited interested parties to submit comments related to the NPRM. These comments are to be considered by the agency in developing the final rules.

DHHS relies on direct input from the National Committee on Vital Health Statistics (NCVHS). In turn, NCVHS works with the designated standards maintenance organizations (DSMOs) to develop specifications for further rules for simplifying administrative procedures and rendering

protected health care information (PHI) private and confidential. The
DSMOs include six standards bodies: NUCC, NUBC, ADA, HL7,
the National Council on Prescription Drug Programs (NCPDP), and
the Accreditation Standards Committee (ASC) of X12N, the EDI
Subcommittee on Insurance Standards.

The federal Administrative Simplification Procedures govern the
entire process, which requires a 75-day period for public comment after
publication in the Federal Register. The final rule, or "report and order,"
usually occurs several months after closure of the comment period.

Currently, there are final rules for transactions and another for
privacy. In addition, there is an existing NPRM for security, which
requires best security practices. The unique identifiers were proposed in
the original transaction NPRM. DHHS has indicated its intentions to
publish NPRMs as soon as possible for the following provider, health
plan, and employer identifiers:

- Enforcement
- Digital signatures
- The electronic medical record
- A workers' compensation first-report-of-injury transaction
- A claims attachment transaction.

The timetables for the publication and effective dates are included later.

The industry has learned to view HIPAA as an ongoing standards-setting
and compliance process. In the future, modifications to existing rules
based on annual updates to the standards will be published. In July 2001,
the Secretary of DHHS, Tommy Thompson published guidelines
interpreting the final privacy rule. The guidelines softened and restated
many of the prevailing extreme interpretations of impact closer to existing
practices. In addition, DHHS issued proposed changes to the final privacy
rule, thus eliminating unintended restrictions to treating patients.

HIPAA will affect covered entities differently. Small physician practices
will feel the greatest relative burdens. To efficiently implement the
HIPAA-mandated standards, the covered entities should keep in mind
that DHHS's intent is to see practical, reasonable, and scalable solutions.

Transactions

HIPAA establishes standards for electronic transactions and for code sets
to be used in those transactions. These standards were selected from the
American National Standards Institute (ANSI) ASC X12N version 4010
transactions. X12N is ANSI's Accredited Standards Committee's EDI
Subcommittee on Insurance.

There was overwhelming industry support for X12N standards for all
transactions except health care claims. The consensus choice for retail
pharmacy claims was the NCPDP standard because of its widespread use.

After considering all advice, the secretary recommended adoption of X12N standards for all but the retail pharmacy claim. The X12N and NCPDP standards met all the criteria developed to measure a standard's suitability. The official implementation guides are freely distributed through Washington Publishing Company (http://www.wpc-edi.com). The transactions mandated in the final transaction rule include:

- Health care claims and equivalent encounter information
- Health care payment and remittance advice
- Coordination of benefits
- Health claim status request and response
- Health plan enrollments and disenrollments
- Health care eligibility benefit inquiries and responses
- Health plan premium payments—payment order and remittance advice
- Referral certification and authorization—request for review and response.

The timetable for implementing the standard transactions is outlined in Table 1-1.

Nonstandard transactions: The standards for the designated transactions apply when those transactions are transmitted electronically but not to transactions performed using paper. Transactions that are conducted electronically but with methods with which the standards cannot apply, such as direct data entry into a health plan's computer using a browser, still must comply with standards for data elements and data conditions. In any case, privacy and security regulations will apply to all exchanges of individually identifiable health information.

All electronic transmissions of a specified transaction from one computer to another must comply with the standards. Electronic transmissions include transmissions using all media, even when the transmission is physically moved from one location to another using magnetic tape, disk, or CD media. Transmissions over the Internet, Intranets, leased lines, dial-up lines, and private networks are all included.

The transaction standards apply only to data transmitted as part of a standard transaction. Data may be stored in any format as long as it can be translated into the standard transaction when required. The proposed security standards, on the other hand, apply to *all* electronic health care information, and the privacy standards extend to cover individually identifiable health information in any form.

Uniform Identifiers

HIPAA mandates the development of unique identifiers in four areas:

- **Provider**: All health care providers will be assigned one national provider identifier (NPI) for life. The proposed rule outlined an

TABLE 1-1

Timetable for EDI Transaction Standards

Transaction	ASC X12 N	NPRM Publication	Final Rule Publication*	Implement By*
1. Claims/encounter				
—Professional	837	3Q98	August 2000	October 2003
—Institutional	837			
—Dental	837			
—Retail pharmacy	NCPDP V 5.1 or batch standard 1.0			
2. Payment and remittance advice	835	3Q98	August 2000	October 2003
3. Coordination of benefits	837	3Q98	August 2000	October 2003
—Professional	837			
—Institutional	837			
—Dental	NCPDP V 5.1			
—Retail pharmacy	or 1.0			
4. Claim status request and response	276/277	3Q98	August 2000	October 2003
5. Enrollment and disenrollment in a health plan	834	3Q98	August 2000	October 2003
6. Eligibility benefit inquiry and response	270/271	3Q98	August 2000	October 2003
—Retail pharmacy	NCPDP V 5.1 or 1.0			
7. Premium payment order/remittance advice	820	3Q98	August 2000	October 2003
8. Referral certification and authorization	278	3Q98	August 2000	October 2003
—Retail pharmacy	NCPDP V 5.1 or 1.0			
9. Patient information/ attachments	275	*3Q1*	*2Q02*	*3Q04*
10. First report of injury	148	*TBD*	*TBD*	*TBD*

*Dates in italics are anticipated dates. TBD indicates to be determined.

enumeration process, the National Provider System (NPS), that HCFA would administer. The 10-character numeric NPI will not contain any embedded intelligence, which could create a major challenge for many organizations.

■ **Employer:** The proposed employer identification number (EIN) is the same nine-position numeric as used by the Internal Revenue Service for tax identification numbers.

■ **Health Plan:** HCFA appears to favor their payer identification definition, but DHHS and the DSMOs have not agreed on how to deal with provider groups versus the individual clinician. A 10-position numeric is being considered.

■ **Individual:** This identifier is perhaps the most controversial component of HIPAA. DHHS officials have stated repeatedly that this number will not be the social security number (SSN), although proposals that include the SSN plus one or more check digits are being considered.

The timetable for implementing the unique identifiers is presented in Table 1-2.

Code Sets

HIPAA standardizes the use of the International Classification of Diseases (9th revision) (ICD-9-CM) for diagnosis codes and inpatient hospital services; a combination of CPT®-4, maintained by the American Medical Association (AMA), and the HCFA's health care procedure coding system (HCPCS) for physician service codes; National Drug Codes (NDC) for drugs; and a significantly changed version of HCPCS for other types of health care services. The switch to ICD-10 is expected to occur eventually, as the industry readies itself for adoption, perhaps as soon as 2003.

HIPAA mandates large code sets to be used for medical data and smaller code sets to be used for other data elements such as race, type of facility, and type of unit.

T A B L E   1-2

Timetable for Unique Identifiers

Identifier	Source	NPRM Publication	Final Rule Publication*	Implement By*
Provider (NPI)		5/7/98	2Q02	3Q04
Employer (EIN)	IRS tax ID number	6/16/98	2Q02	3Q04
Health plan		2Q02	3Q02	3Q04
Individual	Will NOT be SSN	On hold		

*Dates in italics are anticipated dates.

Currently, two general code sets are required for recording medical data:

- HCPCS, which contains three levels:

    Level 1: Captures physician services using the CPT®-4 code set

    Level 2: Contains codes for products, supplies, and services not included in CPT®.

    Level 3: Local codes, includes codes created to meet local needs

- ICD-9, which classifies both diagnoses and procedures.

Level 2 of HCPCS contains codes for dental services and medications as described here:

- Dental services: The "D" codes in the HCPCS system are dental codes created by the ADA and published as current dental terminology (CDT). However, in HCPCS, the first digit, "0," in CDT is replaced by a "D" to eliminate confusion and any overlap with certain other CPT® codes. The ADA has agreed to replace their first digit with a "D." Implementation is required by October 2002.

- Drug codes: Since the NDC system is more precise (11 characters) and is updated more frequently, the rule intends that it should become the national coding standard for inpatient hospital services and retail pharmacies replacing the HCFA HCPCS ("J" or drug codes). Implementation is required by October 2002.

    Due to early assessments and criticisms of the use of NDC codes for inpatient medications and other pharmaceuticals, they will not likely be required. They will, nonetheless, be required for outpatient retail pharmacy prescriptions.

    Note: The NCVHS has submitted a recommendation to eliminate the requirement for "J" codes in the inpatient environment. It is likely that this will be accepted; however, at this time, the standard remains in place.

Level 3, local codes, will be eliminated. A national process will be established for reviewing and approving codes that are needed by any public or private health insurer. All lines of business are affected by the elimination of local coding. Most state Medicaid programs see elimination of the local codes by the original October 2002 deadline as a major challenge.

Organizations may meet these requirements by either transmitting and receiving the standard code sets or submitting nonstandard code sets to a clearinghouse for conversion into standard code sets and receiving standard code sets through the clearinghouse. Either approach will require linking nonstandard code sets to the standard code sets.

Security Requirements

HIPAA, in recognition of the importance of protecting confidential health information, has specified two methods of protection: security practices and privacy standards. Security practices are largely unregulated, and privacy laws vary widely from state to state.

The proposed security rule is organized into five areas. The first three are intended to guard data integrity, confidentiality, and availability. The fourth is to guard against unauthorized access to data that is transmitted over a communication network. The fifth area (electronic signatures) will not be a part of the final security rule; instead, it will be a separate rule with its own NPRM.

- Administrative procedures: To guard data integrity, confidentiality, and availability with documented formal practices covering contingency plans for system emergencies, policies on access control, formal termination procedures, and protection of data.
- Physical safeguards: Covers media controls and security on physical computer systems and plant and equipment.
- Technical security services: To protect, control, and monitor information access, such as access control, audit controls, consent for use and disclosure, data authentication, and user identification.
- Technical security mechanisms: Includes processes for preventing unauthorized access, integrity controls, and message authentication for data that is sent over a network.
- Electronic signature: Includes recommendations for, but does not require the use of, electronic signatures for any of the HIPAA transactions. These standards may not be part of the final security rule but instead may be released as a separate rule at a later time.

The rules are comprehensive but technology-neutral in how they should be implemented. It is left up to each individual health care organization to determine the best approach for achieving compliance. Each organization will have to assess its own security risks to determine an appropriate plan of action.

With regard to enforcement, the Joint Commission on Accreditation of Healthcare Organizations (JCAHO) and the National Commission on Quality Assurance (NCQA) will probably incorporate HIPAA security guidelines as part of their future accreditation criteria. The Office of Civil Rights will be responsible for enforcing the privacy provisions. Little else is known regarding enforcement at this time, ie, before publication of the final rule. Observers understand that the enforcement rule will become effective at the point of implementing the transaction rule.

Privacy Requirements

Congress failed to meet the August 21, 1999, deadline for passing a health information privacy law. As a result, then-secretary of DHHS, Donna Shalala, was required by HIPAA to issue privacy regulations to define appropriate and inappropriate uses and disclosures of health information and how patient rights are to be protected. Final privacy rules were published in December 2000, with an effective date of April 14, 2001, and a compliance date of April 14, 2003. Among many other provisions, the rule:

- Allows health information to be used and shared for treatment, payment, and normal health care operations with minimal restrictions as long as patients consent to that use
- Allows health information to be disclosed without an individual's authorization for certain national priority purposes (such as public health and oversight), but only under defined circumstances
- Requires written authorization for use and disclosure of health information for other purposes
- Creates a notice of privacy practices to inform people of how their information will be used and disclosed
- Requires covered entities to develop and implement internal policies and procedures related to protecting individually identifiable health information
- Requires covered entities to implement new or revised business associate agreements to ensure an end-to-end chain of trust regarding the exchange of PHI
- Provides individuals with the right to access and copy their protected health information, the right to amend disputed information, and the right to receive an accounting of disclosures of their protected health information under certain circumstances.

The regulations do not directly apply to many other entities that collect and maintain health information, such as life insurers, researchers, and public health officials. The covered entity will need to contractually require its uncovered business associates to comply with the rules. The final rule is significantly more restrictive than the proposed rule in that the final rule extends protection to individually identifiable information in any form (including paper and oral communications). The March 2002 proposed modifications to the privacy rule eliminate the requirement to have patients sign a consent to use their health information for the purposes of treatment, billing, and normal operations.

Penalties

HIPAA sets severe sanctions for noncompliance. Penalties for violating patient privacy standards are substantial, with monetary fines and, in some extreme cases, imprisonment. Fines are as described here:

- The civil monetary penalty for violating transaction standards is a fine up to $100 per person per violation and up to $25,000 per person per violation of a single standard per calendar year.
- The criminal penalty for knowingly misusing an individual's identifiable health information can be a fine up to $250,000 and/or imprisonment for up to 10 years. In particular, the sanctions include:

—A fine of not more than $50,000 and/or imprisonment of not more than 1 year.

—If misuse is "under false pretenses," a fine of not more than $100,000 and/or imprisonment of not more than 5 years.

—If misuse is with intent to sell, transfer, or use individually identifiable health information for commercial advantage, personal gain, or malicious harm, a fine of not more than $250,000 and/or imprisonment of not more than 10 years.

Although the civil penalties for violating the standard transaction provisions do not appear onerous, DHHS has indicated that there are 42 ways to do so. As a result, the total financial penalty could exceed $1 million per annum.

In the case of the criminal penalty, the final rule did not clarify who would be imprisoned. However, the common understanding is that it would be a member of the entity's executive team or the chief executive responsible for compliance.

Impacts

The impacts of the HIPAA rules for administrative simplification will be widespread and complex. All health plans, provider organizations, clearinghouses, and other health care commerce players must understand the details of HIPAA to make required changes to their systems, business practices, policies, and procedures. Additionally, HIPAA sets new privacy and security requirements for handling and safeguarding individually identifiable health information transmitted or maintained in electronic, paper, or any other form. The legislation explicitly states that the security and privacy mandates are not limited to the transaction types listed in this article but also include all individually identifiable health information.

For virtually all health care-related organizations (especially providers, health plans, and information technology [IT] vendors), becoming HIPAA compliant will be a multiyear, costly, institution-wide effort required by federal law, federal regulation, and related regulatory and accreditation bodies within the next 2 to 4 years. The effort for most health care organizations will be comparable to recent Y2K preparations.

The WEDI Annual[1] estimates that it will cost large hospitals from $100,000 to $500,000 to implement the transaction segment of HIPAA. This estimate seems low given the fact that some large health plans have completed assessment plans that call for between $50 and $70 million in remediation effort. In spite of the costs, HCFA estimates that health plans will save $1.6 billion per year and providers $1.5 billion per year starting in 2002.

Implementing HIPAA will affect how large- and medium-sized health care entities organize and staff for achieving and monitoring compliance. HIPAA also affects how small independent providers manage both electronic transactions (claims, referrals, eligibility, remittance advices, payments) and medical records. HIPAA's requirements will cause significant changes in process, organization, technology, and staffing in the area of claims, referral, and eligibility management in all organizations.

HIPAA mandates will require substantial changes in the policies, processes, and administration governing patient-specific health information. Similarly, they will require updates of all information systems that use or collect patient data as well as the introduction of new system features and functions.

Coordinating and co-implementing HIPAA-mandated changes among providers, health plans, and IT vendors, largely, those in claims management processes, will minimize the cost, confusion, and disruption involved in the transition. Because HIPAA covers most health care organizations, compliance itself is substantially a noncompetitive issue. However, variations in the value achieved while becoming compliant could produce significant variations in reducing EDI administrative costs that would affect the ability of entities to compete.

GENESIS OF HIPAA AND THE EVOLUTION OF THE STANDARDS BODIES—A CAUSE FOR CHANGE

Before HIPAA, organizations could collect, store, and transmit health care information in any format that they preferred. Most often, they were restricted to the formats negotiated with their partners. No standards existed to guide organizations in how to store, process, exchange, or secure data. Management and clinical information software and databases differed from organization to organization, even if purchased from the same vendor.

The lack of standard data formats (currently, more than 450 electronic claim formats) to support electronic data interchange has proven to be a barrier that is too costly and complex for most organizations to overcome. As a result, the use of EDI has been primarily limited to communicating claims and, to some degree, remittance advices. Yet, to be successful in submitting claims, many organizations have to rely on clearinghouses to communicate with their trading partners. This claims-processing Tower of Babel has left a history of tremendous confusion and errors due to inconsistencies in data elements, code sets, and identifiers.

In November 1991, Joseph Brophy, then-president of Travelers Managed Care and Employee Benefits Operation, and Bernard Tresnowski, president of the Blue Cross Blue Shield Association went to Washington, DC, to meet with DHHS Secretary Louis Sullivan, to discuss administrative simplification. The intentions of the forum were to address the cost of the current health care system from an administrative perspective and identify the steps needed to migrate the industry to greater usage of EDI and unique national identifiers.

As a result of the meetings, Mr Brophy and Mr Tresnowski volunteered to lead a health care coalition of providers, payers, and public organizations, including federal and state entities, to write a report on the current state of the industry and to develop recommendations. In turn, WEDI was organized.

WEDI had the daunting task of creating their first report to present to the secretary of DHHS within 6 months. The first report was presented to the Secretary in July 1992. A follow-up report was commenced to provide greater detail regarding the recommendations that were presented in the first report. They released the second report in early 1993.

These reports represented a consensus of the industry regarding the current state of EDI and included comprehensive recommendations to develop standardized transactions and unique identifiers. The second report indicated what the cost of compliance would comprise and the opportunity for realizing benefits. The report presented a positive financial return on investment in the standards for the health care industry. This report was the first of its kind in the industry. It served as a foundation for the administrative provisions of the Clinton Health Plan in 1994, later the Kennedy–Kassebaum legislation in 1996, and the HIPAA provisions. Many legislators who worked on the provisions, including Senator Hobson and others in Washington, along with their staffers, referenced the WEDI reports of 1992 and 1993 as the framework for many of the HIPAA provisions. WEDI currently has more than 160 member organizations. The organization has been named as an advisor to the secretary of DHHS regarding HIPAA.

A number of key individuals have fostered the development and movement toward administrative simplification in the health care community. Congressmen who have developed, promoted, and passed key provisions that have acted as a catalyst for administrative simplification include Stark, Hobson, Kennedy, Kassebaum, and others. William Braithwaite, MD, PhD, senior policy advisor of DHHS, has been a key advocate and leader of much of the development within the federal government. Many others from across the industry, too numerous to mention, have spent significant hours and efforts in developing the standards and the many HIPAA provisions.

In 1991, the ASC X12N Insurance Subcommittee was formed under the auspices of ANSI. A small group of people initially founded the committee that formed the Healthcare Task Group. This voluntary committee had a vision to create a set of electronic EDI standards that could be used to eliminate all proprietary formats that were then in use. Over the next 8 years, the committee grew dramatically, gathering broad-based representation from the health care community, including the public and private sectors comprised of payers, providers, federal and state agencies, and other key stakeholders.

ASC X12N uses a consensus-based decision-making process to approve new transactions. Most transactions take between 2 and 5 years to be approved. This committee developed all nine transactions that are outlined in the HIPAA provisions. A very dedicated group of individuals had the fortitude and vision to develop and maintain these transactions. Maintenance changes to the HIPAA transactions data can be made annually. The committee then recommended that the secretary of DHHS consider the new provisions.

The NCPDP is the other standards development organization (SDO) that is mandated to set standards for use by pharmacies as part of HIPAA. The standard transaction is the electronic pharmacy interactive claim, which currently experiences an annual volume of more than 1 billion transmissions. NCPDP has developed and maintained a number of other key transactions. It is also an ANSI-accredited organization.

There are other SDOs that both develop and maintain standards and create the data content, which is garnered from their various health care constituencies. Other key SDO organizations include HL7 and the ADA. All SDOs participate in the DSMO process mandated by HIPAA to maintain all of the approved standards.

Two other organizations that are part of the DSMO process include the NUBC, chaired by the American Hospital Association (AHA), and the NUCC, chaired by the AMA. The AHA and AMA groups meet several times annually to review data content requests and assign the changes to the appropriate SDO. Collaboration among the SDOs is critical and has been viewed as a major benefit to the industry.

Other organizations that have played key roles include the Association for Electronic Health Care Transactions (AFEHCT) and the Electronic Healthcare Network Accreditation Commission (EHNAC). AFEHCT has been a major influencer in the passage of HIPAA and has lobbied aggressively to promote administrative simplification on behalf of clearinghouses and value-added networks (VANs). EHNAC is an accreditation organization for clearinghouses and VANs. It developed the first HIPAA transaction compliance program to assist the industry in achieving implementation.

The organization that is currently reviewing, developing, and recommending new standards and requirements to DHHS is the NCVHS. NCVHS continues to hold hearings on new provisions and key implementation issues. They make recommendations regarding new transaction standards, privacy and security provisions, electronic medical records, and other clinical areas. NCVHS is designated in the HIPAA legislation to make recommendations to the secretary of DHHS. DHHS then issues NPRMs, which seek public comment prior to final rules being issued.

Currently, the industry is assessing its needs and requirements to meet HIPAA compliance provisions. Organizations are also commencing implementation of the key provisions, and many industry organizations are assisting the industry to achieve compliance. WEDI has developed a program called the Strategic National Implementation Process (SNIP), which is focused on addressing three domains: training and awareness, security and privacy, and transactions. The SNIP forum has significantly helped the industry to develop national benchmarks, models, case studies, policies, procedures, and major white papers to assist with implementation. The group is also creating and coordinating regional initiatives to ensure a consistent and common approach for the industry. SNIP is promoting both local and national forums to assist with HIPAA implementations.

Finally, Medicare and Medicaid are also aggressively moving toward implementation of the HIPAA provisions. These organizations have been actively involved in the various industry forums to develop the HIPAA provisions and have influenced their development and the data content requirements.

The evolution of administrative simplification over the past 11 years has been challenging and rewarding. HIPAA compliance is a major undertaking for the health care industry, but it will provide significant opportunities to achieve savings and change the way the industry conducts business. Another key opportunity is for the industry to create alliances to achieve compliance and realize some of the benefits that can be achieved. HIPAA has been developed by a consensus of public and private health sector stakeholders.

REFERENCE

1. Workgroup for Electronic Data Interchange Steering Committee. *1993 WEDI Annual Report.* Reston, Va: Workgroup for Electronic Data Interchange; October 1993.

Transactions: Benefits, Impacts, and Information Technology Investments

Currently, there is a variety of spins on the implications of the Health Insurance Portability and Accountability Act of 1996 (HIPAA). Most of them, however, neglect to recognize the vision underlying the proposed rules regarding administrative simplification required by subtitle F of the 1996 act. A thorough review of the proposed rules for electronic data interchange (EDI) transactions, the implementation guides, and the original act provides ample edification of the intended beneficial impacts. While enabling the basic tenet behind health insurance portability, these effects involve both the internal and business-to-business processes of the covered entities (health plans, providers, clearinghouses, pharmaceuticals, laboratories, and home health agencies) and sponsors of covered lives. The gains to the industry should be major—the Workgroup for Electronic Data Interchange (WEDI) estimated net savings of more than $3 billion in the third year after the implementation date and almost $15 billion in the fifth.

This chapter highlights both the impacts on businesses and the opportunities for significant returns on investments in HIPAA compliance. Early initiators should realize a competitive advantage. The review of the HIPAA standard transactions, identifiers, code sets, and security explains the impacts and opportunities. Note that although the proposed transactions represent segments of health care commerce, all must work together within a framework of interrelated business processes and systems to be effective. Figure 2-1 illustrates the typical interrelationships of the covered entities with regard to the likely uses of the standard transactions.

The impact on business operations is significant. In fact, 60% to 70% of HIPAA impacts will be on business operations and 30% to 40% on information technology (IT) solutions. Thus, the intention of this chapter is to reflect on the business changes resulting from HIPAA compliance and the realizable benefits. The review of each transaction will address the impacts and opportunities of business operations as well as investments in strategic IT solutions.

FIGURE 2-1

HIPAA Transactions, Stakeholders, and Major Processes

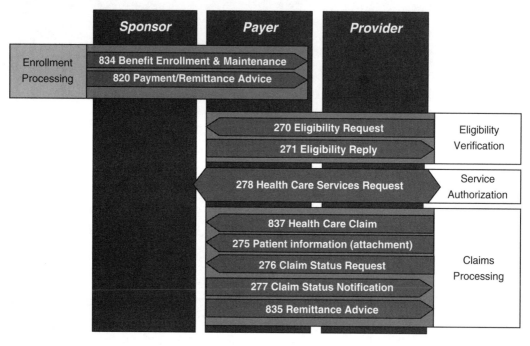

AUTOMATING CLAIMS SUBMISSION (ANSI X12N 837)

The core revenue and expense driver of the "back offices" of health plans and physician practice management groups is the voluminous stream of diverse claims for professional, acute care, and other medical services. Of the eight transactions to see final ruling in August 2000, HIPAA mandated four of them to process claims. At the heart of these transactions is the electronic claim explained and assessed herein.

The health care claim billing transaction is used to submit claims to payers and coordinate the payments when a patient is covered by more than one health plan. This transaction replaces the current dental Health Care Financing Administration (HCFA) inpatient UB92, and professional fee 1500 claim forms. Today, these forms are typically sent as either hard copy or in a proprietary electronic format. For retail pharmacy claims payments, HIPAA requires a different standard transaction already widely used.

To coordinate benefits, HIPAA requires the sequential processing of claims. In cases where patients have multiple health care coverages, each of the patients' payers must reimburse the providers for their portion of the fees before the patients receive a statement for their portion. (There is a major flaw in the legislation requiring the coordination of benefits. The regulations currently exclude third-party liability entities [ie, workers' compensation, casualty and property insurance], which process the same patient medical information required for claims payment.)

Impacts and Opportunities

As a result of having to accept claims in the standard electronic format, providers and payers will no longer process most of the various forms of paper claims and other electronic formats. Currently, the commercial payers generally receive about 60% of their claims electronically, but only about 5% are HIPAA compliant. Some of the 40% of claims submitted in hard copy are from small plans not covered by HIPAA. In any case, the payers must, in large part, gear up to satisfy the various HIPAA transaction requirements.

Implementation of the new standards presents a number of challenges. Business processes will need to accommodate the following:

- New standard values for the data elements such as sex, type of facility, diagnostic and procedure codes, and ethnicity
- More data elements than currently exchanged
- New business rules to ensure:
  —Reversal-of-payment errors
  —Preservation of the original claim, its included service items, and the adjudication history.

The upshot of the changes outlined above will be new work flows as well as new or updated policies and procedures. Payers will probably need to develop new online processing functions and features to handle the additional data elements and the underlying business rules required for each data element.

HIPAA also requires that covered entities and their partners exchange the HIPAA transactions over a secure network when the transactions contain patient-identifiable data. As a result, all covered entities must negotiate trading partner agreements ensuring an end-to-end "chain of trust" for their business-to-business patient information exchanges. These and other security, confidentiality, and privacy impacts will be reviewed more thoroughly in later chapters.

Businesses can and should be able to differentiate themselves in the health care marketplace and derive value from their investments in the implementation of the claims payment transaction. As a result, some key direct and secondary opportunities for competitive advantage and benefits include:

- Greatly accelerated cash flow for providers due to shorter cycles of accounts receivable
- Enhanced customer service for payers and large provider groups by promptly accepting and acknowledging receipt of claims
- Better compliance with claims payment performance standards set by the health plans, which share risk with capitated provider groups that serve managed care covered lives
- Streamlined and more productive work flows with ability to concentrate efforts on exceptions

- Significant productivity and revenue improvements due to enhanced automated claims adjudication (The claims transaction provides all the data necessary for automatically approving or denying claims when linked to stored referral, eligibility, provider contracts, fee schedules, and benefit files.)
- Timely encounter reporting to health plans.

IT Investment Options and Strategies

Senior management will need to work with their IT departments and legacy system vendors to assess the costs and benefits of relevant IT strategies and investments. The possible IT solutions driven by the claims-processing changes include the following:

- Use of clearinghouses to possibly avoid significant reengineering of systems
- Reliance on current IT vendors to ensure complete compliance
- Implementation of interface engines or translators.

For in-house developed and maintained claims systems:

- Provider systems must produce the claims-billing transaction with data elements from multiple sources.
- Self-insured employer (Employers are otherwise exempt from HIPAA.) and payer systems must accept the transaction, store the required data elements, and respond in a timely manner when presented with a health care claims status inquiry.
- New business rules will need to be designed and programmed to support both the core HIPAA processing rules as well as enhanced referral and claims automatic adjudication.

IT infrastructure investment options include:

- A review and an update of the enterprise data model to source, store, and interrelate new and old data elements across diverse application files for integrated back-office processing
- An update of interfaces to or systems integration of referral, eligibility, patient management, facility discharge, data warehouse, and electronic medical record systems
- An update to software purchasing criteria with a request for proposal and information from vendors and software development methodologies to ensure HIPAA-compliant applications and infrastructures
- Design and implementation of an EDI systems architecture
- Leveraging of compliance within a corporate-directed Internet-based e-Commerce strategy.

Several of the current physician practice management and managed care systems provide many of the above features and functions as well as comprehensive "rules-based" automated claims adjudication. The perspective of this writer is that those features have not been fully utilized by either payers or large physician practice management organizations. Moreover, one could reasonably conclude that as many as 80% of claims could be automatically approved or denied accurately. As a result, HIPAA may be the catalyst for realizing the real power and payoffs of automatic claims adjudication.

AUTOMATING CLAIMS STATUS REQUESTS AND RESPONSES (ANSI X12N 276/277)

For various business reasons, providers, laboratories, and third parties responsible for processing health care claims frequently need to determine the status of their submitted claims. Employers, on behalf of their employees with employer-sponsored health care coverage, will also inquire as to the status of submitted claims. Currently, inquirers have to make repeated phone calls only to encounter a maze of bureaucracy or they send a series of faxes or letters and wait patiently for responses.

Health plans and other HIPAA-mandated payers process these inquiries via multiple, paper-driven work flows and respond typically days later via various nonelectronic media. Frequently, the payer must request additional supporting documents from a provider before approving any or all services submitted for payment in the original claim.

Determining the status of claims and responding to the requests for status require considerable manual processing. Generally, claims departments reluctantly provide such customer services. They are hesitant to divert their claims processors from the primary responsibilities of determining services qualified for payment in a timely, accurate manner. Rather than manual processing, HIPAA requires health plans and providers to use a pair of standard electronic transactions for status requests and responses. Covered entities must implement both transactions; they cannot merely implement the request transaction without the ability to send or receive the response.

Claims payers who have implemented electronic processes to respond to claims status inquiries have significantly reduced operating expenses. A 1998 study of payers reported that the cost of manually processing a request ranges between $4 and $8. Providers' costs tend to be slightly higher. In contrast, costs for processing automated claims status using Web technology are approximately 30 cents per inquiry. In another case, a Blue Cross Blue Shield plan reported a cost reduction of $6.60 by automating claims status and eligibility requests.

Impacts and Opportunities

Health plans, third-party administrators, and capitated providers alike can realize improved efficiency and effectiveness in their claims operations. Implementing these information exchanges should result in significant beneficial impacts on business operations. After a complete implementation, there is little reason for manual intervention when responding to unsolicited electronic requests for the status of an entire claim or particular service items within a claim.

To enable full and accurate communication of claims status, the existing systems and processes must conform to the claims statuses prescribed by HIPAA. These statuses include the following types of claims:

- Pre-adjudicated (In some claims areas, pre-adjudication equates to a "logged in" status where the claim is prepared for adjudication.)
- Pended
- Suspended
- Denied
- Approved—prepayment and post-payment.

Many "pended" claims contain service items that have been approved or denied and other items that may still require adjudication. Often, these items require either further internal research or more information from the entity submitting the claim. In the latter case, the transaction enabling the electronic response to a claims request can also be used to request the supporting attachments. To electronically process claims attachments, DHHS plans to publish the rule for claims attachments described in a later chapter.

Reengineering the business operations for claims status tracking can result in both financial and qualitative benefits. Provider and payer claims areas will not only realize a significant reduction in staff but should also be able to focus its core competencies on accurately denying or approving claims. Customer service, in turn, is heightened as responses to requests are made on a timely basis and requests for more information are streamlined and reliable.

Payers may respond by either batching up responses and transmitting the batches at a later date or responding in a quasi real-time mode in less than a minute per the implementation guide. In any case, the payer must respond immediately with a message acknowledging receipt of the request.

As payers become more efficient in their claims-processing operations, providers will benefit from an overall improved cash flow. Although payers will end up paying for claims sooner than they did in the past, they will be able to breathe more easily as they comply with regulated payment turnaround standards and minimize the likelihood of contested claims.

IT Investment Options and Strategies

To realize the benefits from automating the claims status checking processes, an organization will need to significantly reengineer its systems. The IT investments include the following options:

- An upgrade of current systems to accept the request for claims status and respond with the appropriate overall claim or service line item status. In addition, the claims-processing system could provide the capability to automatically trigger a request for status information whenever appropriate.

- The implementation of a "front-end" EDI subsystem to compile the appropriate standard request or response transaction. The organization can either use a clearinghouse to create standard transactions, implement an interface engine that is maintained internally, or devise their own system to map and translate data elements.

- Development of an Internet solution to embrace these transactions aligned with a Web-based e-Commerce strategy.

- The implementation of a work-flow subsystem that interfaces the existing claims system and meets the rules inherent in the claims statuses mandated by HIPAA.

Since many health care organizations rely heavily on vendor-based turnkey solutions, they must soon insist that their software vendors address the options described above. Large organizations should be able to strongly influence the vendors to make the appropriate upgrades. In other cases, the vendors' users' groups or regional alliances can exert the necessary pressure. HIPAA compliance has a significant price tag. The investment in automating claims status processing, however, should benefit the bottom line and ensure competitive advantage to the early initiators.

AUTOMATING CLAIMS PAYMENTS/ REMITTANCE ADVICES (ANSI X12N 835 AND 820)

The final claims paying, receiving, and posting processes are relatively complex, challenging, and fraught with inefficiencies. Typically, after adjudicating submitted claims, payers send payments to either a provider's designated bank lock box or directly to the provider's back office. Payers also usually send an associated remittance advice (RA) directly to the provider to report the adjudicated amounts of each paid claim. RAs can arrive as a hard-copy listing or, less frequently, as some form of nonstandard electronic record. At this point in the RA process, the provider must analyze the payments to discover those claims they believe were incorrectly underpaid or not paid. Then, they must decide whether to contest the payment, submit a claim for the remaining amount to a secondary payer, or determine the patient's responsibility for payment.

Since the claims payment posting process is labor intensive, automation should provide immediate cost savings. Currently few health care back-office systems permit the automatic processing of RAs. The number of systems able to do so is increasing steadily as the deadline for HIPAA compliance approaches. In 1993, WEDI estimated that the payer's costs to process a typical RA with 15 claims payments ranged between $6.75 and $15.00. By automating the RA and payment posting processes, the payer's costs for the same RA were estimated to vary between $1.65 and $4.25. Large capitated physician practice management groups should realize similar reductions in costs. In the WEDI study, hospitals reported savings of almost three full-time equivalents by automating the posting of claims payments.

HIPAA mandates that payers adopt a standard transaction, which enables most of the above processes. This transaction is the most sophisticated of all those mandated in August 2000 and it is clearly pivotal to enabling health care e-Commerce. Via the health care claims payment and RA transaction, a covered entity can perform the following functions:

- Transmit the details of an RA by indicating the amount paid for a claim and each of the invoiced individual services.
- Initiate an electronic funds transfer to the bank specified by the provider. Note that the electronic RA can be sent to either the provider's bank or the provider directly. The payer's bank can transmit the debit or credit payment and RA information within the automated clearinghouse electronic funds transfer (EFT) transaction to the provider's bank.
- Predetermine the benefits associated with a planned medical procedure.
- Make dues payments for covered lives. Although ANSI X12N 835 claims payment could be used for dues payments, the ANSI X12N 820 premium payment transaction is more likely to be used in conjunction with the ANSI X12N 834 benefit enrollment and maintenance transaction.

In addition, when implementing this transaction, HIPAA requires adherence to several related business rules affecting the following:

- Bundling and unbundling of billed procedures
- Balancing claims, service line items, and transactions
- Reversing and correcting payments
- Including interest and prompt payment discounts.

Thus, whereas this transaction can be useful for automating several key claims processes, it also opens the door for new and so far unexploited processes to further streamline claims processing. At the same time, business partners must standardize key business rules. In particular, when attempting to coordinate benefits among two or more payers, the primary payer can use this transaction to confirm a secondary payer's benefits before moving the claim forward. Providers can also use the transaction to confirm expected reimbursements for planned future services.

Few payers have undertaken any form of EFT inherent in the implementation of this transaction. Even fewer provider organizations have developed the ability to accept electronic payments and RAs. The value of implementing this transaction depends largely on the ability of back-office systems to incorporate the rules and inherent features.

Impacts and Opportunities

Implementation of electronic claims payment posting will necessitate a thorough review of current policies and procedures with an eye to automating most of them. The reengineering of processes will permit claims departments to focus on confirming and explaining the exceptions in payments. The implementation can be a catalyst for driving further efficiencies by using the transaction to predetermine benefits and accept dues payments from subscriber sponsors such as employers, trust funds, or associations.

The key challenges to a successful implementation include:

- The adoption of the business rules for bundling and unbundling services and balancing the entire claim, service line items, and batched transactions
- The ability to post payments by claim line item and reflect the explanation for the payment
- The establishment of EFT agreements with banks and business partners
- The building of information systems functions to process all the other refund, crediting, reversing, correcting, interest charging, dues payment collecting, and prompt payment discounting features.

The investment in complying with HIPAA's mandates should realize value in the following areas:

- Greater efficiency and effectiveness in the payment posting and reconciliation processes
- Enhanced cash flows that benefit providers because of direct electronic payments
- Greater accuracy in estimating outstanding liabilities via predetermination of benefits
- Heightened payer customer service in light of timely, more accurate, and better-understood payments
- Competitive advantage to those payers first offering standard electronic payment posting and RAs and to providers who can effectively process them.

IT Investment Options and Strategies

All HIPAA transactions require the establishment of an EDI platform. This transaction, however, is the most versatile and goes to the heart of effective electronic health care business-to-business relationships. As a result, payers and providers should start soon to consider the broad implications and paybacks of an investment in its implementation. Their options and strategies include the following:

- A thorough restatement of their enterprise data model to consider all business function and data relationships enabled by this transaction in conjunction with other transactions mandated by HIPAA.
- Extensive modification of current legacy systems to support the various business rules and uses engendered by the transaction.
- Reexamination of the ability of current back-office applications to take advantage of the transaction. In turn, the affected business areas should consider undertaking a thorough systems-selection effort to determine whether there are better e-Commerce application architectural approaches available in the marketplace.
- Development of capability to improve point-of-service eligibility verification by combining the use of this transaction or the premium payment transaction to accept subscriber dues and capitation payments with the electronic eligibility roster transaction mandated by HIPAA. Routinely updating the provider's electronic eligibility records means having the appropriate co-payment information available at the time the patient arrives for service.

Payers and providers dependent on vendor turnkey systems need to question their vendors on how and when they expect their products to be compliant with HIPAA EDI standards. In the future, the complete chain of claims processing depends on increased automation to significantly improve the efficiency, accuracy, and quality of both financial information and business partner relationships.

AUTOMATING REFERRALS AND AUTHORIZATIONS (ANSI X12N 278)

Automating referral processes should result in significant improvements in the day-to-day practice of medicine. Patient satisfaction and physician satisfaction will both improve. With a visionary strategy and the appropriate spin-off enhancements, payers and physician management groups should experience strengthened financial stability.

The basic episode of care begins with the primary care provider (PCP), be it an emergency room, urgent care center, or scheduled encounter. When the PCP does not possess the expertise to deal with a problem, he or she must refer the patient to a relevant specialist. PCPs responsible for patients covered by managed care contracts must, in most cases, seek authorization from the patient's health plan. One of the greatest sources of patient and physician dissatisfaction lies in this referral and authorization process. For instance, it is common for a patient who has been referred to a specialist to arrive at the specialist's office on the date and time scheduled only to be turned away because the payer had not yet

authorized the service. Alternatively, the payer's utilization review body denies the service about 5% of the time and the visit is cancelled. Subsequently, the denial is appealed and overturned 50% of the time, resulting in a much-delayed, medically necessary visit.

There are interesting future revenue or liability impacts tied to fee-for-service referrals. Out-of-network referrals represent significant purchased medical services liabilities to payers when those specialists are not at risk for the patient's medical services. Note that payers can be either the health plans or independent provider associations (IPAs) and medical groups holding managed care contracts with health plans. The challenge to IPAs and medical groups is to be able to accurately forecast those liabilities. Conversely, for the larger single or multi-specialty groups authorized, referrals represent future revenues as well as a commitment to perform the approved services.

In turn, knowing the status of a referral is paramount to both provider and patient. Specialty providers or their office managers enjoy being able to electronically inquire about the status of their referrals. An electronic authorization inquiry reduces the time spent from an average of 2 to 3 minutes to less than 30 seconds. To challenge the providers even further, there tends to be a limit to the number of inquiries per referral that can be made in a given time period.

In this pre-HIPAA environment, about 40% of referrals are submitted electronically, either by interactive voice-response telephone systems or a proprietary system provided by the payer. Whatever electronic means available to the providers substantially not only decreases the actual inquiry time but also reduces the time to obtain an authorization by 50% or more. There is a dramatic reduction in the cost to submit a request for a referral using EDI. Data from the 1993 WEDI report[1] showed the average cost for both providers and payers to be about $1.40 per request. With automation, the referral cost decreased to $0.17. That cost reduction reflects freeing up approximately 5 to 7 minutes of staff time.

Barriers to accessing care are a major source of dissatisfaction to patients covered by managed care. Timely referrals and authorizations would help to ameliorate that source of grievance. Recently, large health maintenance organization (HMO) and managed care payers have responded with "open access" or point-of-service options obviating the need for a primary care physician referral. Under these plans, patients are able to self-refer. Some data suggest that the pattern for self-referral is similar to that using the traditional gatekeeper model. However, the premium for self-referral plans is higher than for a standard HMO benefit. In addition, employers prefer the less expensive option for their employees with the apparent controls of the "gatekeeper" approach. As a result, the industry will depend on the use of specialty service and other referral requests and on utilization review entities to authorize requested services for the foreseeable future.

The impacts and opportunities of implementing electronic referrals and authorizations are examined below.

Impacts and Opportunities

Automation of referral processes benefits the delivery system directly. It is remarkable that the industry has fairly well neglected exploiting the value of electronic referral solutions. As indicated above, an automated referral sets in motion the delivery of effective care and, if done well, a timely and accurate reimbursement process. The referral and authorization transaction standard actually requires two logically different transactions: one to issue the request and one to respond to the request. A subsequent claims payment is greatly expedited when there is a referral in the system tied to that claim.

There is a cost to enabling the HIPAA-mandated standard referral requests and authorizations; however, specialty providers and medical groups with large managed care patient populations should consider the following impacts and opportunities:

- Improved quality of care due to timely and unrescheduled delivery of the full continuum of services, including dental and home health providers. When the automation is coupled with an emphasis on the automatic approval or denial of requests, the entire process is significantly enhanced. Payers should relieve their utilization review entities from the burden of processing the bulk of requests that are subsequently approved.
- Improved provider productivity for similar reasons as well as lower referral costs
- Enhanced patient and provider satisfaction by assuring appropriate access to care and uninterrupted services. Providers and their office staffs should find the ability to send requests, receive authorizations, inquire as to status, request extensions, and appeal denied requests significantly simplified and more accurate.
- Improved cash flow as subsequent claims for reimbursement require less research for the original service requests and justifications.
- Improved ability on the part of payers and providers to forecast future liabilities and revenues.
- Improved ability for managed care organizations to capture valuable medical management data for analytical purposes such as protocol development, outcomes evaluations, and general "best practice" profiling.

The realization of these benefits requires up-front investment in business process and systems reengineering, as outlined below.

IT Options and Strategies

Because the referral process is at the hub of providing effective, efficient medical care, those contemplating its automation should consider the strategic implications. Entities can realize

competitive advantage by taking the broadest possible view
of opportunities:

- Upgrade current core back-office systems to enable the transmission and
  receipt of the HIPAA service request and authorization transaction. For
  many, this upgrade will require a close partnership with their existing
  application vendor. The upgrades should include the following features:
  —Automatic authorization or denial of services
  —Automatic referral status inquiry and response
  —Ability to link authorization parameters to subsequent claims
  —Automatic determination of the gross and net revenue associated
    with the requested services
  —Ability to request the full continuum of services, including dental
    and home health, in addition to the standard requests for acute
    care pre-certification and outpatient specialty care
  —Ability to automatically request extensions and initiate appeals to
    denied services
  —Ability for contracted physicians to easily check the status of referrals
- Integrate referral and claims processing into an enterprise-wide
  customer service initiative
- Employ Internet technologies to streamline the referral-requesting
  and status-checking functions. Consider the many new Web-based
  health care system solutions that are surfacing at Internet speeds.
- Add-on niche referral and claims services review and validation products
- Revisit and reengineer the enterprise data model to ensure an
  effective and efficient implementation of new EDI capability and the
  features specified above. Determine the best EDI and work-flow
  "engine" solutions. Remember to focus on exception processing.
- Reengineer the entire spectrum of referral and utilization review
  processes.

Again, automation of the referral process can be the key to both
bottom-line and above-the-line improvements. More importantly,
it is a major step toward an advantage in the effective delivery of quality
medical services. Overall, competitive advantage these days lies in
enhanced patient and provider satisfaction, where automated service
referrals have a tangible impact.

AUTOMATING ELIGIBILITY REQUESTS AND RESPONSES (ANSI X12N 270/271 & 834)

An efficient eligibility-checking process is key to both the delivery of and
payment for medical services. For most providers, however, existing
processes remain a deterrent to responsive and streamlined patient
contact and cost-effective back-office processes. HIPAA mandates

electronic eligibility checking, and all health care stakeholders, including consumers, will benefit. Covered entities must implement both the ANSI X12N 270 and 271 transactions; they cannot merely implement the request transaction without the ability to send or receive the response.

To notify payers of their enrolled employees, sponsors would typically use ANSI X12N 834. Payers can also use it to inform their managed care provider groups of their covered members. Ideally, the sponsors or payers would transmit the record of enrollees with the ANSI X12N 820 to pay the respective dues or premiums.

Knowing a patient's eligibility at the point of service benefits provider, payer, and patient. With timely enrollment data, providers can register patients with relatively few hassles. At the same time, they can receive prompt and accurate payment of both co-payments and any charges for procedures during the visit. In turn, nonmanaged care payers should realize improved cash flow and reduced customer service workload.

Current eligibility processing between payer and provider is enigmatic. Other than retail pharmacies, also covered under HIPAA regulations, providers often do not receive timely eligibility and plan benefits confirmation. Instead, they must rely on monthly enrollment information delivered by mail that details current subscribers and dependents. Some providers may receive batch electronic transmissions of the same information.

Many providers have to then use the printed listing at the point of service to identify eligible plan members and covered services. Other providers are able to update their patient management systems with the electronic data. Many providers lack confidence in the data and want to avoid a negative impact on customer service at registration time. As a result, they frequently resort to verifying eligibility a night or two prior to a patient's visit.

To confirm a patient's enrollment with a payer at any point in the care chain necessitates significant clerical time. The 1993 WEDI study estimated that it costs a provider $2 for each eligibility verification, either using bulky enrollment printouts or resorting to phone inquiries. Payers spent about half that amount. Providers frequently seek verification more than once for each managed care patient: once, one or two nights prior to a scheduled visit and, again, when they receive a claim for an out-of-network referral.

Using the electronic eligibility data presents significant challenges. In the current environment, few payers provide the data in the same record formats. Most of them frequently change the layout of the records. Many of the files arrive unreadable and require retransmission or reshipment by mail. Electronic eligibility is, nonetheless, supported to varying degrees in the leading practice management systems. In some cases, the functionality is not tied well enough to the benefits coverage, limiting the ability to electronically determine patient financial liability.

In response, HIPAA mandates a standard electronic record for eligibility information. Transmissions can be sent in either batch or quasi real-time. Providers can request eligibility confirmation whenever necessary, including at the point of service.

The eligibility, dues payments, and capitation processes are frequently unsynchronized. The lack of synchronization makes it difficult for providers to reconcile capitation payments against the managed care enrollment listings. Such reconciliation is impossible if payments are not calculated by the payers and sent to the providers with an associated extract of enrollments. A combination of HIPAA transactions transmitted simultaneously would enable accurate reconciliation.

Payers currently appear to be working collaboratively to facilitate the eligibility status checking process. They may even establish regional and national network services to providers, employing the mandated transactions before HPAA requires them to do so. The impacts and opportunities associated with the implementation of electronic eligibility are reviewed below.

Impacts and Opportunities

Inefficient patient management and back-office business operations mark nonelectronic eligibility processing. Difficulties determining insurance coverage can cause long lines at the point of service. Although patients are probably not deprived of services, customer satisfaction suffers greatly. In the provider's back office and payers' claims areas, claims for payments to specialty providers can pile up awaiting specific clarification of the correct payer and benefits.

Business operation improvements can be realized after significant investments in electronic eligibility transactions. The impacts and opportunities are the following:

- Streamlined appointment scheduling and point-of-service registering processes, reducing waiting on the phone and in lines
- More efficient and effective staffing in scheduling, registering, reviewing referrals, and claims processing.
- Improved cash flow and reduced bad debt due to better eligibility and benefits data at the point of service. Providers can reliably demand payment for co-insurances and uncovered or partially covered services.
- Enhanced ability to determine coordination of benefits based on information from the patient.
- Enhanced ability to reconcile dues payments with payers.

Automating eligibility would clearly eliminate many manual interventions and the resulting delays in gaining access to care. With the appropriate automation of enrollment data in the back office, automating adjudication of the preponderance of referrals and claims would become a reality.

IT Investment Options and Strategies

Ascertaining a person's health care insurance eligibility represents the key to obtaining necessary medical services. In turn, subsequent referral and claims payment processes are improved when complete and accurate policy data is available electronically. All these administrative, medical management, and financial functions are inexorably linked. Thus, to maximize the opportunities described above, organizations should embark on a strategic business reengineering initiative that extends throughout the enterprise.

The IT options and strategies include the following:

- Upgraded legacy applications that transmit and receive the HIPAA-mandated eligibility transactions, rendering all related processes more efficient. Work with vendors to integrate the eligibility, referrals, and claims processing functions. Ensure that benefit plans are fully defined in the system using standard CPT-4 (common procedural terminology) codes for procedures.

- Acquisition of a new integrated system having complete HIPAA electronic data interchange compliance.

- Acquisition of emerging Internet-based integrated systems and applications in conjunction with the organization's e-Commerce strategy. Consider impacts of engineering the Web-based features with existing legacy systems. Frequently, it is difficult to integrate Internet access into existing direct patient processes.

- Establishment of an EDI strategy involving a comprehensive review of the required enterprise data model to determine availability of mandated data elements, their formats, their sources and destinations, and the related business rules.

- Effective utilization of application interface engines, translator tools, and clearinghouses accessing and storing data located in diverse systems to facilitate the appropriate electronic exchange of transactions.

There are ways to modestly implement the HIPAA-mandated transactions. A simplistic approach might be described as a minimally feasible solution. For instance, an organization could receive the enrollment information accepting the HIPAA transactions and print off multiple copies of the electronic data. The listings could then be used as usual without altering their business operations. Such an approach would be "penny wise and pound foolish." In contrast, given a strong organizational commitment to maximize the value of reengineering related business operations, organizations should realize significant savings, improved revenues, and competitive advantage.

AUTOMATING CLAIMS ATTACHMENTS (ANSI X12N 275)

As presently processed, attaching documents in support of invoices for services is a challenging, time-consuming process. Automating the sending of clinical reports will greatly improve the efficiency and effectiveness of the review and approval of complex claims. The resulting automation of clinical data is a definite precursor to the effective creation of a portable medical record that is accessible to all of a patient's providers.

In order to pay some health care claims, payers, health plans, insurance companies, fiscal intermediaries, or physician practice management groups will sometimes require additional medical information in support of the invoiced services. Most of these instances involve acute-care hospital stays or outpatient surgical services. The payers will typically request clinical information regarding the results of diagnostic procedures and special tests such as lab results and diagnostic imaging consultation reports. Frequently, approvals for the payment of ambulance services will necessitate requests for missing or inadequately documented information.

HIPAA architects have clearly endorsed, but not yet formally proposed, the use of standard electronic transactions to request and respond with claim attachment information. They will likely propose the adoption of the standard in the second or third quarter of 2002. Although the transaction may provide process improvements for a low percentage of claims, it reflects a key initial step toward inter-entity sharing of computerized medical record information.

At this time, sharing of clinical information between payers and providers is a slow, cumbersome, paper-driven process. Although much information is exchanged electronically within medical centers and sophisticated community health care information networks, very little medical record data is shared electronically between business partners. The absence of health care business-to-business transaction standards reflects a major deterrent to more frequent exchanges.

Some entities have enabled electronic sharing of medical information with, particularly, claim processors and case managers through remote online terminal access to legacy systems. By permitting external partners legitimate access to local databases, the sharing entities expose themselves to significant risks. Unless the access is carefully restricted, most of an organization's health care systems' files are susceptible to unauthorized and inappropriate browsing.

Upon reflection, the specific HIPAA endorsed transaction might be seen as most valuable in the former less managed care-centric world. In today's environment, payers are committed to meet claims payment turnaround compliance standards and do not concern themselves as much with services provided under full capitation agreements.

While the HIPAA endorsed transaction standard may be seen as responding to prior demands, it also satisfies current needs.

The transaction requires payers and providers to enable the efficient sharing of clinical data required for effective overall medical management. In the future, the transaction should facilitate timely and effective collaboration between providers across the care spectrum. Moreover, WEDI is working with government agencies and industry stakeholders to develop standards for the electronic patient record. These architects envision an all-inclusive longitudinal patient record readily accessible nationally to payers and providers.

A related technology trend of note involves the advent of XML (Extensible Markup Language). XML enables the sharing of information contained in electronic documents as actual data—the same data mandated by HIPAA. So, in two years when health care business partners must comply with the currently proposed HIPAA EDI standards, health care XML solutions may become a reality. The HL7 (Health Level 7) standards body (whose transaction standards form the basis for exchanging claims attachments) is also responsible for the development of XML standards for the health care industry.

Following is a summary of the impacts and opportunities associated with the electronic exchange of claims attachments.

Impacts and Opportunities

The benefits of implementing the claims attachment transactions will be realized in simplifying claims payment processes and, perhaps more dramatically, in accelerating the efficiencies and effectiveness of the delivery of medical care. Thus, it is envisioned that the early adopters of the standard will benefit in many ways not previously targeted nor anticipated by the HIPAA architects. Some of the short- and long-term impacts and opportunities flowing from this electronic transaction follow.

- Significant reengineering to make the provider clinical and billing systems, and payer claims payment processes more efficient and effective by automating the request for clinical diagnostic data and the response containing the appropriate medical data.
- (All covered entities should investigate "non-HIPAA standard" uses of the transactions. With further reengineering of processes and systems, it appears useful for referral and second opinion requests, and, possibly, "out-of-area" emergent or other consultations.)
- Minimization of delays in processing complex hospital claims.
- Improved data quality as current medical diagnostic results are retrieved directly from the respective clinical systems.
- Enhanced medical record databases since information is retrieved and collected electronically. As a result, decision support capability improves.
- Useful experience with tools to authenticate and authorize access to patient-identifiable medical data.

Compliance with the electronic claims attachment transaction reflects an excellent investment in an infrastructure enabling the controlled exchange of medical record information. The related IT investment options and strategies are reviewed below.

IT Investment Options and Strategies

The investment in electronic claims attachments will bring about a significant reduction in the cost of processing a complex claim and claims that fail reasonable edits for appropriateness. It is, however, unclear whether benefits realized will exceed the implementation expenses. The value proposition for this transaction must be considered as a function of a long-term and unified health care e-Commerce strategy. In that context, the overall value of implementing all the HIPAA-mandated transactions collectively is greater than the value realizable by each transaction individually.

There are several IT investment options and strategies worth considering:

- Acquisition of new vendor systems that can successfully demonstrate full return on investment based on compliance with all HIPAA transaction standards.
- Active collaboration with one's existing administrative and clinical systems vendors to maximize short- and long-term gains.
- Establishment of an EDI strategy based on a thorough determination of an enterprise-wide data model.
- Implementation by providers of an HL7-compliant interface engine or transaction mapper and translator. At a minimum, the providers' IT departments will need to interface relevant clinical systems per HL7 transaction standards.
- Payers will need to build interfaces to accept and process the HL7-compliant claims attachment information.
- Alignment of forward-thinking electronic patient-record and e-Commerce strategies with the opportunities presented by this and the other HIPAA-mandated transactions. Consider Web-based solutions that integrate well with existing legacy systems.
- Reassessment of decision-support systems strategy, content, and priorities as more clinical data can be made available.
- Establishment of a digital signature initiative to validate the authenticity of the clinicians' electronic reports.

HIPAA has not yet formally proposed the use of the electronic claims attachment transaction, but it will likely do so in 2002. Some health care industry pundits might suggest that the transaction is based on a need that has largely come and gone. In addition, in light of emerging XML technology, the current transaction standard may not be the most effective in the long run. The current standard is the propeller for exchanging clinical data between entities, whereas XML will possibly be the jet engine. Nevertheless, the electronic exchange of clinical information across multiple and diverse provider systems will be the critical enabler for the envisioned national portable and computerized patient record standard. As recounted above, this transaction will enable some targeted benefits. At the same time, its implementation should provide the early adopters with significant unforeseen opportunities and market advantages.

AUTOMATING THE BENEFITS COORDINATION VERIFICATION (ANSI X12N 269)

HIPAA staff has announced their intention to propose the use of the ANSI ASC 269 Health Care Benefit Coordination Verification Request and Response EDI standard transaction. This transaction is one of four soon to be published via one or several proposed rules. The other three transactions include the first report of injury, claims attachments, and physician credentialing. The benefit coordination verification transaction standard effectively enables nearly 100% electronic processing of claims. The goal of the transaction is to eliminate the cumbersome manual process used by secondary payers to determine what was adjudicated and paid for by prior payers.

The benefits coordination verification transaction includes several features:

- Permitting the inquiring payer to indicate for which benefits it needs an explanation of benefits (EOB).
- Requiring that the secondary payer indicate whether there is a patient's authorization to coordinate benefits on file.
- Establishing a reference "trace" number to permit linking the particular inquiry to its response.

Payers cannot use this transaction to correct claim information. If the primary payer does not acknowledge that the specific service information is valid, the secondary payer must contact the provider to obtain the right information.

Currently, it is a significant challenge for secondary payers, be they health plans, insurance companies, third-party administrators, or medical groups with large managed care populations, to determine their reimbursement responsibilities. The volume is significant. Approximately 30% of patients in the past have had at least dual coverages. The challenges begin at the time they receive a claim from a provider. First, they need to identify the primary payer. Often that information is only available on a UB92 claim form as comments in a free-formatted field not captured by the internal claims system. Once detected, the claims processors must contact the primary payer (or the secondary payer if it is the tertiary payer) in regulated time frames to ascertain what were the EOB and the payment. Typically, the information exchange requires several phone calls, faxes, and possible mailing of supporting claims documentation.

No party in the existing claim processing cycle is immune from disappointment when trying to coordinate benefits. In many cases, payers must resign themselves to pay for all covered services and then continue to pursue reimbursement from the secondary payers. As a result, payers will overpay their portion and consume significant staffing resources to recover those overpayments. As a result of these inefficiencies, providers experience unnecessarily lengthy revenue recovery cycles and inefficient billing processes. In many cases, patients who believe their claims have been significantly mishandled must undertake the arduous task of convincing their payers that this has occurred.

The ability to electronically request and receive the appropriate claims information completes the electronic processing chain of claims. By using the standard transactions, providers can electronically send both claims and selected clinical attachments to one or more payers at the push of a key or click of a mouse. The EDI 835 health care claims transaction will contain all payers that the providers have identified for a specific patient. The providers can electronically receive claims payments at their financial institutions with the EOB remittance advice. At the same time, or in sequence, all of their patient's payers can accurately and efficiently determine their payment responsibilities. Unfortunately, most payer and provider claims systems cannot assist in realizing the benefits of automating the full set of EDI transactions. Also, the providers are still burdened with obtaining all of the patient's benefit plan coverages.

In spite of this, both providers and payers will benefit from reduced manual processing burdens, more accurate claims adjudication and reimbursements, and further reductions in accounts receivable. Some of the general impacts and opportunities derived from the implementation of this transaction are described below.

Impacts and Opportunities

This transaction is only useful after the covered entities have im-plemented the ANSI ASC 837 Health Care Claim and the 835 Health Care Claims Payment standard transactions. Effective and efficient coordination of benefits will not occur until the payers invest in the benefit coordination verification standard transaction.

Key impacts and opportunities realized by investing in this transaction include the following:

■ Significant business operations reengineering to streamline the coordination of benefits processing.

- Improved cash flow and reduced accounts receivables to payers meriting a reimbursement; providers should also benefit further from an improved cash flow.
- Fewer errors in payments and subsequent corrections
- Increased investments in upgraded and enhanced systems as outlined later.
- Fewer claims held beyond state-regulated or other mandated time frames for payments.
- More subscribers satisfied with the accuracy and timeliness of resolving their claims.

The benefits cannot be realized without investing in IT solutions as described below.

IT Investment Options and Strategies

Although the covered entities need not comply with this transaction standard at the same time that they must implement the transactions already adopted by HIPAA, it should be included in their HIPAA implementation initiative. Key IT options include the following:

- Entities with in-house IT development staff should:
  —Ensure that that the direct and indirect business rules affected by the transaction become part of their enterprise-wide data model.
  —Consider the implementation of an interface engine, a comprehensive package for mapping and translating EDI transactions, or the use of a regional or national clearinghouse.
- Other entities will need to collaborate with their IT vendors to ensure eventual compliance with this standard. Their systems should enable the more efficient and effective business processes resulting from use of the transaction.
- All entities should develop an integrated e-Commerce and HIPAA EDI transaction strategy.

Effective and efficient electronic claims processing runs to the heart of health care e-Commerce. Integrating all the HIPAA published and proposed EDI transactions into an entity's front- and back-office business processes and systems will result in greatly simplified administrative processes, as HIPAA and its supporters intended.

REFERENCE

1. Workgroup for Electronic Data Interchange Steering Committee. *1993 WEDI Annual Report*. Reston, Va: Workgroup for Electronic Data Interchange; October 1993.

Standard Identifiers

Efficient health care claims and referral processing relies heavily on the accuracy of several key entity identifiers: the health plan, employer, provider, and patient. To facilitate health care e-Commerce, the Health Insurance Portability and Accountability Act (HIPAA) architects have mandated the standard health care transactions and have proposed the use of these identifiers within those transactions.

The least contested identifier of the four listed above is the employer identifier. Each employer, frequently referred to as a sponsor, will be identified by his or her tax identifier, the employer identification number (EIN). Although the use of a health plan identifier is not controversial, it has apparently been difficult to determine which entities should be defined as a health plan. Until clarified, the HIPAA staff will not publish a standard format.

The industry has clearly supported the issuance of a standard provider identifier in order to simplify the physician identification process. In addition, the centers for Medicare & Medicaid Services (CMS), formerly the Health Care Financing Administration (HCFA), has testified that there is significant opportunity for fraud in the current environment. Clinicians and their groups can now bill using a different identifier based on the specialty of the services and the location where service was delivered. Medicare, itself, requires a different provider identifier number (PIN) that is dependent on where the clinician delivers care. The ability to identify and authenticate the proper providers in order to approve claims and referrals is, as a result, problematic.

The only identifier that will not be mandated in the near term is the patient identifier. The debate on what would be an acceptable person identifier is deadlocked and frequently strident. Notwithstanding the deadlock with the patient identifier, the other three were met with a subdued acceptance.

A provider will have many identifying numbers in addition to their social security number, licensing accreditation number, and their own tax identification number. Even at the smallest provider group, the back-office billing system will require yet another identifier. Most systems will automatically generate a new identification number the first time the provider is set up in the system. Imagine the confusion this creates in a larger multiple-entity hospital-based delivery system with enterprise and departmental systems. Each physician will probably have a separate internal identification number in the provider master file of each clinical system. In turn, as recounted above, the clinician frequently has a different identifier for billing purposes for each specialty and patient care location.

Many provider groups historically have designed their providers' identifiers to assist in pricing services. For instance, a group of providers might agree to a specific fee schedule with some limited exceptions. The provider group's back office might handle those exceptions by slightly modifying the provider number for the affected clinicians. For that reason and others, many provider numbers have "intelligence" built in to them. The proposed HIPAA format would eliminate the ability of those groups and their systems to directly take advantage of the attributes of the previously assigned number.

The managed care payers, in particular, tend to compound the provider identification problem. They will generate a special identifier for each physician enrolled in a preferred or exclusive provider benefit plan for use by the health plan's subscribers. Thus, there is substantial opportunity for not only fraud and abuse by misguided providers but, also, for inefficient claims payment processes. Without a standard provider identifier, such inefficiencies are bound to persist, costing every entity along the referral and claims-processing chain valuable resources and possibly inconveniencing the affected patient.

IMPACTS AND OPPORTUNITIES

The implementation of each proposed identifier will differ. Once the health plan identifier has been resolved, its implementation along with the employer identifier should be straightforward. In most cases, the business processes should remain the same. Depending on the architecture of the provider, health plan, or clearinghouse legacy systems, the greatest impacts will be on the relevant master files.

In contrast, the implementation of the provider identifier will encounter significant challenges. The resulting benefits will be felt over time as fewer referrals are denied and fewer claims are rejected for presumed incorrect provider identifiers. At the same time, entities can simplify the process required to validate the specific providers.

The process of obtaining the new, unique PIN will be centralized and managed by a national provider system (NPS). Initially, all Medicare providers will receive their new number first. Entities requiring the new standard identifier will be able to inquire directly to the enumerator for the number. The NPS will maintain the national database in perpetuity, thus eliminating some of the problems physician credentialing services experience in keeping their files current and accurate.

Most provider groups will require significant changes to their legacy systems in order to ensure continuity between the previous identifiers and the new national provider identifier (NPI). In light of that challenge, providers, particularly large multidivisional and other hospital-based groups, should address their "person" identification and authentication strategy. Large integrated delivery networks should take the opportunity to review all relevant systems accessed by their providers with an eye to simplifying the process of identifying a provider across all internal systems.

The principal opportunities and impacts of implementing the standard physician identifier are highlighted here:

- For Medicare administration, elimination of a significant opportunity for fraudulent claim submittal.
- Requirement to link the new NPI to all previous and actively used provider identifiers.
- Reduction in inefficient referral and claims processing due to the frequent inability to identify a correct provider.
- Requirement to establish a process to obtain the NPI and maintain any associated physician-specific information needed by the NPS.
- Reengineering of legacy systems to use the identifier correctly in all claims-processing activities.

By mandating a standard NPI, the HIPAA authors have acknowledged the current challenges to accurate and legitimate billing for health care services.

IT INVESTMENTS AND STRATEGIES

All HIPAA-covered entities will need to invest prudently in the implementation of the new NPIs. There will be some impacts on business processes, but the greatest impacts will be on the setup and configuration of legacy systems. The physician identifier must be included in all provider master files and linked to almost all prior identifiers. Given that widespread impact, the organizations should consider a long-term architectural change to permit a centralized master "person" index. Most health care delivery systems utilize as many as six interfaced clinical applications. As a result, physicians require access to most of them. Thus, a single point of entry, which manages and controls access to those systems, should greatly enhance the usability of those systems.

The significant information technology investments and strategies are outlined below:

- Work with existing patient management, clinical systems, and physician credentialing vendors to determine how they intend to support the new provider identifier.
- Develop an enterprise-wide, multiple system, long-term strategy to simplify both the identification of providers and the access control of providers to all relevant systems. In the strategy, include the

HIPAA standard transaction requirements and the enterprise's e-Commerce strategy.

■ Consider an integrated master person identifier architecture in order to identify patients, employees, providers, and subscribers. Evaluate the existing vendor products as to fit within the enterprise's suite of applications. Consider, also, their ability to simplify the access control to multiple systems while meeting the HIPAA security regulations.

The investment in satisfying the HIPAA provider identifier standard can lead to significant overall claims and referral process improvements. In addition, a uniform "front-end" process to identify individuals and control system access should aid the enterprise in its addition of new systems. Although an enterprise can implement and benefit from the PIN standardization without much regard to the other HIPAA mandates, it is prudent to include the requirement in a general strategy.

chapter 4

Benefits and Return on Investment

Health Insurance Portability and Accountability Act (HIPAA)-covered entities need to thoroughly assess their current state of compliance, including a vision of their optimal future state of business operations, to maximize their opportunity to invest in HIPAA solutions. The greatest benefits will flow from streamlining manual processes directly affected by the standard electronic data interchange (EDI) transactions, code sets, and identifiers.

This chapter addresses the benefits and return on investment (ROI) based on a simplified model of health care services and payment processes.

To really maximize benefits, payers and providers should consider aligning their e-Commerce strategy with their HIPAA compliance. In addition, there are significant benefits to incorporating the industry's best physician practice management and back-office practices in the future vision.

CARE SERVICE AND PAYMENT MODEL

The services and payment-processing model highlighted below provides a broad look at many of the health care events from the perspective of the health plan enrollee and, subsequently, the patient. The events marked with an asterisk (*) can be significantly influenced by a commitment to maximize the benefits of complying with the HIPAA-mandated standards. Many HIPAA-influenced events and several others indirectly affected by HIPAA may see further benefits when folded into an e-Commerce strategy.

Health Care Service and Payment Events

1. Employee researches and selects health plan.
2. * Employer enrolls employee with health plan.
3. * Employer initiates monthly dues premium payment.
4. * Health plan notifies primary care physician (PCP) or physician group of enrollment.
5. Employee selects PCP.
6. * Health plan member makes appointment.

7.   Health plan member visits physician.

8.   * Patient pays for services. Depending on benefit plan, physician may submit claim to health plan.

9.   Physician may order diagnostic services or prescribe medications (and supplies).

10. * PCP refers managed care patient to specialist.

11. * PCP, specialist, and patient may check on status of referral.

12. Specialist requests medical history and physical from PCP.

13. * Health plan authorizes, denies, or pends referral and notifies the specialist.

14. * Patient makes appointment with specialist.

15. Patient visits specialist.

16. * Patient pays for specialist services.

17. * Specialist submits claim to payer (either PCP at risk for the care or the health plan).

18. Specialist may order diagnostic services or prescribe medications (and supplies).

19. * Patient makes appointment to visit diagnostic services.

20. Patient receives diagnostic services.

21. * Patient pays for diagnostic services.

22. * Patient goes to pharmacy, or optometrist, or durable medical equipment vendor and pays for items.

23. * Specialist or group may check on status of claims payment.

24. * Health plan may require supplementary claims information. Specialist or physician group provides it.

25. * Health plan authorizes or rejects part or all of the specialist's claim.

26. * Health plan notifies specialist or physician's group of claims adjudication and pays specialist's claim.

27. * Health plan may coordinate claim payments with secondary payers (including property and casualty third parties).

28. * Primary payer may pay their portion and transmit coordination of benefits (COB) claim to secondary payer.

29. Physician orders patient to Be admitted to hospital.

30. * Hospital may require pre-certification and concurrent authorizations for extensions of hospital days.

31. * Patient gets admitted.

32. Patient receives inpatient services.

33. * Patient is discharged and pays for services.

34. * Hospital and providers bill health plan.

35. * Health plan may require supplementary inpatient claim information.

36. * Health plan authorizes or rejects part or all of inpatient claim.

37. * Health plan notifies hospital and physician of adjudicated claims' statuses and pays claims.

38. * Health plan may coordinate inpatient claim payments with secondary payers (including property and casualty third parties).

39. * Physician may prescribe home health services.

40. * Physician, patient, and home health agency may check status of home health service request.

41. Home health requests medical history and discharge planning from hospital.

42. * Health plan authorizes home health.

43. Patient gets home health services.

44. * Home health service agency bills health plan.

45. * Home health service agency may request status of claim.

46. * Health plan authorizes home health claim and pays claim.

47. Patient may receive emergency care.

48. * Emergency room (ER) verifies patient's eligibility (injury may be result of work on a job).

49. * ER bills patient or health plan for services; patient would file claim with health plan.

50. * ER or patient may check status of claim payment.

51. Health plan may request medical treatment record from ER.

52. * Health plan may bill third party for injury on job, in a vehicle, or some other third party.

53. * Health plan pays ER claims.

To realize the most benefits, payers and providers need to incorporate the HIPAA-mandated standards within a vision of the industry's best practices.

Many of the necessary operational changes will reduce or eliminate manual paper handling and status-checking procedures. To accrue even modest benefits, the entities must also enhance or reengineer their supporting computer applications.

For instance, to significantly benefit from an EDI request for a referral authorization, the payer's systems must be able to process the information using computer-based rules and algorithms. The preponderance of requests can be automatically approved. Upon approving the request, the system should respond to the requesting physician with minimal or no manual intervention. On the provider side in the inpatient setting, case managers should be able to easily initiate EDI requests to the payer for certifying days in the hospital.

Below is further examination of the service and payment events in this care model and the related best practices and benefits that should be included in a future vision for HIPAA assessments. Subsequently, they will identify symbiotic e-Commerce solutions to further eliminate or streamline inefficient services and payment processes. Finally, using the entity's standard cost, revenue, and workload performance metrics and prevailing benchmarks, entities can evaluate their returns on investing in HIPAA-influenced benefits.

BEST PRACTICES AND BENEFITS

Payers and provider organizations can mutually benefit from aggressively complying with the HIPAA-mandated transactions, code sets, and unique identifier standards. Working together and in their own interests, they can minimize and possibly eliminate significant manual referral, claims, enrollment, and eligibility processing activities. As explained below, when the covered entities pursue a set of enabled best business practices, there are many profitable opportunities. Using existing workload, revenue and expense data, the covered entities can reasonably estimate their return on the investment in HIPAA standards.

To truly maximize the benefits of satisfying the HIPAA regulations, organizations must broaden their strategic business process and information technology (IT) visions. The best practices and benefits highlighted herein reflect those directly stimulated by compliance with HIPAA. Chapter 5 uncovers further benefits derivable from emerging advanced application features and Internet-stimulated solutions.

The previously outlined care service and payment model provides the template for uncovering the benefits of implementing the standard transactions, code sets, and identifiers. For those events identified as directly benefiting from a strategic implementation of HIPAA, the following review highlights the specific HIPAA standards, the quantifiable benefits, and the best practices.

Enrollment and Eligibility

On the same day an employee enrolls in, disenrolls from, or changes a benefit plan, the employer can automatically notify the selected health plan and make the electronic payment. Whether done daily or weekly, the health plan receives a timely payment, thereby avoiding manual check processing. Moreover, as long as the enrollment transactions are synchronized with the respective dues payments, the health plan and capitated provider group can accurately reconcile capitation revenues.

In turn, the health plan can automatically notify its contracted providers of the enrollment changes, thus avoiding processing hard-copy listings and tapes at both ends. The provider's practice management system becomes automatically aware of the eligibility of the subscriber, the dependents, and their benefits. Such timely notification will minimize the now frequent calls from new enrollees making their first contact only to discover that their selected provider is unaware of their enrollment.

Appointment Making

When the enrollee calls to make an advanced appointment, the provider's staff will be able to confirm eligibility in one of two ways. Either the enrollment information will be available on their system or the appointment clerk will request an electronic eligibility response from the payer. If the business partner agreement includes the use of real-time requests, the provider's staff, much like the pharmacy technician, can verify eligibility and benefits within seconds. Based on the eligibility information, the appointment clerk can inform the patient of their likely financial responsibility for the ensuing visit.

Point of Service

At visit time, the patient service representative can, with certainty, determine the patient's eligibility and confirm their co-payments and fees for services. They can receive the payments before and after the encounter with the physician, thus avoiding arduous patient billing efforts. Ideally, the provider's system could automatically issue a claim or encounter record to the particular payer once the physician had recorded the correct ICD-9 coded diagnoses and ICD-9 or CPT®-4 coded procedures.

Referrals

When the PCP needs to refer a managed care patient to a specialist, the physician's office can automatically make the referral request to the payer's utilization review department. The health plan should be able to immediately authorize or deny over 90% of the requests. For those requests either denied, pended, or not initially responded to, the provider can use their management system to either contest the denial or routinely request the referral status.

The referral process can be automated to avoid untimely manual processes and all of the related telephone and faxed status requests and responses. Specialists will also improve their productivity and finances by avoiding the all-too-frequent canceling and rescheduling of appointments.

Specialist Visit

When the patient visits the specialist, the specialist's practice management system can use the standard eligibility request and response transactions to confirm the patient's benefits and financial responsibilities. Like the PCP's office, they can reliably collect patient payments at the point of service. Additionally, they can issue an electronic claim to the relevant payer within hours of the visit.

Diagnostic Services

Although diagnostic imaging and laboratory services are normally covered under most managed care and preferred provider policies, the associated business office processes can be automated using the standard HIPAA eligibility and claims transactions.

Claims Status Checking

The PCP's, specialist's, and diagnostic services' offices can electronically request the status of any outstanding electronically submitted claim. The payer's claims system can respond in real-time or within 24 hours to the bulk of those requests. As a result, both the providers' and payers' offices can focus primarily on resolving complex claims, thereby avoiding significant customer service calls and unnecessary claims processor interruptions.

Additional Claims Information

For complex claims that require research and analysis, the utilization review staff could electronically request additional information in its claims status response. In turn, the provider can take advantage of a soon-to-be mandated transaction to aggregate and submit the requested additional medical information to the payer. Although useful for a small proportion of claims, primarily institutional ones, both parties can avoid significant manual and prone-to-loss medical record processing.

Upon manual or computer-system verification of the electronically provided additional information, the payer can electronically notify the provider that the claim has been adjudicated. The payer can then electronically pay the claim and transmit the remittance advice to the provider.

Coordination of Benefits

If payers become aware of other patient health plan coverages, they can electronically pay what they believe is their responsibility and submit a detailed claim to the secondary payer. Although the ability to coordinate benefits requires significant discovery efforts on the part of the payer, the electronic COB transactions enable timely, reliable claims processing between payers. Payers will improve their cash flow by using the COB electronic claims to receive timely payments. In fact, they most likely will recover more payments as a result of the appropriate systems and process reengineering.

Hospitals, Dentists, Home Health Agencies, Emergency Rooms, Pharmacies, and Suppliers

Most of the same benefits accrue to other providers and vendors such as hospitals, dentists, home health agencies, emergency rooms, pharmacies, and durable medical equipment vendors. Hospitals and admitting physicians can request and receive pre-certification for hospital stays when the patient's coverage requires one. While performing concurrent stay reviews, case managers and hospitals can request extensions to the stays and approvals for additional procedures.

Hospitals are also excellent candidates for electronically providing additional claims information because they typically operate the necessary clinical department systems.

Hospitals benefit by their ability to do the following:

- Minimize or eliminate untimely manual pre-certification and concurrent review authorization requests.
- Minimize manual, error-prone processing of supplementary claims information.
- Minimize the provision of unauthorized and contested services.
- Improve cash flow by reliably requesting payment of patient's financial responsibility either upon admission or discharge.

Recap of Best Practices

To best take advantage of EDI requires rethinking all core business processes and service levels. The primary advantage that compliance with HIPAA EDI standards provides is avoidance of the slow turnaround inherent in manually preparing and handling paper forms, the inefficient customer service calls, and postal service delay. As a result, health care entities, particularly health plans, can institute "same day" or 24-hour turnaround service for most of their key transactions.

The other specific best practices referred to above include:

- Point-of-service payment collection due to real-time eligibility and benefits determination
- Electronic customer service to handle enrollment, referral, and claims status checking
- Electronic funds transfers and automatic posting of sponsors' dues and providers' claims payments to their patients' accounts
- Electronic submittal of additional claims clinical information
- Automatic reconciliation of managed care capitation payments with the associated payments
- Electronic coordination of benefits.

Based on these best practices and service levels, the same entities will reduce inefficient staffing, minimize nonpayroll expenses, and improve provider productivity. As a result, they can establish effective exception-oriented policies and procedures.

In sum, organizations can realize the benefits and best practices outlined above if they undertake a well-conceived and committed HIPAA implementation. There are further benefits and good business practices to be gained through non-HIPAA–driven initiatives to upgrade back-office and practice management automation and to implement an e-Commerce strategy. The next discussion will consider those solutions in the context of the health care service and payment model.

ALIGNING HIPAA WITH e-COMMERCE AND ADVANCED AUTOMATION STRATEGIES

The HIPAA provisions for standard transactions, code sets, unique identifiers, and security lie at the heart of health care information exchange. Covered entities must consider how to best benefit from implementing HIPAA standards. At the same time, other technologies and approaches are converging to enable effective and efficient health care e-Commerce. At the forefront is the Internet with its inherent low transaction cost, standards, and ubiquity. This review highlights the add-on benefits and best practices associated with use of the Internet and other convergent technology trends.

The discussion follows the general flow of the care service and payment model. Except for the actual delivery of hands-on clinical services, HIPAA and the emerging and converging technological solutions will foster paperless, timely, and customer-focused administrative processes.

Enrollment and Eligibility

There is a movement by employers toward empowering personal health care benefits decisions using a program of defined contributions. In response, employers and Internet "brokers" can provide automated health care enrollment. Employers and other health care coverage sponsors will likely profit from setting up secured, "self-service" Internet kiosks to enable the selection of benefits. Internet health care brokers can help enrollees select the plan that best suits them and meets their financial constraints.

In fact, the broker can assist enrollees in selecting their primary care physician and later their specialists. To do so, they can offer online physician credentialing data. The National Provider System prescribed by HIPAA will be established to control the issuance of unique physician identifiers and to become the primary source for reliable physician information.

Once a health plan is selected, the online benefits service can issue the relevant HIPAA electronic transactions to initiate coverage and the dues payment to that payer. The payer can then automatically notify the appropriate medical group of the enrollee's eligibility for services.

Appointment Scheduling

"Self service," Internet-enabled, future appointment scheduling may eventually become a standard solution. If online scheduling services can integrate effectively with the local practice management system, providers will be able to reduce their dependency on appointment service representatives. To be most effective, the process needs to access the most current eligibility information.

Point of Service

The most critical time to access eligibility information is at the point of service. To best take advantage of the HIPAA transaction standards, the practice management system needs an intelligent module to generate a patient invoice and a clean claim. These modules are similar to an incoming claims adjudication "engine," which needs to process many different inputs. In particular, it must deal with clinical information, possible multiple coverages, provider contracts, fee schedules, and service charge master and eligibility data to determine financial responsibilities. Once implemented, the module ensures accurate patient payments before the patient leaves the clinician's office and timely, accurate claims submissions.

Key input to the adjudication process is the provider's noting of the diagnoses and procedures performed. Providers cannot be expected to know the HIPAA-mandated standard ICD-9 and CPT®-4 diagnostic and procedure codes. Smart tools are emerging to address the timely determination of the correct codes.

Referrals

Effective outpatient referral processing requires the ability to translate the physician's request for services into terms or codes understood by the payer's benefit plan policies. Few practice management systems enable these translations or include support of the HIPAA standard referral transactions. Emerging Internet-enabled referral request solutions using accepted clinical guidelines can facilitate recording the appropriate terms or codes, thereby enabling intervention-free and near real-time referral requests and authorizations.

The challenge to providers is to integrate an Internet-enabled solution with their host system. To best process subsequent claims for services, the host system needs to retain the referral information.

Specialist Visit

A specialist requires the same capabilities as a PCP. However, they need to rely more heavily on claims processing. For each visit, it is likely that they will need to submit a claim to a payer. To generate a timely and accurate claim with minimal claims staff intervention, they need the aid of an integrated software module to clean the claims. The providers can acquire these modules either from their core system vendor or other vendors who can interface their products with the core system vendor's claims-processing functions.

Claims Status Checking

Internet-enabled claims status checking can be performed effectively without a direct interface to the host claims-processing system. The HIPAA-mandated claims status response transaction simply returns the status of both the entire claim and individual service items. It is possible that payers will join together to provide eligibility, referral, and claims status checking via the Internet. In the future, patients and providers will be able to inquire electronically about the status of their claims, thereby significantly reducing their customer service burden.

Additional Claims Information

Frequently, providers are aware of information required to support their claims. In those cases, they can routinely send the additional claims information transaction with the electronic claim. To efficiently and effectively assemble this information from their clinical department systems, providers should take advantage of so-called "interface engines." These engines can retrieve the pertinent data and create the standard attachment transaction. In the future, an increasing amount of clinical information will be transmitted automatically.

Eventually, most HIPAA EDI experts expect that the ANSI X12N and Health Level 7 (HL7) data standards maintenance organizations will enable the provision of attachments for referrals.

Claims Payments and Coordination-of-Benefits Processing

Payers will need to take advantage of rules-based claims adjudication engines. To be most effective, they must make referral authorization results available to the engine. Emerging claims engines need to integrate with the host system to be effective. A well-configured claims adjudication engine will result in less provider, claims processor, and utilization review intervention in pricing the claim.

To ensure accurate claims and to minimize fraudulent claims, payers need code-checking capability. Such modules have been available for several years and can integrate well with many of the existing physician practice management systems. Some can be used at the point of service to validate diagnosis and procedure coding; most can be used for claims processing.

Large claim processors and health care delivery systems can take advantage of work-flow "engines" to coordinate the processing of referrals and claims. Work-flow engines can route transactions to relevant work areas based on key parameters that reflect the nature of the record or its status. Work-flow engines need to interface efficiently with the incoming record-handling process of the host systems.

Hospitals, Dentists, Home Health Agencies, Emergency Rooms, Pharmacies, and Suppliers

Hospitals are excellent candidates for many of the following solutions:

- Interface engines or "translators"
- Work-flow engines
- Code checking
- Claims adjudication of outgoing claims
- Internet-enabled claims status checking.

In addition, large health care systems are often created through mergers of health care enterprises using disparate patient management, clinical department, and billing systems. They can benefit from the implementation of shared master file solutions. For instance, large health care systems need to ensure the correct identification of patients, employers, health plans, and providers across many different computer systems. They can implement a "front-end" master patient- and entity-indexing system to retrieve and incorporate the correct identifier, thereby maximizing the accuracy of referral and claims transactions.

Hospitals and integrated delivery systems can also take advantage of the interface engines (or translators) to build and submit the standard HIPAA transactions.

Recap of the Benefits and Best Practices Converging with HIPAA Impacts

The solutions described above present a powerful synergy when aligned with a HIPAA implementation strategy. Several of the Internet-based solutions provide "self-service" capabilities for health care consumers who wish to be responsible for their care. The consumers can make intelligent choices about the plan and doctors they select; they can monitor the status of their enrollments, specialty referrals, and claims. Payers and patient sponsors can significantly reduce their enrollment and patient inquiry service expenses while their customers participate more actively in their health care and payment processes.

Many other symbiotic solutions should greatly improve the quality of data while reducing the need for manual interventions and highly specialized decision-making. If effectively implemented, HIPAA standards and the convergent technological solutions will shift the industry focus from administrative overhead to the actual delivery of services and employment of best clinical practices.

DERIVING THE RETURN ON INVESTMENT

Since the passage of HIPAA, the projected costs and benefits of complying with the Administrative Simplification Provisions have varied significantly. The Workgroup for Electronic Data Interchange reported the original estimates of annual net benefits from compliance with HIPAA were $1.6 billion. Since then, the Department of Health and Human Services (DHHS) published the final Privacy Rule. Two important privacy implementation reports, one commissioned by the American Hospital Association and the other by the Blue Cross Blue Shield Association, estimate that compliance with the privacy provisions would cost as much as $22.5 billion over the first five years. DHHS now reports that the cost of implementing HIPAA could be $17.6 billion, with $29.9 billion of benefits over the next 10 years. It is also estimated that savings associated with integrated HIPAA and Web-enabled health care back-office solutions will total over $50 billion by 2008. Clearly, there are no consistent and accurate estimates of either the costs or the benefits; nevertheless, the health care industry overall should benefit from HIPAA and related Internet solutions.

A thorough assessment of what is required for compliance is necessary to determine how any individual entity will benefit. The following discussion illustrates how to apply the general benefits highlighted in this chapter to one's organization in order to derive an estimate of annual and total net benefits. Once the organization has determined the likely annual costs to implement the HIPAA standards in conjunction with its Web-based initiatives, it can derive a critical measure of its return on those investments. In fact, some organizations may choose to see whether they can make the business case for an aggressive, integrated HIPAA and e-Health care implementation. With reasonably collected estimates of costs and benefits, such a first look-see is feasible.

Benefit–Cost Models

In general, a benefit–cost model is similar to a business plan and must include the following components:

- A time frame over which management needs to determine results. Five years is reasonable.
- Monthly or annual estimates of investments, benefits, and ongoing expenses.

- Benefits estimated by using either business process reengineering (BPR) expectations or accepted industry benchmarks. Benchmarks usually reflect the industry's best practices on similar initiatives.
- Forecasted business metrics, such as the volume of claims or referrals, to be used with the benchmarks to estimate benefits.

The benefit–cost analysis typically culminates with the calculation of an ROI as a measure of the interest rate required to at least recover the original investment and maintenance expenses. Some larger-scale benefit–cost analyses include multiple criteria for justification. In those analyses, the ROI and costs become just two of several criteria weighed together to rank alternative solutions.

Benefit Model

For HIPAA, the benefit–cost analysis would address all of the following components:

- Each standard transaction the organization must comply with and the resulting process changes
- The code-set conversions
- The unique identifiers
- Security and confidentiality—technical and administrative mechanisms, policies, and procedures
- Privacy.

As demonstrated previously, the quantifiable benefits highlighted were predominantly the following:

1. Reduce the payers', employers', and providers' costs of changing health plan enrollment.
2. Reduce the providers' cost of determining eligibility.
3. Increase the providers' collection of co-payments and service charges at the point of service.
4. Reduce the providers' and payers' costs of processing referrals.
5. Reduce the payers' cost of responding to requests for status of claims, referrals, and eligibility.
6. Reduce the payers' and employers' costs of processing premium payments.
7. Reduce the providers' and payers' costs of processing claims payments, including the processing of claims attachments.
8. Reduce the payers' cost of incorrectly paying claims.
9. Improve the providers' productivity and revenue by increasing the timeliness of referral authorizations.
10. Improve the providers' revenue by increasing accuracy of their claims.

11. Improve the hospitals' revenue by increasing timeliness of authorizations for extensions of stays and additional procedures.
12. Improve the payers' revenue by enhancing ability to coordinate benefits with secondary payers.

To build the benefits model, the organization needs to determine or estimate the metric associated with each benefit. For instance, for benefit 1 above, the payer or provider needs to document the current and projected volumes of enrollment changes. Instead of receiving and processing the enrollment information via diverse media, the payer can plan to use the standard HIPAA ANSI 834 transaction (assuming the employer or sponsor agrees to use the standard). An acceptable benchmark for the use of an electronic enrollment is a savings of $0.67 for the payer and $1.35 for the provider.

Benefits can also be estimated by taking a BPR approach. The BPR approach requires understanding of the current costs for the affected business areas. Instead of using industry benchmarks, the organization can take a particular stance regarding operational changes. BPR specialists propose three levels of business change:

- A 10% to 25% improvement by minimally adopting the new standards.
- A 25% to 50% improvement with concerted cross-departmental efforts to benefit from enhanced electronic information exchanges.
- A 100% to 500% improvement due to an aggressive operational transformation in core business practices.

The benefits model is the more difficult one to build. Frequently, the data are not available in the form required. As a result, the analyst is compelled to settle for estimates based on reasonable assumptions. For example, in a case where referral request volumes are unavailable, it is worth recalling that the number of outpatient referral requests is tied closely to the number of outpatient managed care claims. Since most managed care plans require a referral request for specialty services, it is reasonable to assume there was a referral request preceding each claim. There is usually a valid means to assume a relationship of a nonexistent metric to an existing one. Some current HIPAA and related electronic processing cost savings benchmarks include the following:

- Claims processing using ANSI 835 and 837—$5.50 per claim
- Referral-request processing using ANSI 278—$1.70 per request
- Claims, referral, and eligibility customer requests—$6.66 per request
- COB claim processing—$5.50 per claim
- Enrollment changes—$1.35 per change
- Eligibility reporting and updating—$1.00 per new or changed eligibility
- Electronic funds transfer of dues and claims checks—$0.80 per check

- Bad debt and revenue improvements—2% as rule of thumb
- Days in receivable—30- to 60-day improvements

In sum, a useful benefits model worksheet would include the following parameters for each benefit:

- The statement of the benefit
- The associated metric description
- One or more assumptions regarding the derivation of the metric or benefit
- The associated benchmark or BPR assumption, as highlighted above
- Sixty monthly or five annual estimates of savings using the metric (including an estimate in overall activity growth)
- Sixty monthly or five annual estimates of savings or improved revenues.

Cost Model

The best cost models are based on an analysis of resources required to make the initial investment and to cover the ongoing expenses. Such cost estimates are made as a result of a thorough assessment of the compliance requirements. However, to perform a pre-HIPAA assessment estimate of the possible ROI, the organization will likely need to rely on its department managers' best estimates of the capital investment and operating costs. Most cost estimates tend to be departmental totals rather than detailed operating expense estimates at the general and administrative accounts level.

The HIPAA investment costs need to include, but are not limited to, the following:

- An internal or contracted HIPAA assessment
- Business process transformation impacts including any consulting services and resulting staffing changes required to comply with all HIPAA provisions
- IT implementation and maintenance staffing or contracted services
- New software and hardware.

The Return on Investment

To complete the analysis, the benefits and costs need to be totaled by month or year, depending on the entity's preference. Assuming annual totals, there would be five cash flow amounts, one for each year. Tools such as Microsoft Excel® can be used to calculate the ROI measure. A resulting high positive interest rate typically means that the benefits significantly exceed the first one or two years' investment. Most organizations require an ROI of over 25% before they are convinced they will benefit from the proposed investment. The skepticism is largely predicated on the historical inability of many organizations in and out of health care to squeeze out savings based on the reduction in staffing.

Payers and large provider associations can benefit from implementing transactions, code sets, and unique identifiers. Smaller provider groups will likely continue to manually process paper claims, referrals, and enrollment information. As a result, the implementation of the Privacy Rule and soon-to-be published Security Rule will result in no cost savings. There are signs, however, that payers may offer their providers incentives to use the payer's Internet claims, referral, and eligibility submission and status-checking solutions. If those offerings come to fruition, even the smaller provider groups may benefit overall from HIPAA.

In the end analysis, when stimulated by HIPAA and the Internet revolution, the health care industry should experience a significant beneficial digital transformation in its business and delivery processes over the next 5 years.

chapter 5

Security

The Health Insurance Portability and Accountability Act of 1996 (HIPAA) mandates both administrative and technical security measures. Leading health care industry security and confidentiality spokesmen such as Dr Ted Cooper,[1] Kaiser Permanente Medical Care Program, have repeatedly emphasized that the proposed rules reflect good business practices. The goal of the security rule is to protect all individual, identifiable health care information against intentional and negligent sharing.

By fostering standards for the electronic exchange of sensitive protected health care information (PHI), the advocates and others understood the potential for much greater access to that data. To counter that fear, the standards makers proposed requiring adherence to security and privacy standards. There are many accredited and internationally recognized security standards. However, if the proposed security provisions become effective, the health care industry will stand alone in self-imposing those standards.

For the past decade, public concerns over the confidentiality and privacy of medical records have been driving the need to legislate good security and privacy practices and measures. Notwithstanding HIPAA's focus on digital health care information, application of the proposed security rules would protect personal records in all forms. Excellent security practices should therefore minimize the risk of public lawsuits and HIPAA penalties as well as enhance an enterprise's reputation with patients, providers, and prospective business partners.

The HIPAA authors classified the security and confidentiality rules into three areas: administrative procedures, physical safeguards, and technical services and mechanisms. This chapter on security will review the following:

- Proposed administrative and physical safeguards
- Proposed technical security services and mechanisms
- Proposed trading partner, business associate agreements targeting end-to-end PHI "chain of trust"
- Proposed use of digital signatures to authenticate computer-based records.

ADMINISTRATIVE SECURITY

The proposed security measures have the most impact on providers. Many large payers and clearinghouses have already deployed robust policies and practices for administrative and physical safeguards. In contrast to provider organizations, payers tend to benefit from having to secure less diverse and fewer records at fewer locations.

Providers are exposed to many types of security attacks. There are typically more locations with more access points, more personnel, and more clients than the payers and clearinghouses. In comments regarding the proposed privacy rules, authorities revealed that medical records are the most widely shared personal data. The records tend to be the subject of concerted interest of employers and insurers (eg, life, automobile, health care) to aid them in their application processes.

The proposed HIPAA rules apply broadly to most internal and external processing of patient information. HIPAA mandates that all processes involving the exchange of patient information between business partners be documented in "chain-of-trust" agreements. Covered entities must insist that their uncovered partners practice the same or similar level of efforts to ensure security and confidentiality.

The act and the proposed security and privacy rules limited the coverage to records maintained in computer systems and generated or exchanged by those systems. However, based on the final privacy rule, all forms of individual identifiable information are now covered.

Entities can most efficiently apply the measures if they do not try to distinguish between the sources of information. For payers, all claims, referrals, and enrollment information must be secured and remain confidential. The amount of covered materials increases greatly for providers. For instance, the rules will require demonstrable security measures covering all components of a patient's medical chart, including online-created histories and physicals, flowcharts, intakes, consultations, diagnostic tests and results, registration face sheets, consent forms, and more. The rules also apply to the use of computer monitors and other patient information visible in public areas.

Security and confidentiality rules affect almost all operating departments and staff. For instance, the rules specify that human resources (HR) departments should orient all personnel to the security, privacy, and confidentiality standards. HR will need to establish policies and procedures directed at employee sanctions and terminations due to security violations. In acute-care settings, the key clinical departments will include medical records, correspondence, and emergency. An enterprise will need to institute a chief security or compliance officer or both, security organization, or compliance governance group to ensure ongoing compliance and mandated reporting.

Impacts and Opportunities

The general impacts are profound and widespread. Implementation of the rules will result in the following impacts:

- New or revised security policies and procedures enterprise-wide
- New or revised administrative authentication and access controls to patients' physical records
- Physical security of all computers and workstations and digital record storage
- New or revised record disposal practices
- Capability and procedures to recover archived or locally stored records
- New disclosures to patients and business partners regarding security and confidentiality practices and expectations
- New or revised business partner "chain-of-trust" agreements
- Routine internal security audits
- Initial and updated security risk assessments
- HR hiring practices to include legal, demonstrable background checks
- Demonstrable sanctioning of those violating policies
- Routine reports of security attacks and resolutions.

Most benefits of deploying rigorous security and confidentiality policies are intangible. After implementing the HIPAA security measures, many organizations should be able to improve their image in the community as a trustworthy institution. In addition, having established a strong security infrastructure, an enterprise is better able to accommodate the newer e-Commerce processes. In any case, the security measures will reduce the risk of major lawsuits contesting an enterprise's efforts to prevent negligent or fraudulent release of confidential information.

In December 2000, the Department of Health and Human Services (DHHS) published the final rule to ensure the privacy of PHI. Although distinctions between the concepts of security, confidentiality, and privacy are not well understood, most authorities agree that privacy cannot be ensured without adequate security. Security forms the base for the effective implementation of the new privacy rule.

IT Strategies and Options

The administrative controls and physical safeguards are focused on people, processes, and work flows. To facilitate the application of new controls and safeguards, enterprises should consider some modest information technology (IT) strategies and solutions. These options would include the following:

- An Intranet corporate repository of all relevant and standard departmental and organizational disclosure and consent forms, policies, and procedures

- Database inventory of all information-sensitive locations and equipment
- A secured HIPAA security, confidentiality, and privacy data warehouse for ongoing reporting
- An integrated smart card or biometric employee identification and access control system that encompasses parking, access to controlled areas such as the inpatient and outpatient chart rooms, and computer systems.

Regarding the latter solution, an enterprise should consider a strategy to integrate all security and confidentiality needs. Access control needs to start at all points of entry, including the parking lot and the front and back doors to any covered location. In light of the public's general concern over the perceived unrestrained sharing of personal records, having a reputation for being an effective guardian of patient information will evolve into a competitive advantage. Also, a strong security and confidentiality foundation will enable a dynamic organization to engage successfully and safely in the newly developing e-Commerce economy.

TECHNICAL SECURITY SERVICES AND MECHANISMS

In addition to extensive administrative and physical security measures, HIPAA requires fundamental technical security services and mechanisms. HIPAA mandates that standard transactions and other computer-generated individual-identifiable information be encrypted between business partners. The technical security rules also cover the dynamic world of Internet information exchange. HIPAA mandates which security services and mechanisms need to be in place but not what tools to use. Implementation of industry standard technical security will enable compliance with the published privacy rule. Also, it will make it possible to engage safely in powerful Internet e-Commerce and chronic disease management initiatives between providers and patients.

Currently, the use of technical security is less rigorous than the HIPAA authors recommend. Most health care organizations rely on the typical sign-on and password user entry for the authentication and access control processes. Some health care information systems allow controls on what data elements can be accessed based on a user's sign-on and password. However, most commonly, the systems will only control access to specific screens. A handful of organizations have implemented some form of biometric user authentication via fingerprint algorithms. Few systems or networks provide the required data encryption. Encryption in health care prevails primarily over the Internet.

Security and privacy have become the number one priority for health care IT departments. The results of the 11th annual Healthcare Information Management and Systems Society (HIMSS) leadership survey sponsored by IBM indicate that the respondents' top concern continues to be the threat of internal breaches of security. Nearly three-quarters of the participating providers think that HIPAA compliance is a top security concern. Fewer than half of the provider organizations have undertaken any security initiative. Many now plan to do so, in large part, due to the looming HIPAA mandates. Fortunately, during the past several years, rugged security tools have been developed for networking, legacy, and Internet applications.

Some security and health care information system vendors already portray their products as HIPAA-compliant. Given that the final security rule has yet to be published, that claim reflects more hype than reality. Even when the rule is published, there will be no official list of HIPAA-compliant tools. Becoming HIPAA-compliant necessitates a thorough understanding of the required features as well as the intent of the authors. In turn, implementation must demonstrate a thorough assessment of the exposures to risk and the rationale behind each solution.

Impacts and Opportunities

The HIPAA technical security rules will affect information systems, local and wide area networks, and Internet connectivity of all covered entities. Providers, again, will feel the impacts most heavily. They have the greatest variety of systems and users. Most medical centers and regional health care delivery systems use at least six different patient administrative and clinical systems. These provider systems also employ a highly diverse set of clinical, paramedical, and administrative personnel. Roles vary as to what health care information they must access. In the current state, user authentication and access control policies and procedures are not closely adhered to. Many poor practices commonly prevail at covered entities. Physical safeguards of protected information sources are more likely to exist than the expected technical security safeguards.

Technical security is correctly regarded as an investment in infrastructure. Nevertheless, well-planned and well-implemented technical security can become a springboard to efficient and effective privacy and commerce between business partners, subscribers, and patients. Key impacts associated with the implementation of the HIPAA-mandated security rules are as follows:

- New or revised policies and procedures regarding the use of network resources and legacy systems
- Audit trails and logs of access to individual identifiable information
- Encryption of online and batch transactions
- Enhanced access controls and user authentication measures (Organizations will need to monitor and react effectively to attacks by intruders.)

- Adequate storage, archiving, and recovery of sensitive information
- Upgrades of server and workstation processors to perform high-speed encryption and decryption
- Upgrades to network services and resources to ensure adequate bandwidth, depending on security approach and configuration (Note that implementation of the HIPAA-mandated electronic transactions will also affect network performance.)
- Challenges to productivity and job satisfaction as new security steps are deployed.

Some of the principle opportunities include the following:

- Avoidance of risk of exposure to the accidental and intended publication or use of protected patient information. HIPAA enforcers will bring civil or criminal suits against abusers, and the organization minimizes the loss of business due to adverse publicity.
- Enhanced ability to safely deploy disease and demand management programs targeting at-risk enrolled populations, linking providers and their patients. Such services provided electronically will improve provider productivity and patients' perceptions of their caregivers and, hopefully, enhance the overall continuity and quality of care.
- Recognition by potential business partners in a high-quality, reliable relationship. That recognition should translate to more timely and effective referrals, claims, eligibility, and payment business transactions.

Compliant technical security measures will promote long-term quality relationships with many stakeholders in the overall health care environment.

IT Options and Strategies

The technical security marketplace has witnessed an explosion in related products and services. There are many solutions now available for internal legacy systems, local and wide area networks, and the Internet. Feasible solutions regarding encryption appear to vary from the adequate to the most sophisticated.

Large organizations are considering an initiative for public key infrastructure (PKI) to tackle the network access and authentication controls. An extensive PKI deployment will likely enable the use of digital signatures for employees and possibly patients. HIPAA may mandate the use of digital signatures in the near future. Several states already permit the use of digital signatures for providers to electronically sign medical records.

Most organizations still need to consider an enterprise-wide strategy to both identify and authorize access to their personnel across all patient administration and clinical systems. Some centralized sign-on applications are available but they infrequently ensure the tracking and levels of authorizations and certifications to be required by HIPAA.

The significant IT options and strategies are highlighted below:

- Collaborate with existing legacy health care information system vendors to determine their approach to ensuring compliance with HIPAA technical security.
- Undertake enterprise-wide security compliance strategy, including administrative measures and physical safeguards. Consider several key options:
  —An integrated "smart card" solution encompassing physical and systems access controls.
  —Implementation of a PKI initiative that lays the foundation for user certification and digital signatures while ensuring access control and data integrity.
  —A centralized master personnel identification and authorization "front-end."
  —Use of a biometric identifier such as fingerprints, voiceprints, retinal scans, and DNA identification. Retinal scans appear to have the greatest merit in the long run because of the inherent challenges in counterfeiting retinas.
  —Use of data center outsourcing to reduce risk by contracting with technical security specialists and managers.
- Determine options for efficient and effective audit trails at the levels to be specified in the final rules
- Carefully assess encryption options to select the most cost-effective alternative
- Include the organization's e-Commerce strategy in the statement of requirements.

The implementation of a class A technical security environment will necessitate a significant investment. The payoffs for addressing those requirements can accrue prior to the deadline for HIPAA compliance. In particular, new Web-based business lines enter the realm of feasibility and opportunity. At a minimum, a technically secure organization is best positioned to offer competitively advantageous confidentiality and privacy services.

BUSINESS PARTNER AND CHAIN-OF-TRUST AGREEMENTS

To greatly minimize the risks of sharing PHI, HIPAA-covered entities and their business partners must comply with the provisions of the proposed security and privacy rules. The provisions regarding third-party processing of PHI will necessitate significant new or revised trading partner agreements along with new related policies and procedures. The intents of the provisions are not in dispute; they reflect good business practices in a sensitive health care environment. Ensuring the end-to-end protection and privacy of PHI will enhance the value of covered entities in the eyes of their communities, members, and patients.

The provisions left many related issues unresolved. The proposed security rule did not flesh out the terms of a chain-of-trust agreement nor did it anticipate the privacy provisions. In fact, its sole example involved a hypothetical relationship between two covered entities that must comply with the security provisions regardless of the rule. In contrast, the proposed and final privacy provisions were more extensive and anticipated the entire spectrum of third-party relationships but they were not clear about the application of the security and confidentiality provisions. This section will review the key clauses for contemplated business partner agreements, related issues, and recommendations for compliance.

The proposed security rule requires a "chain-of-trust partner agreement"; whereas the final privacy rule spells out the general terms of a "business associate contractual agreement." These are overlapping concepts but with different emphases. The chain of trust focuses on the protected exchange of patient-identifiable health care data, while the business associate agreement addresses potential privacy violations associated with the use and disclosure of shared PHI. Most HIPAA authorities agree that the soon-to-be published security and the final privacy rules will reflect a consolidated set of business associate agreement terms.

In the health care industry, there are many types of business relationships. Typical partnerships include, but are not limited to, the following:

- Vendor relationships such as:
  —Information technology
  —Suppliers
  —Consultants, including auditors
  —Outsourcing agreements binding outsourcer to expressed and implied industrial performance standards
  —Clearinghouse, claims, statement, and third-party administrator processors requiring technical specifications for the exchange of PHI
  —Claims repricers
  —Eligibility identifiers
  —Couriers
  —Medical record storage and waste managers
  —Billing collections agencies
  —Patient transporters
  —Medical transcriptionists
  —Attorneys
  —Internet content and application providers
- Joint ventures
- Alliances and affiliations

■ Medical services, which can be extremely complex but assumedly do not address the security and privacy of PHI

■ Private accreditation organizations.

Most of the common relationships necessitate sharing of PHI, often without consideration of the security and privacy of the information. As can be noted in the above list, many of the contracted partners are not HIPAA-covered entities. Moreover, some relationships are significantly downstream from a given covered entity responsible for the PHI. Only the privacy provisions attempt to tackle those "downstream" relationships between noncovered entities processing PHI. The principal considerations are reviewed below.

Key Considerations

It appears that HIPAA security and privacy authorities are already blending the chain-of-trust and business partner agreements into one set of general guidelines. For instance, the Security Summit's January 26, 2000, "Draft HIPAA Security Summit Guidelines"[2] documents broadened chain-of-trust guidelines. Davis Wright Tremaine proposes standard contract points in a document drafted for the Los Angeles HIPAA Forum, titled "Preliminary Guidelines for Business Partner/Chain of Trust Agreements."[3] (Their model business associate contract addenda and "placeholder provisions" are available in Appendix D.) Many of the points included in the above documents are interpreted below.

The key considerations for chain-of-trust business partner agreements include:

■ The covered entity binds the business partner (BP) to abide by the current and future HIPAA security, confidentiality, and privacy standards regarding PHI. The agreement would cite the relevant HIPAA business partner provisions.

■ The agreement between the parties limits use and disclosure of PHI to what is permitted in the agreement or contract.

■ A BP must similarly bind their BPs.

■ The terms should limit the sharing of PHI to that which is minimally necessary.

■ The agreement should address the procedures the parties will follow once the PHI is no longer useful depending on the nature of their relationship. The terms should cover the return or disposal of PHI.

■ The agreement needs to consider sanctions regarding violations of the agreement.

■ The covered entity should consider serious sanctions upon violation of the security and privacy provisions.

■ The agreement needs to leave open the possibility to amend and update the terms as HIPAA regulations evolve.

The objective of the proposed terms is to apply the same level of compliance to both the covered entity and all business partners linked by the PHI.

Issues

The final security rule and likely subsequent DHHS guidelines may resolve the following issues:

- *Are HIPAA-defined business partner agreements necessary between covered entities?* The proposed chain-of-trust provisions suggest that they are. Undoubtedly, to do business together, the two covered entities have executed a contract defining their relationship; however, they are, by mandate, both required to comply with the HIPAA provisions.

- *How can the covered entity certify that their chain-of-trust business associate agreements are HIPAA compliant?* The privacy rule goes much further than the security rule in defining compliance. However, the rule, among other issues, did not clarify its relationship to the security provisions' chain-of-trust agreement.

- *Can the contracting parties agree to a compact set of umbrella clauses binding the parties to the rules? Or do they need to identify key security and privacy components pertinent to the nature of their relationship?* The approach of most covered entities will be to develop or obtain standard business associate terms and conditions that can be easily agreed to as contract addenda. Realistically, many agreements will require terms tailored to the business relationship.

- *Although it is clearly intended that the burden of enforcement fall on the covered entity, how far out on the chain does their responsibility extend?* Covered entities must insist that their business associates require their business associates to comply with HIPAA's mandates on the exchange and use of PHI. Those "downstream" relationships are difficult for the original covered entity to enforce.

- *How does the covered entity confirm third-party compliance?* If they reasonably suspect that a partner is noncompliant, they must enforce the related agreement. As a result, they may need to require on-site certifications of compliance.

- *Will business arrangements with diagnostic affiliates require a chain-of-trust business partner agreement?* Providers are generally exempt from having to comply with the business associate agreement provisions while treating patients. They must, nevertheless, comply with security, confidentiality, and privacy provisions.

Recommendations

Thorough compliance with HIPAA regulations requires enterprise-wide participation. In particular, to ensure secure and private transactions with all affected business partners, organizations need to undertake the following:

- Include counsel in any HIPAA assessment; empower them to understand the HIPAA regulations and resolve any outstanding issues. They should become aware of the eventual availability of model agreements through professional societies, forums of industry leaders, or law firms with a HIPAA practice.

- Identify all third-party relationships.

- Assess the need for chain-of-trust business partner agreements based on the nature of the relationship; consider simple umbrella terms in low-risk relationships. Otherwise, use tailored terms based on the key considerations outlined above.

- Use best security practices for those third parties accessing PHI on one's own host systems.

- Insist on open third-party site assessments, ongoing compliance reporting, and complete disclosure, depending on the nature of the relationship.

- Amend agreements to include the most stringent health care industry privacy policies after ensuring HIPAA compliance.

- Amend all existing and interim business partner contracts to include HIPAA compliance requirements.

There are obvious challenges to implementing chain-of-trust business associate agreements. Most HIPAA provisions reflect good business practices, which should already be incorporated in existing contracts. Organizations committed to adopting the best security and privacy policies will derive both a trusted relationship and competitive advantage within their community.

DIGITAL SIGNATURES

The implementation of digital signatures should result in efficient and effective processing of electronic forms of prescriptions, medical notes, reports, and contracts. Electronically signed documents will provide timely completion of business agreements and reduce fraud. For these reasons, the HIPAA authors originally proposed promoting and setting standards for digital signatures on health care documents not covered by the HIPAA transaction standards.

Federal standards would likely preempt the differing state standards and limitations. They will, however, be a challenge to implement. In addition, the proposed HIPAA requirements for digital signature are primarily technical in nature and do not address when and who should use them.

HIPAA sponsors had intended to include the digital signature requirements as part of the planned security and confidentiality rules. They revised that approach, however, and will publish a separate rule for digital signatures. To successfully promulgate rule-setting standards for digital signatures, they face several major challenges from:

- Accelerating pressures to facilitate Internet e-Commerce by having a federal standard that preempts current state limitations.
- Evolving technological initiatives where digital signatures must operate. For instance, PKI initiatives and other encryption/decryption strategies will provide platforms for digital signatures. Also, certificates of authority will likely be involved with the authentication of digital signatures.

Digital signatures already play a major role in health care. Until the onslaught of business-to-business (B2B) e-Commerce via the Internet, they have been predominantly used to expedite physician attestations of notes and reports required for billing or further services.

Among other uses of the physician's signature, the Centers for Disease Control and Prevention relies on signed reports for their cancer registry. The physician's signature normally vouches for the content of the report and indicates that the record should become permanent. Medical records professionals (or health information managers) use electronic signatures to indicate that a set of records has been well maintained in their possession and should be complete. Some states have approved digital signatures for use on medical records. However, among other processing bottlenecks, there is still a delay in processing claims requiring signed clinical report attachments.

On August 22, 2000, President Clinton signed into law the "Electronic Signatures in Global and National Commerce Act"[4] (popularly termed E-Sign) was signed into law. Although the Internet e-Commerce community welcomed the law, it is unclear how its benefits will accrue to the health care industry. For instance, the law applies specifically to interstate commerce and therefore voids the states' handwriting and hard-copy requirements. At this time, however, state provider licensing regulations seriously constrain the delivery of interstate health care services. In turn, encrypted electronic data interchange transactions transmitted over a secure connection as mandated by HIPAA do not require digital signatures. In any case, E-Sign does establish a backdrop favorable to the eventual elimination of intrastate limitations.

To be HIPAA compliant, digital signatures would have properties similar to handwritten signatures as follows:

- They authenticate and vouch for the content of the record.
- The signer or user of a digital signature cannot deny his or her signature.
- They would be tied to a specific date.
- They could be countersigned.
- There can be more than one signature per record.
- They would be associated with a particular purpose.

In health care, where digital signatures are allowed by state law, providers often "sign" their transcribed medical reports or electronic documents by means of a secured sign-on and password. Most often, the transcription or medical record system permits only one signature per document. The system uses an indicator in the record to acknowledge that the physician has signed the document.

Sometimes the "signature" is encrypted to prevent alteration. The system then prevents the document from being modified. Any other technical features would likely prevent the record from being used by other systems and thus become "non-interoperable" per the proposed standard. It would seem that the current state of health care applications and technology is challenged in accommodating the soon-to-be-prescribed digital signature requirements.

Impacts and Opportunities

With the advent of profitable B2B Internet commerce, digital signatures will enable new efficiencies between supply chain partners. They will be useful for timely authorization signatures on product and service agreements. In health care, they will enable the electronic exchange and storage of documents that have previously remained in paper form because a signature was required. In addition, they can aid in HIPAA's intention to eliminate fraud.

Other specific impacts and opportunities include the following:

- Investment in a proper security infrastructure to support digital signatures (It is noteworthy that to best secure digital signatures they should not be kept on local workstations thereby necessitating a comprehensive network-centric solution.)
- Upgrade of applications to recognize and accept the signatures
- Reduction in delays of processing referrals and complex claims through elimination of supporting paper medical reports
- Timely, accurate, and reliable filling and modifying of prescriptions, enhancing patient satisfaction
- Timely product and service agreements, enhancing vendor cash flows and contractor's ability to initiate projects on schedule
- Speedier delivery of care where official authorizations are required
- Improved quality of medical records and downstream delivery of care
- Improved provider productivity and quality of care due to new modes of provider and patient care relationships
- Timely and reliable ordering of ancillary diagnostic service requests
- Fostering of telemedicine programs as states relax restrictions on interstate delivery of health care services.

IT Options and Strategies

A digital signature is, by definition, a technical object. Investors in digital signatures should ensure that their solution is based on their business requirements and the technology platforms to support them.

The reliable implementation of digital signatures in compliance with the proposed HIPAA features is not a trivial task. The issue needs to be addressed as a component of an enterprise-wide security and confidentiality initiative. Current usage of digital signatures will not likely meet the HIPAA standards.

Providers face the most compelling and complex technological challenges. In order to ensure the authentication capability of a large number of responsible parties, they must contend with many incomplete technical solutions available in the commercial market. The primary maturing technologies include PKI, XML (extensible markup language), and certificates of authority. The certificates of authority provide a third-party authentication of the user, much like a driver's license is used in many face-to-face transactions. The practices of secure, confidential, and private health care depends on knowing exactly who is electronically signing a clinical document, and therein are both the challenge and the promised payoffs.

REFERENCES

1. Dr Ted Cooper is one of the authors of the Computer-Based Patient Record Institute's *HIPAA PRI Security Toolkit,* which includes presentation materials and a thorough statement of security policy and procedures. See www.cpri-host.org.

2. *Draft HIPAA Security Summit Guidelines.* Version 1.2. Presented at: HIPPA Security Summit. Baltimore, Md: Oct 11–13. Available at www.smed.com/hipaa/draft.pdf.

3. Davis Wright Tremaine LLP (San Francisco, Calif). Preliminary guidelines for business partner/chain of trust agreements. Presented at: HIPAA Forum, Los Angeles, Calif. Available at www.HIPAAUSA.com. Accessed July 26, 2000.

4. Electronic Signatures in Global and National Commerce Act ("E-Sign"). P.L. 106-229. Passed by both houses on June 30, 2000, and signed into law Aug 22, 2000.

chapter 6

Privacy

Early adopters of the final HIPAA privacy standards among health care enterprises likely will experience a competitive advantage by ensuring the confidentially of sensitive patient and member information. This chapter reviews the final privacy rule, the industry's debate over its new requirements, the ensuing May 2001 federal guidelines and March 2002 Privacy Modification NPRM promoting a practical interpretation of the rule, the possible information technology (IT) investments and strategies for compliance, and ways for providers to adopt many of the provisions prior to the HIPAA deadline.

The Department of Health and Human Services (DHHS) published the Privacy Modification NPRM in order to fulfill its promises in the earlier May 2001 federal guidelines to clarify the final privacy rule and to respond to outstanding industry interest groups' criticisms. Several modifications surprised those following the transformation of the national health privacy legislation. DHHS limited the comment period to 30 days. In light of the likely heated debate over the proposed changes, DHHS may not be able to publish the final rule until the summer of 2002.

The proposed privacy modifications may affect the December 2000 final privacy rule as noted in bracketed material throughout chapter.

GENERAL IMPACTS OF THE PRIVACY RULE

Heightened practices to ensure privacy will come with a significant investment in reengineered business processes. Providers, health plans, and electronic data interchange (EDI) clearinghouses will have to comply with the final HIPAA privacy rule. It lays out profound impacts on current practices. These impacts include the following:

■ Exempting the provider from meeting the "minimal necessary" standard to use or disclose protected health care information (PHI) needed to treat, bill, or perform normal health care operations. Thus, if a clinician, in the course of treating a patient, reasonably believes that a referred consulting physician who has obtained the patient's consent to use PHI should have access to the entire patient record, he or she should feel comfortable in meeting the terms of the final rule.

- Ensuring patients' rights to access and amend their medical records.
- Providing an "accounting of disclosures" to third parties to the patient's PHI. The covered entities must maintain records for up to 6 years. Providers do not have to report uses or disclosures made to third parties prior to the April 2003 compliance date. [The proposed modification eliminates the need to account for all external disclosures. The provider must be able to account for all external disclosures not specifically authorized by the patient.]
- Defining and limiting permitted disclosures and uses of a patient's records. Entities will need to identify in policies and procedures who needs routine access to categories of PHI and under what conditions. Providers need to make "reasonable efforts to limit PHI to the minimum necessary. . . ." Providers must also institute a formal HIPAA employee privacy-training program analogous to the security training required in the proposed security rule.
- The final rule goes to great lengths to define the efforts needed to de-identify PHI.
- The final rule establishes the criteria for a valid patient authorization.
- Permitting patients' restrictions on who, and under what conditions, can access their records. However, providers do not have to agree to the restrictions.
- Requiring an initial consent to the provider's use or disclosure of PHI for the purpose of treatment, payment, and health care operations. Providers may withhold treatment if the patient refuses to agree to the consent. [The proposed modification would eliminate the need for the initial consent. Providers have the option to require consents, but they cannot decline treatment if a patient refuses to sign the consent.]
- Notifying patients or members of the entity's privacy policy. The notice-of-privacy policy must be a separate document, ie, it cannot be combined with the consent to use or disclose PHI for treatment, billing, or administration. The patient must be informed about the entity's privacy policy. If the covered entity operates an Internet Web site, they may notify its members and patients of their privacy policy via the Web site. [The proposed modification requires that the provider undertake a "good faith" effort to have the patient review the privacy policy notice and acknowledge having read it.]
- Defining the general requirements of a business associate agreement. The final rule relaxed the requirement that a covered entity must ensure the compliance of its business associate. Instead, they must respond appropriately whenever they become aware of a violation. [The proposed modification would extend the deadline for executing the business associate agreements until April 14, 2004, a 1-year extension.]

■ Defining the conditions for the uses and disclosures of PHI for marketing and fund-raising purposes. [The proposed modification would require patient authorization for the use of PHI for marketing purposes, but it removes the patient "opt-out" provision for approved marketing uses.]

■ Requiring the designation of a privacy official.

■ Defining the right and process to file a complaint with the secretary of the DHHS.

American Health Information Management Association's (AHIMA's) Policy and Government Relations Team performed one of the best operations-focused analyses of the final privacy provisions. Readers are encouraged to review their report, "Final Rule for Standards for Privacy of Individually Identifiable Health Information."[1]

PRIVACY AS A NATIONAL CONCERN

In response to the proposed rule, health care industry stakeholders reacted with many polar and forceful comments. In spite of their adverse reactions, health privacy was and still is in the public spotlight. As a backdrop to the publication of this federal health care privacy policy, representatives of the 106th Congress have proposed at least 15 new bills directly addressing medical information privacy. The previously proposed HIPAA provisions reflected most of the privacy protection themes encoded in those bills.

One of those bills mandating new privacy regulations, the Gramm–Leach–Bliley Act (GLB), was enacted into law in 1999. The Federal Trade Commission published GLB's Title V final privacy rule May 24, 2000, requiring banks and insurance companies to adopt a privacy policy and notify their customers by July 2001. Although it was widely understood that health plans, particularly HMOs, would also be covered, California's Department of Corporations exempted them.

The public's current attention to its right of privacy in and out of health care is probably due to published incidents of misuse of personal information via the Web. There is also a palpable public sentiment that breakthroughs in DNA technologies will provide health plans opportunities to deny coverage or employers opportunities to deny employment to someone with a detected genetic flaw. People are reluctant to divulge all of their medical problems when they sense that the information cannot be kept private. In their introduction, the authors of the privacy rule acknowledged that the Association of American Physicians and Surgeons had indicated that 78% of its members reported withholding information from a patient's record due to privacy concerns. Another 87% reported having had patients request to have information withheld from their records.

CURRENT STATE OF PRIVACY IN THE HEALTH CARE INDUSTRY

The health care industry has always held confidentiality and privacy of medical records as core values. Physicians need not be reminded of the dictates of the Hippocratic oath in which they commit that "Whatever . . . I see or hear, in the life of men, which ought not to be spoken of abroad, I will not divulge, as reckoning that all such should be kept secret." Hospitals limit access to patient charts to persons with a clear need to know. Clinics typically keep records under constant vigilance and well secured after-hours. Teams implementing hospital and integrated health care network systems have consistently configured restrictions on the user's ability to access celebrity or other sensitive information.

Although patients are usually informed about the possible use of their information and can have access to their records, they do not now have rights to amend their records, neither to restrict who can access them nor to obtain a disclosure of those accessing them.

There has been one recent major industry effort to confirm a patient's right to privacy. In 1999, a coalition of various stakeholders, including health plans, physicians, nurses, employers, disability and mental health advocates, and accreditation organizations as well as experts in public health, medical ethics, information systems, and health policy, adopted a set of "best principles" for health care privacy.[2] In July 1999, the Health Privacy Working Group published its "Best Principles for Health Privacy."[3]

ESTIMATED COST OF PRIVACY COMPLIANCE

HIPAA-covered entities have always invested in ensuring the privacy of medical records. To comply with HIPAA, however, they will have to step up their investment. Much of the additional expense will include process improvements, new policies and procedures, and ongoing employee training. The biggest expenses for compliance are projected to be those related to required changes in technology infrastructure.

The secretary of DHHS has estimated the overall costs of implementation to be $17.6 billion over 10 years. Two major industry-sponsored cost studies of implementing health care privacy legislation have estimated significantly greater costs. Their cost estimates ranged from $4 billion to almost $43 billion. In the fall of 1999, the Blue Cross/Blue Shield Association commissioned the Robert E. Nolan Company Inc to perform the first major cost analysis.[4] In December 2000, the American Hospital Association (AHA) engaged First Consulting Group (FCG) to assess the costs to implement the proposed privacy rule.[5] FCG did estimate significantly lower costs than Nolan did. Both summarized the estimated costs over 5 years as displayed in Table 6-1.

T A B L E   6-1

Estimated 5-Year Costs to Implement Proposed Privacy Rule

Cost Component	Blue Cross/ Blue Shield Association Report, million dollars	AHA Report,* million dollars
State law preemption	0	351
Business partner contracting	†	2,364
Minimum necessary use (consents, authorizations, and disclosures) and training	11,040	101
Infrastructure,† includes business contracts	23,400	19,384
Medical and referral management	4,400	
Patient right to amend medical record	4,000	
Other		325
Total* FCG reported low end costs of $4,003M	42,840	22,525

Source: Information compiled from *Blue Cross Blue Shield Association Report*, 1999 and *American Hospital Association Report*, 2000. Note: Blank spaces indicate no comparable estimated dollars.

According to a follow-up assessment requested by AHA after the final rule was published, the industry respondents indicated little or no reduction in estimated costs. Realistically, the guidelines for the final rule should result in a reduction of the estimated privacy implementation costs. Although compliance with the privacy rule will require a significant investment in IT and business process changes, hopefully, it will be much less than the lower estimate above. To mitigate against taking on unwarranted expenses, HIPAA officials are asking only for reasonable and diligent efforts. Other impacts and opportunities are outlined below.

IMPACTS AND OPPORTUNITIES

All covered organizations will have to reduce their vulnerability to intrusions into their members' and patients' records. The greatest onus of compliance with the privacy rule will fall on the providers, large and small. The obvious business impacts and opportunities associated with the privacy provisions are as follows:

■ Many new and revised policies and procedures covering:
  —Ongoing employee in-service training to ensure compliance with the "minimally necessary" standard
  —Establishment of a privacy officer, who may also be the chief security officer, required by the proposed security rule

—Disclosure of a notice of privacy practice and privacy policy to patients and their formal acknowledgment

—Procedures to log and save most accesses of a patient's records for uses to provide treatment, bill, or perform administrative operations

—Procedures to document and possibly honor a patient's restrictions on disseminating any part of his or her medical records. The organization does not have to agree to any restriction. If they do agree to restrict access, they must be capable of fulfilling that restriction.

- Improvement of medical data for allowable disease, demand and outcomes management research and analysis

- Significant efforts to grapple with the "gray areas" of the rule. (Fortunately, providers have barely 1 year now before they are required to implement the entire rule. During this period, there may be further clarifications and industry collaboration to surface unintended adverse effects of the provisions.)

POST FINAL RULE PUBLICATION DEBATE

After publication of the privacy rules and before the extended comment period ends, key professional organizations and business associations lobbied strongly against several of the provisions, including:

- AHA expressed concerns in a letter to the US president concerning the reasonableness of many of the requirements and the costs to implement them. Their extensive comments can be found on their Web site as well as the HIPAA Advisory and Workgroup for Electronic Data Interchange Web sites.

- The Blue Cross/Blue Shield Association advocated strongly on behalf of the providers to extend the transaction and privacy deadlines.

Other representative industry comments included the following:

- From the *New York Times*:[6] New Privacy Rules Are Challenged," the Health Care Leadership Council (HCLC) (50 chief executive officers from large health care companies) indicated that:

—They were concerned with the new feature requiring doctors, hospitals, and other health care providers to obtain a general written consent before disclosing their medical information, even for routine purposes like treatment or payment of claims.

—Providers need to retain consent forms for 6 years. HCLC is worried that providers would have the "privacy police" looking over their shoulders.

- The global leader of PriceWaterhouseCoopers' privacy practice stated that [their] "clients in the health care industry need to be alarmed . . . [they] are light-years away from complying . . . ."[7]

■ Janlori Goldman, Director of the Health Privacy Project at Georgetown University (Washington, DC), argued, "the administration did lots of hard work trying to make it a strong privacy law but also workable for the health care industry, and I think it has done that."[8]

■ Psychiatrist Charles Welch, MD, vice president of the Massachusetts Medical Society was quoted as saying, "Doctors and patients will be able to talk about the illness and its treatment freely and openly in an atmosphere of trust."[9]

■ William Winkenwerder, MD, executive vice president for Health Care Services at Blue Cross/Blue Shield of Massachusetts commented, "We support these regulations and believe they are important for the country."[10]

■ Local Massachusetts health executives felt that "Most area hospitals and HMOs will easily absorb these costs. Many . . . have already implemented some of the changes."[11]

■ Local Massachusetts physicians were most pessimistic in noting that, " . . . smaller physicians' practices, especially those with fewer than 10 doctors and those in rural areas, will be drastically hurt, perhaps put out of business."[12]

Some interpretations of the privacy rule, however, appeared extremely dire to key HIPAA and health care privacy proponents. To counter many of the prominent unfavorable versions of the provisions, the Health Privacy Project of the Institute for Health Care Research and Policy of Georgetown University, Washington, DC, published their paper "Myths and Facts about the Federal Medical Privacy Regulation" in early April. The complete text is included in Appendix F.

In response to the intense pressure to significantly amend or overturn the rule, Tommy Thompson, secretary of DHHS, opened up a comment period of 1 month. Somewhat surprisingly, after the comment period the Bush Administration allowed the final privacy rule to become effective without any immediate changes after the hearings. DHHS, however, issued federal privacy rule guidelines that interpret and clarify some of the provisions. In addition, DHHS indicated they would seek rule changes for certain provisions they saw as having unintended results hampering the providers' ability to treat patients.

THE MODERATING EFFECTS OF THE FEDERAL GUIDELINES

The federal guidelines interpret the impact of the provisions closer to current industry privacy and confidentiality practices. The guidelines affirm the general commonsense interpretation promoted by such HIPAA leaders as Bill Braithwaite, senior advisor on health information policy, and others. In general, they illustrate the intention at the federal level to enable effective medical care while prescribing ethical and professional privacy and confidentiality standards. Many of the guidelines demonstrate how covered entities can benefit if the initial significant estimates of privacy implementation costs are reduced. The guidelines clarified the prevailing misperceived or unintended impact of the privacy rule, as highlighted below. The guidelines clarified various aspects of the privacy rule:

■ Reduced efforts on behalf of covered entities to monitor business associate agreements. They will, nonetheless, need to respond energetically to violations and breaches brought to their attention.

■ "Broadened" treatment referral and indirect services processes. For instance, a laboratory department or service does not need to obtain patient consent prior to completing an order for a diagnostic test.

   —Consents need only be obtained by a provider one time and are to be effective until revoked.

   —Exempted health plans and clearinghouses from obtaining consents.

   —An intended rule change will enable pharmacists to fill first-time patient prescriptions without having a consent on hand.

■ Clarified the application of standard of determining what is "minimally necessary." Entities will need policies affecting internal PHI exchanges and computer system authorizations to access PHI.

■ Typical treatment-oriented oral communications (including intern and resident training rounds) from disclosure provisions and physical alterations of patient rooms are not subject to the privacy rule.

■ Effectively limited disclosure tracking to external releases of PHI.

■ Clarified what is required in the patient authorizations for release of PHI.

The guidelines addressed several of the five AHA "pressing" concerns recently presented in a letter to President Bush. Those concerns, summarized in AHA's privacy cost report and quoted below, included:

■ The requirement to obtain written consent for standard uses of information

■ Restrictions on the amount of information that can be shared among providers for purposes of treatment

■ The huge paperwork burden created by business associate contracts

■ Impediments to discussions among caregivers and patients

■ The need for advisory opinions to identify conflicting state laws.

The guidelines did leave the following areas weakened, unsimplified, or unqualified:

■ State versus federal privacy preemption

■ Marketing uses of PHI. For the purposes of marketing and fund-raising, the covered entities must provide the patient with an "opt-out" capability. To use PHI for marketing, the rule is restrictive.

■ To lesser degree, disclosure tracking and reporting. Providers still need to adopt specific best practices to minimize the effects of these processes.

■ Content of the privacy policy.

The issue of state preemption principally revolves around the question of what constitutes more stringent regulations of privacy. For example, HIPAA requires that patients have the right to see and amend their medical records. If the state regulation is not contradictory and affords a greater right of access to the patient, then state law regulates.

   The complexity of dealing with state law makes resolving a possible violation very challenging. In particular, most states have many laws that could impact privacy of health information. California has more than five applicable statutes. The morass is further complicated by the likelihood that for any electronic exchange, a covered entity may involve business associates in several states. In addition, there are other federal laws and agencies affecting privacy and confidentiality, such as those in the following list, which are provided in the discussion within the privacy rule:

■ The Privacy Act of 1974
■ The Freedom of Information Act
■ Federal Substance Abuse Act—Confidentiality
■ Employee Retirement Income Security Act of 1974
■ The Family Educational Rights and Privacy Act
■ Gramm–Leach–Bliley Act
■ Various federally funded health programs' requirements
■ Food, Drug, and Cosmetic Act (Federal Drug Administration)
■ Clinical Laboratory Improvement Amendments
■ Other mandatory federal or state laws
■ Federal disability nondiscrimination laws
■ US Safe Harbor Privacy Principles.

THE CLARIFICATION AND SIMPLIFICATIONS OF THE PROPOSED PRIVACY MODIFCATION RULE

DHHS issued the Privacy Modification NPRM on March 21, 2002, and published it in the Federal Register on March 28, 2002. The proposed privacy modifications left most of the final privacy rule intact. In its most controversial revision regarding patient consents to use PHI for treatment, billing, and normal operations, DHHS reverted back to the original Clinton administration proposal that consents to use PHI for treatment, billing, and normal health care operations should be optional. It allows for providers to require consents but doing so is at their discretion. Moreover, providers may not decline treatment when the patient refuses to sign the consent.

The criticisms to the proposed modifications come primarily from the patients rights' groups well represented by the Health Privacy Project, the former secretary of DHHS, Donna Shalala, and the office of Senator Ted Kennedy. Senator Kennedy plans to hold hearings particularly of the proposal making the consents to use PHI optional. The Health Privacy Project felt that the change was "destructive."[13] In general, those who advocated maintaining the consent requirements, such as *USA Today's* editorial board, felt that operational efficiencies were held more valuable than the right to privacy.[14]

Other industry groups, such as the American Hospital Association, were pleased by the changes. In an article in the *Report on Patient Privacy* published a few weeks ahead of the publication of the proposed privacy modification rule, Bill Braithwaite, former senior advisor on health information at DHHS, argued against the final privacy rule's insistence on collecting the patient's consent with the provider's ability to decline treatment if the patient did not agree. He stated, "there are many circumstances in which the consent mandate is unrealistic given the intricate complex relationships that make up the health care delivery system. Put succinctly, it has no meaning and clearly isn't workable."[15]

Donna Shalala expressed the hope that DHHS would be able to strengthen the proposed good faith notification of a patient's right to privacy.[16] She was also disappointed that the marketing provisions diluted the restriction on what could be provided to a patient regarding possible treatment or medications without a patient's authorization.

The proposed privacy modifications also included the following changes:

- Require providers to use good faith efforts to obtain the patient's acknowledgment of having reviewed the notice of privacy policy. Providers must be able to explain why those good faith efforts may have failed.

- Enable providers to refer and schedule patients with specialists or other health care entities without requiring the referred to provider to first obtain a patient's consent. Additionally, pharmacists would not need a consent before providing medications.

- Enable hospitals and health care systems to share PHI with their affiliated providers and diagnostic service entities for their billing purposes.

- Defer to state regulations regarding parent or guardian access to an unemancipated minor's patient records.

- Soften the "minimum necessary" requirement for the use of disclosure of PHI to accept incidental disclosures resulting from possible overheard oral communications.

- Accept indirect identifiers for research data. The proposed modification requests further industry inputs regarding how to adequately de-identify data while allowing effective use of the data.
- Restrict the marketing use of PHI to those patients who have authorized such use.
- Postpone the compliance with the business associates agreements for 1 year.

Other than the above and several technical or modest wording changes, the mandates of the privacy rule remain the same. The Bush administration has clearly demonstrated its support of national privacy legislation. At the same time, it attempts to address the compelling industry criticisms of operational inefficiencies in the final privacy rule.

IT INVESTMENT OPTIONS AND STRATEGIES

Confidentiality and privacy reflect core values for health care enterprises. They should therefore drive many of the requirements for an enterprise-wide security strategy that includes IT. Organizations must anticipate that most of their legacy and newer Web-based member- or patient-oriented systems will need to be enhanced to comply with HIPAA.

Technologies to address the implications of both the likely federal legislation and HIPAA are still maturing. For instance, the September 11, 2000, copy of *INFO WORLD* has this headline: "Privacy Spurs Innovation."[17] Internet-centric health care entities will need to consider investing in some of the emerging privacy solutions for the Web. To enforce privacy on current legacy systems, most organizations will need to work with their existing vendors or internal IT departments.

Some of the IT investment options and strategies to ensure privacy include the following:

- Work with existing vendors or internal staff to determine the HIPAA privacy compliance strategy that includes the following features:
  - —Make audit trails and logs easier to manage. The logs of both authorized and attempted accesses to identifiable health care information must be stored for disclosure efficiently and effectively.
  - —Integrate new features such as acknowledgments that patients have been provided the privacy policy and that they have agreed to receive the privacy policy electronically.
  - —Record each patient's restrictions on accessing his or her records.
  - —Enhance access controls to reflect the patients' restrictions. The solution will likely be complex and expensive to develop.
- Assess new entrants in the security, confidentiality, and privacy arenas for their Internet applications requiring the identification and authentication of those accessing protected health care information.

■ Ensure that an enterprise-wide security strategy includes the requirements for privacy, confidentiality, and e-Commerce initiatives.

A solution that realizes the benefits of HIPAA while minimizing expenses requires a combined global, creative, systematic, and practical approach:

■ **Global, not suboptimal thinking**. Consider all of HIPAA, particularly the widespread systems and business process benefits of the standard transactions, code sets, and unique identifiers.

■ **Systematic**. Structure the analysis to include many objective and subjective factors.

■ **Creative**. Include ways to take advantage of existing systems and processes.

■ **Practical**. Consider what is reasonable given a specific risk.

Below are two scenarios illustrating the implementation of new disclosure and consent tracking processes. The goal is to highlight efficient and effective solutions for privacy compliance.

Scenario 1: Disclosure of Medical Record Information

In the hospital setting, the correspondence function of the Department of Health Information Management (HIM) is typically responsible for obtaining all authorizations and providing external releases of patients' records. The guidelines target the external releases to be tracked in order to be able to disclose them in a reasonable amount of time after a patient's request. Frequently, other areas in the hospital, such as social services and discharge planning, might release medical information. The providers will need system enhancements to record the specific authorizations and disclosures and report on them later.

To meet the guidelines, the covered entity must insist that HIM control both the authorizations and releases. If that is not feasible for timely performance reasons, the entities need HIM to provide oversight, leadership, and training. The department's computer system needs to be enhanced to note the elements required for authorizations specified in the guidelines.

This proposed solution has the advantages of building on current practices, reflecting the patients' rights, minimizing system reengineering, and maintaining controls where they should be.

Scenario 2: Consent Tracking [Revised in light of proposed privacy modifications]

To obtain the initial HIPAA-compliant acknowledgments of having received the privacy policy and estimate related costs, the Nolan study presumed 100% mass mailings, pursuing nonrespondents and recording the consents. New, legal counsel-approved privacy policy forms are required as a means to record patients' acknowledgments. In addition, the provider's computer system needs an additional ability to note the patients' review of the privacy policy.

A possible solution is to obtain the patients' reviews of the privacy policy as they visit their providers. Currently, at the time of admission and sometimes at outpatient registration, providers already require the recording of consent for treatment and assignment of benefits. The consent is kept in the patient's chart.

The admitting or registration staff often navigates through 6 to 12 computer screens or windows to complete the following steps:

- Identify patient
- Confirm patient and demographics
- Obtain and confirm insurance plans and benefits
- Obtain and confirm guarantor information
- Obtain and confirm subscriber information
- Confirm primary care physician, allergies, drug reactions, and other medical information
- Confirm contact and next of kin
- Confirm employer and related information
- Obtain the patient's wishes to have the hospital stay remain confidential, if applicable.

Thus, the privacy policy acknowledgments could be obtained at the first patient encounter or the first time there is a need to use the patient's information. As a result, another computer screen or window would be added to the admitting or registration process. The staff would record, one time only, that the patient has reviewed the privacy policy. The actual form can be signed and placed in or on the patient's chart. Electronic patient signatures in the computer system are valid.

This additional step in the admitting and registration process may seem burdensome. However, with implementation of HIPAA standard enrollment and the point-of-service eligibility transactions, most of the following data can be available for new and recurring patients prior to any encounter:

- Patient demographics
- Insurance company and health plan
- Guarantor and subscriber demographics
- Contact information
- Employer data.

Effective systems engineering can enable staff to bypass the step to collect the privacy policy acknowledgment until the authorization expires or the patient wishes to revoke it. By implementing a strategy to record most acknowledgments upon the first encounter or a need to use PHI, the ongoing implementation costs are both reduced and more evenly distributed.

Again, the solution builds on current processes, simplifies them, and takes advantage of a growing body of professionally endorsed privacy policies. Both scenarios highlight the need for an integrated reengineering strategy to minimize the undisputed significant costs of implementing HIPAA.

The HIPAA privacy rule will engender enhanced business practices. Nevertheless, efficient compliance operations will depend on both pragmatic and strategic solutions. Ensuring privacy in health care reflects good business practices. Moreover, it improves the quality of care, the associated patient records, and medical research by fostering trust between a provider and his or her patient.

EARLY PARTIAL ADOPTION OF THE PRIVACY STANDARDS

The privacy rule includes both a set of standards and related implementation specifications. Most of the implementation specifications are clearly stated but devoid of details. The dilemma for providers is where and how they must make changes in order to comply. Providers are probably now vulnerable to patient complaints regarding both unintended and intentional unauthorized disclosures of PHI. As a result, providers can and should fix many of their privacy gaps prior to the deadline. Early implementation of specific privacy solutions reduces the risk and softens the eventual impacts as the deadline to comply approaches. The following section highlights both the risks of noncompliance for all covered entities and the relatively inexpensive, easy security and privacy fixes for hospital and physician office settings.

The degree of overall risk of HIPAA noncompliance varies considerably by the type of covered entity, as projected in Table 6-2.

TABLE 6-2

Overall Risk by Type of Covered Entity

Covered Entity	EDI	Security	Privacy
Health plans, third-party administrators, repricers	Medium to high	Low to medium	Low to medium
Clearinghouses	Low	Low	Low
Integrated delivery networks and regional health care systems	Medium to high	Medium	High
Hospitals and medical centers	Medium	High	High
Clinics and small physician groups	Low	Medium	High
Large physician groups	Medium to high	Medium	High

Clearinghouses

The clearinghouses are at the least risk for EDI noncompliance largely because they are motivated to stay ahead of the other entities. Because they are principally technology-based their primary security concerns will involve wide area network encryption and user authentication services. Few, if any, have business associate agreements requiring either online or hard-copy access to protected health care information.

Health Plans

Most health plans have significant experiences with EDI and secured physical sites and computer systems. Nevertheless, many have numerous provider and clearinghouse partners. In addition, they are burdened with HIPAA-mandated EDI standards to automate the coordination of benefits. However, most Blue Cross/Blue Shield plans have developed their own systems tailored to their pre-HIPAA needs. Thus, in spite of their long history with health care EDI, the health plans need to assess their compliance risks.

Health plans should address the complex testing challenges in their assessments. Many health plans are facing hundreds of EDI interfaces to be tested across as many as eight different transaction standards in less than a year.

The payers additionally need to address new privacy provisions. Although the impact of the privacy rule on them is likely to be widespread, their environments are much less complex than those of providers.

Providers

All provider organizations will have to seriously augment both their security and privacy practices. With regard to EDI, the larger provider organizations have had some experience with proprietary transaction definitions and, possibly, in the supply chain arena, the standard payment transaction.

Many providers have also become dependent on vendor-supplied solutions for their EDI compliance. To optimize the vendors' intended HIPAA enhancements, providers must assess their own business processes to evaluate the best ways to utilize the proffered solutions. Testing with the numerous payer trading partners will be one of the most critical areas to address in a risk assessment.

Large provider organizations will encounter major challenges when striving to understand and plan for implementing the mandated security and privacy regulations. Acute-care facilities are particularly at risk for breaches of privacy standards. They are typically complex settings with numerous points of entry, diverse visitors and types of employees, and areas where PHI is used or maintained. They are, of course, the principal repositories of protected health care information. Large and small providers will require careful assessments of their current environments to determine the most effective and reasonable solutions to meet the HIPAA security and privacy provisions.

On the one hand, small providers may be at low risk for implementing whatever EDI solutions their practice management system vendors may provide. On the other hand, they are unlikely to benefit greatly from the widely promoted productivity and revenue gains foreseen for the HIPAA EDI implementers. To benefit at all, they must take a systematic assessment of their needs and options. Some may regrettably feel that it will be simpler to resort to paper claims, thereby avoiding the impacts of HIPAA altogether.

For their security and privacy assessments and implementations, small providers are likely to benefit from tools, templates, and the implementation wisdom of their affiliates and professional societies. Many templates and tools should become readily available via the Internet as the industry progresses toward compliance.

EARLY PROVIDER SOLUTIONS

Dr Cooper, Kaiser Permanente, in the July 31, 2000, AISHealth.com in their e-mailed *Business News of the Week*,[18] recommended that solutions be crafted from the perspective of how we would want our mother's PHI handled. No entity can anticipate all the ways that PHI can be abused. As Dr Cooper indicated, "Every permutation that can happen will happen." The goal is to develop compliance solutions that can reasonably anticipate and address them. It is likely that many vulnerabilities exists. The solutions highlighted below for acute-care and physician settings provide short- and long-term opportunities to minimize them.

Acute-Care Settings

Hospitals, medical centers, and regional delivery networks are most burdened by the need to engineer new consents, health care privacy notices, record keeping, and business associate agreements. They need to thoroughly assess existing processes and contracts before undertaking extensive enterprise-wide implementation solutions. Before deploying those strategic privacy initiatives, they can solve some basic lax policies and processes.

The likely remedies include the following:

- *Entry points* such as cafeteria doors, loading dock areas, and doors kept ajar for smokers require stricter observance by security and reminders to employees to keep locked.
- At those entry points, *all* personnel must demonstrate credentials, as would be required of any other visitors.
- Core computer system policy changes
  —Policy reminders to all staff to avoid use of the core computer systems to determine the health status of friends, relatives, and other acquaintances. Other new or restated policies should encourage all staff to log off the systems whenever they are drawn away from their workstation.

—Limit dial-up access to systems

—Remove system access privileges immediately upon termination of an employee

—Eliminate generic and shared sign-ons and passwords

- At all areas using or keeping PHI, such as the medical records departments, patient examination areas, admitting, registration, billing, cafeteria, elevators, and satellite facilities, staff need to:

—Require authorization for access from all visiting personnel

—Restrict use of and visual access to white boards, confidential fax transmittals, and patients' history and physical clipboards

- Nonmedical record departments such as discharge planning, social services, case management, and utilization review will likely need in-service training on disclosure policies and procedures regarding the use of PHI fax transmittals and the provision of records to transporters.

- Copies of PHI such as ancillary orders, IV and specimen labels, copied clinical reports, and face sheets require formal, effective destruction procedures. Facilities will likely need to invest in inexpensive shredders and secured disposal units. In addition, they should immediately review the contract with their record disposal services to ensure confidentiality of the materials they handle.

- Access to data repositories for research, marketing, or fund-raising purposes requires some form of patient authorization and formal process to obtain permission to use the PHI.

Physician Entities (as a covered entity or as a business associate)

Although many small physician practices might conceivably avoid the HIPAA regulations by using only paper for billing eligibility and referral processes, their business partners will likely obligate them to do so through the HIPAA business associate agreements.

Physician offices are vulnerable to unintentional and flagrant use or abuse of PHI. The privacy rule mandates the types of solutions outlined below. An asterisk identifies the relatively inexpensive, easy-to-implement solutions.

1. *Hanging or other record storage files must be lockable.
2. *Offices and areas where PHI is used or stored need locks and a practice of locking those areas when appropriate.
3. *Marketing concerns require restrictions on sharing PHI.
4. *Documents must be effectively destroyed. Physicians must review and amend contracts with services responsible for destroying patient records.
5. *All clinical personnel must be sensitive to conversing about patients in patient waiting areas and on elevators.

6. *Phone conversations regarding eligibility, referrals, and medications must take place where they will not be easily overheard.

7. *The design of sign-in sheets, patient check-in, and bill-paying lines must be configured so as to avoid possible unintended observing and overhearing of PHI.

8. *Patient clipboards with histories and physicals, physician notes, and other PHI records must be protected from casual viewing. There should be a blank cover sheet. Also, they can be consistently turned around in wall pockets.

9. *Telephone memo notes from patients should be safeguarded.

10. *White boards should not be used when they can reveal more information than merely a patient's name. Some HIPAA authorities do not recommend the use of white boards anywhere a visitor might observe them.

11. *Offices should strive for clean counters, avoiding any risk of divulging PHI.

12. *Terminals used for checking in, scheduling future appointments, and bill paying need to be configured so as to avoid easy visitor observation.

13. *Eligibility listings should be used only by those with a need to know and stored at night under lock and key.

14. *Faxes containing PHI to and from any business partner should be safeguarded. Staff must employ safe faxing procedures, ensuring that the authorized person receives faxes. The office staff needs to authenticate the identity of anyone calling in for PHI.

15. *Other oral and recorded exchanges of PHI must be guarded.

16. *Policy reminders to all staff to avoid using core computer systems to determine the health status of friends, relatives, and other acquaintances. Other new or restated privacy policies should encourage all staff to log off the systems whenever they are drawn away from their workstations.

17. *Limit any dial-up access to systems.

18. *Remove system access privileges immediately upon termination of an employee.

19. Ensure that the physician practice management system enables screen time-outs and uses both a sign-on and password for authorizations to view what is minimally necessary. Physicians should see to the effective use of these three security functions.

20. E-mails exchanging PHI require encryption.

21. Staff must be trained in best privacy and confidentiality processes. Physicians may need to consider upgrading the skill levels and experience requirements of their clerical staff.

22. Personnel must be disciplined for violations of privacy standards.

23. Each office must designate someone to be responsible for privacy and security measures and processes.

24. The office must eventually undertake the good faith effort to obtain acknowledgments of having reviewed the privacy policy regarding the one-time-only consents for the use of PHI for payment, treatment, and normal operations and retain them indefinitely.

25. Authorizations for the disclosure of PHI, much akin to current formal consents to release PHI for specific purposes, will need to be deployed and retained for 6 years.

26. Physician groups should start investigating the availability of standard notices of privacy policy, which will need to be provided to patients, posted in patient areas, and also retained for 6 years.

27. Physicians will also need to track authorized disclosures, both oral and written, and be prepared to provide an accounting of them to patients.

28. Physicians will eventually need to establish alternative means to communicate confidential information when requested.

29. Physicians should become sensitive to what is "minimally necessary" use of PHI within an office based on roles such as nurse, office manager, medical records manager, nurses' aides, and general clerical assistance.

30. The office will need to take stock of all their current written and verbal contracts with partners requiring the use of PHI. Eventually, physicians will need to include new terms and conditions that either obligate themselves or their partners to comply with the privacy and security provisions.

The proposed security and final published privacy standards reflect good core business practices. As a codified set of industry standards, they open providers to the potential risk of aggressive litigation even before the HIPAA compliance deadlines. Providers should address the spirit of the rules as soon as possible to minimize their short-term vulnerabilities and longer-term implementation impacts. As noted above, many of the policy and procedural changes can be achieved easily as long as the provider is committed to a culture of confidentiality and privacy.

REFERENCES

1. American Health Information Management Association Policy and Government Relations Team. Final rule for standards for privacy of individually identifiable health information. Available at www.ahima.org/search/index/html. Accessed August 28, 2001.

2. Foubister V. AMA panel releases ethics guidelines on patient privacy. *American Medical News.* Feb 19, 2001. Available at www.ama-assn.org/sci-pubs/amnews/pick_01/prsc0219.htm. Accessed May 2, 2001.

3. Health Privacy Working Group. Best principles for health privacy. Health privacy project. July 1999. Available at www.healthprivacy.org. Accessed Jan 20, 2001.

4. Robert E. Nolan Company. Cost and impact analysis. Common components of confidentiality legislation. Fall 1999. Available at www.renolan.com/healthcare/privacy.pdf. Accessed Aug 14, 2001.

5. First Consulting Group. The impact of the proposed HIPAA privacy rule on the hospital industry. A report prepared for the American Hospital Association. Dec 2000.

6. Pear R. New privacy rules are challenged. *New York Times.* Dec 21, 2000.

7. Pear R. New privacy rules are challenged. *New York Times.* Dec 21, 2000.

8. Goldman J. Privacy for patients. *Online News Hour.* December 20, 2000. Available at www.pbs.org/newshour/bb/health/july-dec00/privacy_12-20htm. Accessed Feb 21, 2001.

9. Mishra R. Privacy rules likely to alter medical terrain. *Boston Globe Online.* Dec 21, 2000. Available at www.boston.com/dailyglobe2/365/nation. Accessed June 27, 2001.

10. Mishra R. Privacy rules likely to alter medical terrain. *Boston Globe Online.* Dec 21, 2000. Available at www.boston.com/dailyglobe2/365/nation. Accessed June 27, 2001.

11. Mishra R. Privacy rules likely to alter medical terrain. *Boston Globe Online.* Dec 21, 2000. Available at www.boston.com/dailyglobe2/365/nation. Accessed June 27, 2001.

12. Mishra R. Privacy rules likely to alter medical terrain. *Boston Globe Online.* Dec 21, 2000. Available at www.boston.com/dailyglobe2/365/nation. Accessed June 27, 2001.

13. Pear R. Bush acts to drop core privacy rule on medical data. *New York Times.* March 22, 2002.

14. AHA News Now. Davidson uses *USA Today* column to air support for privacy rule changes. Available at www.ahanews.com/asp/NewsNowDisplay.asp?PubID=2&ArticleID=465. Accessed March 28, 2002.

15. Braithwaite B. Braithwaite: People are confused by those who are misinterpreting the rules. *Report on Patient Privacy.* 2002;2:1–2.

16. Shalala D. A loss to medical privacy. *New York Times.* March 30, 2002; Op-ed column.

17. INFO WORLD. *Privacy Spurs Innovation.* (Front Cover) Sept 11, 2000.

18. Cooper T. Business News of the Week. E-mailed to the author from www.AISHealth.com. July 31, 2000.

HIPAA Assessments: Best Practices and Key Compliance Challenges

BEST PRACTICES

Health Insurance Portability and Accountability Act of 1996 (HIPAA) covered entities and their business associates should begin assessing their HIPAA compliance needs. Many payers have already performed some kind of assessment, but most providers have not.

Payers are definitely further along than providers in several respects: they have already implemented some of the key electronic data interchange standard transactions, and they tend to have secure facilities and internal networks. Nonetheless, many payers have undertaken comprehensive third-party assessments to obtain objective findings, recommendations, budget estimates, and tactical plans to become HIPAA compliant. As a result, the industry can start to take advantage of the lessons learned and best assessment practices.

As the industry progresses to meet the October 2003 transaction deadline and the April 2003 privacy deadline, the assessment options will increase. There are three general approaches to a HIPAA assessment: (1) third-party assessment, (2) self-assessment, or (3) a combination third-party and self-assessment. Some large integrated delivery systems have proposed having a third party perform an assessment at an initial site and then using their trained staff to perform the remaining assessments. Many physician groups, which comprise the bulk of the clinician community, will likely wait until there are proven self-assessment tool kits available. In addition, those providers strongly affiliated with local medical centers may benefit from the medical centers' experiences and eventual tools or guidelines for compliance.

Leading HIPAA consultants have recently put forward several best practices to maximize the value of an assessment.[1-3] In the future, as the Strategic National Implementation Program (SNIP), sponsored by the Workgroup for Electronic Data Interchange (WEDI), works with local SNIP groups and regional forums, it will disseminate a series of white papers and best practices. In the interim, the industry needs to focus on materials that are currently available. For example, the HIPAA forum of southern California and the privacysecuritynetwork, have developed HIPAA assessment proposal templates (see Appendix E).

The current set of best practices relates to the outcomes, structure, and processes of HIPAA assessments. In general, full assessments of all HIPAA components need to address a broad set of outcomes:

- Comprehensive HIPAA executive management orientation and governance group and project team training. Ideally, the organization could acquire the training curriculum and tools and tailor them to its ongoing HIPAA compliance training program.

- Comprehensive documentation of the current state and inventory of the transaction-related systems, business processes, security and privacy practices, policies, and procedures, including all business partner and vendor agreements.

- Complete statement of HIPAA regulations affecting the organization and the future vision of the organization's commitment to HIPAA and converging Internet e-Commerce initiatives.

- A thorough set of findings and recommendations regarding where there are deficiencies and how they should be addressed.

- Depending on the organization's concerns about the value of implementing HIPAA solutions, recommendations for three levels of solutions: a "minimalist" compliance, an aggressive maximization strategy, and a hybrid "optimal" approach.

- Estimation of all resources required for the possible three levels of investment in HIPAA compliance, including the new ongoing demands on staff and systems support. The estimates can be fine-tuned as an organization focuses on its priorities for transforming its businesses. When focusing on opportunities, the organization should take steps to measure the likely changes in staffing requirements.

- A plan to become compliant in the required time frames once the organization decides on its preferred level of investment.

The findings and recommendations should include a structured analysis of all security risks, including estimates of vulnerabilities. This security risk assessment is not only required by HIPAA, it is also good faith evidence of an organization's commitment to compliance.

Benefit–cost analyses are an important possible outcome of an assessment. They can be used to preview the return on investing in HIPAA and to differentiate the potential levels of investment. Subsequently, they are useful for deciding on alternative strategies for maximizing the benefits of specific HIPAA and e-Commerce solutions.

The assessment's structure is key to its success. HIPAA assessments should include the following components:

- Sponsorship from the chief executive officer and the senior executive team on down

- A governance group or steering committee chartered with seeing to successful compliance with the HIPAA provisions (The governance group needs an operating budget and one or two full-time staff.)
- A multidisciplinary team, with most key operating areas represented on the governance group (In particular, a HIPAA assessment requires participation of an organization's legal counsel and regulatory compliance office.)

Legal counsel must eventually attend to the following:

- Developing standard terms and conditions in existing and future contracts consistent with the requirements of the business associate provisions
- Interpreting the interplay between state and federal laws and regulations
- Composing HIPAA-mandated chain-of-trust business associate agreements
- Reviewing and approving new policies regarding disciplining and terminating employees based on HIPAA violations
- Crafting new documents and policies required by the privacy provisions for, among other things, patient rights
- A well-structured and effective project architecture to ensure participation and leadership at all levels of the organization
- For some organizations, independent verification and validation of the results of a partial or complete HIPAA assessment
- A well-crafted, detailed, and tailored work plan.

To support the HIPAA compliance efforts, organizations should request automated tools that will function as a knowledge base and repository of collected information. A superior tool would be able to support the implementation efforts in tracking progress toward remedying deficiencies. The manner in which the assessment team works toward meeting the assessment goals is vital for its success. The best HIPAA project management processes include:

- Frequent routine communications at all levels of the project (Most communications should be documented in status reports and interim management reports.)
- Effective reporting and addressing of issues as they arise
- Effective knowledge transfer between consultant and client
- Routine teaming and meeting with other stakeholders in the local, regional, and national communities
- Diligent ongoing access to, review of, and use of free materials and updates available via the Internet.

Many organizations will not have sufficient resources to undertake an assessment on their own. Fortunately, an increasing number of examples of requests for proposals for a HIPAA assessment are becoming available. Before using any of them, the HIPAA project lead should ensure that they include the components described above. Although many consulting firms can provide comprehensive services, there are "best-of-breed" alternatives, particularly in the security and privacy arenas.

Small provider groups may be able to wait until there are proven self-assessment and implementation guidelines available from their professional associations or other reliable sources. In the interim, they need to become aware of the likely impacts and address changes where appropriate. It is worth being as practical as possible, noting that the Department of Health and Human Services (DHHS) intends for the impacts of meeting the HIPAA regulations to be reasonable and scalable.

Recommendations for Compliance Initiatives

Covered entities should, at a minimum, undertake the following initiatives and strategies:

A. *Designate a HIPAA sponsor that reflects the entire organization.* The sponsor should institute a HIPAA governance group and appoint a HIPAA leader. Legal counsel and other regulatory compliance personnel should participate.

B. *Take advantage of the free HIPAA resources available on the Internet.*

C. *Participate at one or more of the several conferences and seminars relating to HIPAA that are sponsored by professional organizations.*

D. *Have the appropriate person in the organization join one or more of the designated standards maintenance organizations,* in particular, WEDI or Health Level 7.

E. *Develop a broad assessment strategy that encompasses all components of HIPAA and any e-Commerce initiatives or business strategies.* There are obvious benefits to realize from implementing the HIPAA standards linked to e-Commerce initiatives.

F. *Consider contracting the assessment process with a consulting firm that has a proven track record with HIPAA.*

G. *Educate all employees as to the organization's solid commitment to meeting the principles and policies embedded in the HIPAA rules.*

The deadlines are approaching and, for large organizations with significant cultural and political inertia against change, they are approaching quickly. Organizations need to ensure quality assessments; there is not enough time to perform a poorly planned, ill-fated assessment. One important result of an assessment will be discovering the most profitable strategy and plan for compliance.

KEY HIPAA COMPLIANCE CHALLENGES

Neither the initial act nor the far-reaching proposed and final rules reveal how the administrative provisions will be enforced. They are equally vague about how to comply. As a result of specifying both civil and criminal penalties, most HIPAA authorities agree that the government intends to vigorously enforce all provisions.

The final privacy rule includes a common set of health care definitions to be used in all Notices for Proposed Rule-Making (NPRM). It also broke new ground by significantly increasing patients' rights. Many providers reacted out of fear that their ability to provide timely, unimpeded medical services was at risk. It is therefore likely that the courts will ultimately interpret some of the final security and privacy rules. The following section reviews 10 key provisions and several remaining challenges to ensuring compliance.

HIPAA-Covered Entities and Distinctions

HIPAA mandates that three types of health care entities comply with the administrative simplification rules: payers, clearinghouses, and providers who perform any of the standard HIPAA electronic transactions. Providers who wish to take advantage of EDI must use the standard transactions; however, they can contract with clearinghouses to send or receive those transactions.

HIPAA Enforcement and Accreditation

DHHS intends to publish an enforcement NPRM. The established accreditation bodies, the Joint Commission on Accreditation of Healthcare Organizations and the National Commission on Quality Assurance, will have roles with respect to HIPAA deficiencies. It is unclear if and to whom they may report the deficiencies, but noncompliance will not initially result in holding back their accreditations. DHHS has recently established an office to oversee federal health care security and privacy measures. They have also stated that the Office of Civil Rights will enforce civil penalties for privacy violations. In addition, the Department of Justice has informed the Office of the Inspector General of its intentions to prosecute HIPAA offenses.

At this point, the covered entities do not know how to assure compliance and avoid capricious enforcement actions or impacts on accreditation. In that regard, the proposed security rule indicates that HIPAA will provide for security compliance accreditation. DHHS has empowered the Electronic Healthcare Network Accreditation Commission (EHNAC) to develop security certification for providers, clearinghouses, and vendors. It is, however, not known what their role will be in determining whether an entity complies with the HIPAA security provisions. EHNAC, via its Web site, will certify whether test batches of EDI transactions comply with the published ASC X12N transaction implementation guides.

In the interim, an organization has various options to determine compliance. One option is to use the services of a competent HIPAA security consulting firm to conduct an assessment. However, after the entity rectifies reported deficiencies, it is unlikely that these firms will contractually attest that the entity is fully compliant. Another option is to perform a self-assessment while involving the entity in national initiatives such as SNIP of the WEDI. In a conversation with the author, Lee Barrett, chair of WEDI, stated that, "an organization has some options today to determine compliance through EHNAC and tools becoming available such as the North Carolina Healthcare Information and Communications Alliance's Early View™ security checklist."[4]

10 Key Compliance Provisions

1) *Risk Assessment*
   The proposed security and confidentiality rule identifies the requirement for a security risk assessment. A risk assessment must highlight an organization's security vulnerabilities and indicate appropriate remedies. It is critical to determine remediation costs and to demonstrate a well-reasoned, good faith approach and commitment to meet the standards.

2) *Documented Human Resource Security and Privacy Policies and Procedures* and *3) Employee Training Program*
   According to the proposed security rules and the final privacy rules, every employee must be trained on new or updated organizational security, confidentiality, and privacy policies and procedures. Examples of changes in practices include:

   a.   Restrictions on public discussions of patients and members
   b.   Prevention of inadvertent viewing of patient information
   c.   Restrictions on sharing any patient-identifiable records
   d.   Clear procedures on internal enforcement of potential violations

4) *Chief Security, Chief Privacy, or Compliance Officer Representing Business Operations*
   The proposed security rule requires a full-time chief security or compliance officer who is also responsible for enterprise-wide security policies. The chief security officer will need to understand the impacts of policies on patient care.

   In addition, the final privacy rule requires the covered entity to designate a chief privacy official. The position of IT security officer will not satisfy this requirement. Regardless of how the organization implements the functions, the designated person should have a firm grasp of normal treatment and business operations as well as the security and privacy requirements.

5) *Reports on Attempted Intrusions and Internal Violations Including Sanctions*
According to the proposed security rule, organizations will need to
implement comprehensive reports on all attempted network and host
system intrusions and other noncomputer system attempts to access
protected health care information (PHI). Although entities need to be
concerned about external intrusions, it is far more likely that
employees and other privileged insiders commit the documented
security and privacy violations. The HIPAA security reports will thus
need to document all alleged internal violations and demonstrate how
the cases were disposed.

6) *Business Partner Trading and Business Associate Chain-of-Trust
Agreements Between Covered and Uncovered Entities*
The proposed security and privacy rules defined two kinds of third-
party business agreements: business associate and chain of trust.
Covered entities must revise existing agreements with other entities,
requiring them to meet HIPAA standards regarding the processing of
PHI. The agreements should include major contractual penalties upon
a breach and terms covering the disposal or return of PHI. In all cases,
the covered entity has the legal burden to be aware of compliance.

7) *Audit Trails and Logs*
The proposed security rule requires covered entities to implement
manageable host-system audit trails and logs to record who accessed
which patient's records and why. It is still unclear what level of detail
will be required. The privacy rule requires that covered entities report
some of those uses and disclosures to their patients and members.

8) *Encrypted exchanges of PHI*
The security rule requires that all PHI messages to third parties be
encrypted. The proposed provisions do not state the form of
encryption necessary, but the Health Care Financing Administration
has documented its requirements for Internet-secured transactions. A
covered entity would be wise to meet those published standards, even
if HIPAA does not prescribe any technical solutions.

9) *Authentication Procedures Determining Who Is Requesting PHI*
As part of the proposed security rule, networks and host systems must
authenticate all users attempting to log in to a health care application
or network. The level of complexity of authentication is left to the
entity, but, at a minimum, the procedure must ensure the identity of
the person logging in. Traditional sign-ons and passwords may suffice,
but generic passwords and accounts will not.
  In addition to authenticating the person logging in, the entity must
ensure that people access only those parts of the system they are
authorized to access. Note that although digital signatures may work
well for network and Internet authorizations, they will not easily be
adapted to legacy mainframe systems.

10) *Patient Consents, Authorizations, Disclosure, and Directives*
   In the privacy rule, patients are provided federal rights to access and
   amend their records and to direct who, and under what circumstances,
   could access them. Covered entities must ensure that they have a
   patient's consent to use or disclose PHI before using or disclosing PHI
   in the course of treatment, billing, and normal operations. If the
   March 2002 proposed modifications to the privacy rule survive the
   30-day comment period and review by DHHS, providers will have the
   option to require patient consents. Instead, they will need to undertake
   good faith efforts to obtain their patients' acknowledgments of having
   reviewed the entity's privacy policy.
       Authorizations are, however, required for most other disclosures.
   Knowing what are acceptable uses or disclosures for treatment, billing,
   or normal operations necessitates an enterprise-wide review of current
   practices. In turn, the covered entity must deploy subsequent
   education and training of what is appropriate.

Challenges to Ensuring Compliance

There are several unresolved issues that present challenges to ensuring
HIPAA compliance, namely:

*State versus Federal Law Preemption and Federal Law versus Federal
Law Conflicts*: There are several concerns: (1) In many instances,
patients' records may be processed in many states; (2) state regulations
can also apply to EDI transactions where there has been no real
analysis; and (3) state regulations on privacy will prevail when they are
deemed more stringent.

There are many federal laws that also affect the privacy and
confidentiality of PHI.

Technology Neutrality of Security Provisions: The HIPAA administrative
simplification rules were designed to be technology-neutral and
therefore do not prescribe specific IT solutions.
Compliance Funding: All compliance efforts will need to be self-
funded since no funds have been designated to assist with
compliance initiatives.
Accreditation and Enforcement: The regulations are silent on how to
ensure HIPAA accreditation. Perhaps there will be clarification in the
enforcement rule.

Most HIPAA experts agree that the costs of compliance will probably
exceed the initial federal estimates. HIPAA standards do, however, reflect
excellent business practices, and early adoption can yield a competitive
advantage.

REFERENCES

1. Phoenix Health Systems HIPAA Compliance Staff. *Steps for Providers: HIPAA Gap Assessment/Risk Analysis.* Copyright 2001–2002. Available at www.hipaadvisory.com/action/compliancee/gapassessments.htm. Accessed May 2001.

2. HIPAA patient privacy compliance guide. *AISHealth.com.* Available at www.aishealth.com/product/HIPAA_Guidehtml. Accessed Nov 2001.

3. Brickler and Eckler LLP, The Quality Management Group LTD. *HIPAA Privacy Self-Assessment and Compliance Guide for Health Care Providers.* Sponsored by the Ohio Hospital Association. Copyright 2001-2002 the Ohio Hospital Association. Available at www.hipaacomplyonline.com. Accessed Nov 2001.

4. North Carolina Healthcare Information and Communication Alliance, Inc. EarlyView[TM]. December 2000. Available at www.nchica.org. Accessed January 15, 2001.

chapter 8

Resources

PUBLIC DOMAIN AND FEE-BASED MATERIALS

To minimize the costs of compliance with the Health Insurance Portability and Accountability Act of 1996 (HIPAA), covered entities need to avail themselves of the emerging public tools, industry alliances, knowledge leaders, and standards bodies dedicated to providing reliable best practices and lessons learned.

Payers, clearinghouses, and most providers now have less than 2 years to assess their needs and comply with the HIPAA transaction and code set standards. The government will eventually publish the final rules for the unique identifiers, security, and confidentiality. All entities will then have 26 months to comply with them.

To comply within that period will be a major challenge—an even greater challenge to those who have adopted a skeptical wait-and-see attitude. Those committed to meet or exceed the requirements can take advantage of the growing amount of available resources to ensure success. At this time, most providers and payers have recognized the need to take HIPAA seriously. Most large payers have initiated or completed their HIPAA compliance assessments, and about a third of the providers have done so. At any rate, 93% of providers responding to the HIPAA Readiness Survey conducted by the Health Care Compliance Association November 2001[1] said they had established a HIPAA committee or task force.

Numerous seminars and conferences are scheduled in the near future for those unsure of how to proceed. Attendance at similar events has exceeded expectations. As of April 2000, 70% of those who responded to the 11th Annual Healthcare Information and Management Systems Society (HIMSS) Leadership Survey,[2] sponsored by IBM, indicated that they plan to concentrate on HIPAA compliance over the next 2 years. In light of the fact that most providers must comply with HIPAA in some way or another, that percentage may reflect both the providers' skepticism about their need to comply and their general lack of awareness about the impacts of HIPAA.

The popular belief is that the cost to comply with HIPAA will far exceed the costs surrounding the Y2K conversion. At the same time, the April 2000 HIMSS leadership survey indicates that fewer health care institutions expect an increase in information technology (IT) budgets in 2000 than reported in 1999. As a result, all HIPAA-covered entities need to invest in and apply cost-effective resources in order to assess the impacts. In addition, after the assessments and before remedying their compliance gaps, they will require proven, level-set, best practices to minimize risks and costs.

There is no dearth of relevant information and emerging tool kits to address security and privacy assessments. Relatively speaking, there is less available to help with assessing deficiencies regarding transactions, code sets, and identifiers. The difference is probably due to the institutional variances in the related business processes and the front- and back-office system configurations. Those variations do not lend themselves to common tools and solutions.

Opportunities to Minimize Risk and Cost of HIPAA Assessments and Compliance

Many HIPAA tools and aids address both assessments and compliance implementations. In general, the bulk of this focused information and tools is available for free or at a nominal cost via the Internet. The most effective way to gather information and useful products is through the emerging regional alliances of health care industry providers, payers, lawyers, and vendors. Examples of the most successful are provided later in this chapter. The opportunities are outlined here.

EDI Transactions and Code Sets

Many tools and knowledge sets currently available from the referenced organizations would be appropriate for all phases of HIPAA compliance efforts.

- The main source of HIPAA information from the federal government is found at www.aspe.hhs.gov/admnsimp. The rules, both in preliminary and final form, are found at www.access.gpo.gov/su_docs/aces/aces140.html.

- The American National Standards Institute (ANSI) X12N Insurance Industry Implementation Guides are available for free by downloading from the Washington Publishing Company Web site, www.wpc-edi.com. These implementation guides include both high-level business process impacts and detailed transaction data content and formats.

- The Workgroup for Electronic Data Interchange (WEDI) has provided several key reports that substantiate the need for EDI standards in health care. Much of the data regarding the metrics for eligibility, referrals, claims, and benefits processing is available from WEDI or the National Committee on Vital and Health Statistics

(NCVHS). Their Web sites are www.wedi.org and www.ncvhs.hhs.gov. NCVHS must also review and comment on any proposed change to the standards. WEDI has initiated a Strategic National Implementation Process (SNIP) as an outreach program to enable the sharing of best practices and lessons learned regarding transactions and security.

- The Data Interchange Standards Association (DISA) is a nonprofit association of international standards bodies that includes, in particular, X12N for the insurance industry. Its Web site, www.disa.org/X12/X12N, is rich in X12N products and services.

- Other HIPAA designated standards maintenance organizations (DSMOs) include:

  —Health Level 7, which is responsible for patient and clinical systems interface transaction standards, including the standards for the ANSI X12N 275 claims attachments. Web site is www.hl7.org.

  —National Uniform Claims Committee

  —National Uniform Billing Committee

  —The American Dental Association, which is responsible for the code on dental procedure and nomenclature referred to as the CDT code set.

- The American Medical Association (AMA) is responsible for the Common Procedural Terminology (CPT®-4) underlying level one of the health care procedure coding system (HCPCS) required by the Health Care Financing Administration (HCFA). HCFA at its Web site (www.hcfa.gov) details its HIPAA initiatives and provides an official HIPAA glossary.

- The Department of Health and Human Services (DHHS) is responsible for maintaining and distributing the International Classification of Disease coding system, ICD-9-CM and HCPCS.

- The Electronic Healthcare Network Accreditation Commission (EHNAC) is an independent, not-for-profit accrediting body. In fact, accreditation represents a major unresolved issue surrounding HIPAA. EHNAC provides a Web-enabled X12N standard transaction format compliance service for a nominal fee from its Web site at www.ehnac.org.

- The DHHS Data Council coordinates health data standards, health information, and privacy policy activities (Web site is http://aspe.os.dhhsgov/datacncl/).

- The Association for Electronic Health Care Transactions (AFEHCT) is dedicated to supporting the use of EDI and to improving and reducing the cost of health care. Technical "white papers" on transaction sequencing, testing, and certification procedures are available at its Web site, www.afehct.org. (AFEHCT's model trading partner agreement is included in Appendix C.)

Unique Identifiers

There are few nongovernmental sources to aid in assessing and deploying the proposed unique identifiers. The health plan or payer identifier awaits a proposed standard. One for-profit enterprise, Managed Healthcare Information Services (www.PayorID.com.), may have compiled the most complete national repository of health plans, insurance companies, and other payers.

Security, Confidentiality, and Privacy

Many materials to aid in both assessing and remediating security and privacy practices already exist. Although many security IT vendors profess their products to be HIPAA-compliant, the security rules have yet to be published. In turn, the security provisions are and will likely remain technology- and vendor-neutral. In the near future, WEDI/SNIP will identify best practice technological solutions and organizations able to accredit solutions.

Professional organizations, regional HIPAA alliances, and other interest groups have developed resources and made them available to their members and Internet users. Several of the early contributions are included herein:

- The Computer-Based Patient Records Institute (CPRI) prepared the CPRI Security Toolkit (at www.cpri-host.org) to help health care organizations develop HIPAA-ready information management and security initiatives. At its Web site, www.3com.com/healthcare/securitynet/ hipaa/index.html, 3COM, a prominent vendor of telecommunication security software and equipment, has made the tool kit available along with sample training materials to educate medical personnel about compliance with information security and patient-privacy rules.

- The North Carolina Healthcare Information and Communications Alliance (NCHICA) has developed an electronic comprehensive security questionnaire termed "Early View." NCHICA represents one of several successful regional communities of HIPAA-affected entities. The Web site is www.nchica.org.

- Beacon Partners Inc published its "Guide to Understanding and Complying with HIPAA Security & Privacy Regulations" in February 2000.[3]

- WEDI is working on a final draft of a white paper on security guidelines.

- The HIPAA Security Summit, which groups vendors and providers, has published a series of updates to their "Draft HIPAA Security Summit Guidelines."

- The Privacy Security Network at www.privacysecuritynetwork.com, in conjunction with the Health Information Privacy Network, provides a set of free products such as the HIPAA Calculator™, an interactive diagnostic assessment, model security policies, and model requests for proposals. Their model business trading partner agreement and request-for-an-assessment proposal are included in the appendices.

■ The AHA provides a model consent form to its members.

■ The American Health Information Management Association (AHIMA) provides many HIPAA resources to its members and visitors to its Web site.

Many other resources are available for those needing to determine how HIPAA impacts them and to assist them in formulating assessment and compliance strategies. For example, Healthleaders.com is a leading provider of content on health care trends and HIPAA impacts. There are others, such as HIPAAadvisory.com and HIPAAcomply.com, that enable registered members to receive unsolicited updates on HIPAA activities. Health care industry organizations like HIMSS and AHA have published online lists of HIPAA resources.

Regional meetings of health care stakeholders probably provide the best opportunities to address one's assessment and compliance needs. At meetings of the Community Health Information Technology Alliance (CHITA) of Washington, the Minnesota EDI Healthcare Users Group, NCHICA, and other organizations, business leaders can meet and collaborate openly on developing HIPAA business templates. Templates for the required chain-of-trust agreement and requests-for-assessment proposals can be developed jointly, shared, and reused at almost no cost. Resourceful HIPAA entities can effectively and efficiently reduce the costs and risks of implementing the provisions if they take the time to investigate what is now in the public domain.

REGIONAL HIPAA-CHARTERED ALLIANCES

Motivated and committed HIPAA-covered entities, professional organizations, business associates, and vendors have coalesced in several states to address their common compliance needs. These alliances represent a new phenomenon in health care and are critical to the industry's successful implementation of HIPAA.

Historically, state or regional professional societies rallied within themselves to address new state or federal regulations. Now, these organizations are working with other stakeholders in sponsoring or providing resources to more inclusive working groups.

HIPAA and e-Health opportunities are the drivers. Both forces necessitate an understanding of critical standards and content, tying the players tightly together. Several local alliances and forums have already demonstrated their value by producing HIPAA tools, templates, and joint strategies for planning and testing.

The health care industry is only now digesting the magnitude of the implications of the HIPAA rules. For instance, the state of California envisions the eventual large-scale need to draw up thousands of trading partner and business associate agreements and test as many EDI transaction interfaces. California is seriously concerned about their ability to meet those needs within the current deadlines.

Small clinician entities that electronically exchange any protected health care information and the larger medical groups will need to comply with HIPAA rules. To do so will require proven economical tools, templates, guidance, and educational materials to ensure efficient and effective implementations of the standards.

There are three types of alliances exhibiting some success:

1. Statewide associations led by a diverse group of industry leaders, including payers, providers, professional societies, governmental agencies, key vendors, and related business groups. Important examples include, but are not limited to, the following:

    - The *Minnesota Center for Healthcare Electronic Commerce* established in 1998 after consolidating e-Commerce projects at the Minnesota Health Data Institute (MHDI), created by the Minnesota state legislature.

    - The *Community Health Information Technology Alliance* (CHITA), a member-driven alliance of health care and technology organizations, both public and private. It is operated under the nonprofit Foundation for Health Care Quality.

    - The *North Carolina Healthcare Information and Communications Alliance* (NCHICA), a privately funded, nonprofit organization that actively promotes the advancement and integration of health care IT.

    - *CALINX (California Information Exchange-Linking Partners for Quality Healthcare)*, a broadly based standards collaboration of California businesses, physicians, health plans, hospitals, and health care systems agreeing to cooperate on implementation and compete on quality.

2. Statewide health care information networks (HINs) led by a partnership of a similar set of key stakeholders. Two successfully active HINs are:

    - The *Utah Health Information Network* (UHIN), a broad-based coalition of insurers, providers, and other interested parties, including state government, who have come together for the common goal of reducing health care administrative costs through standardization and EDI.

    - The *New England Healthcare EDI Network* (NEHEN), a consortium of regional payers and providers who have successfully piloted a secure e-Commerce solution.

3. National, not-for-profit associations with a mission to support key national health care initiatives. Three such groups include:

   ■ *Massachusetts Health Data Consortium* (MHDC), founded in 1978 by the state's major public and private health care organizations. The consortium collects data, publishes comparative reports, promotes electronic standards, and educates through information exchange events and research.

   ■ *The Rx2000 Institute*, a nonprofit institute headquartered in Minnesota. Its mission is "to ensure that critical information reaches the healthcare community regardless of size, funding or technological sophistication." Its membership, fees for service, foundation grants, and vendor sponsorships support the institute.

   ■ *Joint Healthcare Information and Technology Association* (JHITA), a collaborative advocacy group of health care informatics professional organizations including:
   —*American Health Information Management Association* (AHIMA)
   —*American Medical Informatics Association* (AMIA)
   —*Center for Healthcare Information Management* (CHIM)
   —*College of Healthcare Information Management Executives* (CHIME)
   —*Health Information and Management Systems Society* (HIMSS).

All share the basic motivating value—collaboration is essential for producing the most effective HIPAA and e-Health environment and interdependent solutions. Walter G. Suarez, MD, MPH, and executive director of MHDI, in his presentation to the second annual HIPAA Summit in Washington, DC, put it succinctly: "There is no competitive advantage to be 'HIPAA ready' if your trading partners aren't."[4] In turn, all associations and regional initiatives share, more or less, the following common objectives, to:

■ Foster electronic commerce
■ Provide sources for education and training
■ Influence and establish EDI and security standards
■ Develop data privacy and disclosure policy
■ Ensure quality health care, measurement, and data repositories.

As these groups have matured, they have found many ways to provide value to their members:

■ Provision of comments to the DHHS on proposed and final rules. Note that final rules are open to modification for at least 1 year after publication. The alliances can exert greater political influence than any one of their members.

- Production of standard assessment requests for services and tools, consent forms, and trading partner and business associate agreements. Since publication of the final privacy rules, many of these alliances have jointly developed and published or endorsed industry best practice and assessment tools. Examples include NCHICA's Early View™ security self-assessment tool, model consent forms and privacy policy statements, and trading partner and business associate agreements.

- Agreements on how to handle or eliminate local codes within the HCPCS coding system and aids for mapping current data elements in billing forms UB92 and HCFA 1500 to the HIPAA-mandated transaction elements.

- Provision of a forum to address state law differences affecting the alliance participants using members from the legal and governmental domains.

- Recommendations on prioritizing and sequencing standard EDI transactions.

- Collaboration with key health care vendors to understand systems reengineering and possible financial options to implement the standards.

- Consensus on and recommendations for compliant security and privacy services, policies, and technical solutions.

- Strategies for testing and certification.

- Plans for ensuring the collection and community use of quality health care information compliant with HIPAA security and privacy provisions.

- Provision of technical consultation services by members belonging to any of the HIPAA-designated DSOs or by those subject matter experts invited to work with the alliances.

- Communications and networking among players who otherwise would work independently to pursue their self-interests.

Some alliances have successfully leveraged their members' symbiotic contributions. For instance, NEHEN has successfully piloted an interoperable network that connects their providers and payers. NEHEN delivers HIPAA-compliant transactions to its members. Its private network allows a secure and high-speed connection for sending and receiving patient data with no transaction costs, simply a monthly membership fee. Early tests show less than 5-second response times for eligibility verifications. In addition, participants see millions of dollars of savings in administrative costs by reducing the time spent manually verifying eligibility and by increasing the accuracy of claims.

Several of the above alliances (ie, MHDC, MHDI, CHITA, NCHICA, and UHIN) have come together to present the concept of a secure

HIPAA-compliant, multistate network called HealthKey. HealthKey is funded by the Robert Wood Johnson Foundation to create a model for public key infrastructure by employing digital certificates for the health care industry. The industry is bound to learn some lessons as well as obtain recommendations emanating from this project.

Although most alliances and local forums of health care business leaders will not undertake projects of such scale, they can benefit significantly by sharing their complementary expertise, stature, and influence. Many alliances should transform themselves into regional WEDI/SNIP platforms. As a SNIP, they will be able to benefit further from SNIP's national focus on sharing best practices, tools, industry inputs to current and future rules, effective success factors, and other aids.

REFERENCES

1. Health Care Compliance Association. Preliminary findings of the HIPAA readiness survey conducted November 2001. Funded by Vinson & Elkins. Available at www.hcca-info.org. Accessed Dec 2001.
2. Healthcare Information and Management Systems Society. 11th annual HIMSS leadership survey, 2000. Available at www.dc.com/hipaa/about.thm. Accessed on Oct 3, 2001.
3. Beacon Partners. Guide to understanding and complying with HIPAA security and privacy regulations. Feb 1, 2000; revised Jan 8, 2001. Available at http://ecom.das.state.or.us/legislative_reports/beacon_guide_to_HIPAA_rev010801c.pdf. Accessed Aug 10, 2001.
4. Suarez WG. Multi-institutional/regional approaches to HIPAA compliance: The Minnesota experience. Presented at: Second National HIPAA Summit; Feb 28-March 2, 2001; Washington, DC. Slide 2.

chapter 9

Training and Ongoing Employee Education

To successfully implement all components of the Health Insurance Portability and Accountability Act of 1996 (HIPAA), education and training must begin early in the project life cycle and significant investments in knowledge resources must be made.

From the outset, HIPAA implementation will require critical subject matter experts to assess one's needs. Moreover, the security and final privacy rules require related internal and ongoing in-service training programs and personnel policies.

Before beginning implementation, a covered entity's executive management must become aware of HIPAA's broad impacts. At this point, most payer and provider management teams are aware of the imminent compliance deadlines. Provider organizations are still biding their time.

Depending largely on the phase of implementation, the four general education and training areas are:

■ Orientation and awareness
■ In-depth training on assessment process, tools, and impacts
■ Specialized HIPAA implementation components
■ Ongoing internal operations.

The diverse affected participants include, but are not limited, to those discussed below.

ORIENTATION AND AWARENESS

■ Potential HIPAA implementation sponsors
■ Executive team, including legal counsel
■ Almost all department managers and supervisors
■ Almost all employees
■ Key business associates not directly covered by HIPAA.

IN-DEPTH TRAINING ON IMPLEMENTATION PROCESS, TOOLS, AND IMPACTS

- HIPAA implementation team
- HIPAA governance group.

SPECIALIZED HIPAA COMPONENTS

- Transactions, code sets, and unique identifiers
  —Affected financial systems managers and staff
  —Interface engine and transaction translator managers and staff
  —Designated implementation team subject matter experts.
  —Legal counsel for chain-of-trust agreement terms.
- Administrative security and privacy
  —Designated implementation team subject matter experts
  —Enterprise security and regulatory compliance offices
  —Human resources
  —Information technology
  —Medical records
  —Utilization review
  —Legal counsel for business associate agreement terms.
- Technical security
  —Designated implementation team subject matter experts
  —Technical security office
  —Network and applications security leads.

ONGOING INTERNAL OPERATIONS

- Departmental
  —Regulatory compliance office
  —Chief security office
  —Human resources.
- Enterprise-wide
  —Almost all employees.

The number of people to be trained in each area varies considerably. For many organizations, the process of orienting most department managers and leads would involve groups of 20 to 50 people. In contrast, orienting the executive team typically involves a handful of personnel. Training most employees could necessitate training thousands. Different modalities are appropriate for specific audiences. Some of the possible modalities include:

- General lectures
- Newsletters (traditional or electronic)

T A B L E 9-1

A Blueprint for Education Strategy

Implementation Phase	Form of Education	Audience	Modality
Pre-project	Awareness and orientation	■ Potential HIPAA sponsors or visionary ■ Executive team	■ Internet mining ■ Local forums or alliances ■ Professional societies ■ Lectures by consultants, vendors, or other informed sources
Assessment	Awareness and orientation	■ Almost all department managers and supervisors ■ Key business associates not directly covered by HIPAA ■ Almost all employees	■ Lectures by consultants, vendors, or other informed sources ■ Newsletters ■ Intranet or private Internet content ■ Lectures in auditoriums, optional
	In-depth training on implementation process, tools, and impacts	■ Implementation team ■ Governance group	■ Tailored lectures and interactive learning provided by consultant, vendor, or other HIPAA specialist
Implementation	Specialized HIPAA components	■ Transactions, code sets, and unique identifiers specialists ■ Technical security specialists ■ Legal counsel for chain-of-trust and business associate agreement terms ■ Administrative security and privacy professionals	■ Classroom with group participation and testing ■ CBT training with measures of progress and achievement ■ Vendor classes and certification ■ Lectures provided by consultants or law firms with HIPAA practice ■ Educational sessions provided by professional societies, HIPAA alliances and forums ■ Self-help via the Internet ■ Educational sessions provided by professional societies, HIPAA alliances, and forums ■ Self-help via the Internet ■ Classroom with group participation and testing

Continued

T A B L E   9-1

Continued

Implementation Phase	Form of Education	Audience	Modality
Ongoing internal operations		■ Most employees	■ Intranet or private Internet training manual with monitoring of progress through materials ■ Internal in-service education program ■ Internal reminders system
		■ Departmental regulatory compliance office, chief security office, and human resources responsible parties	■ Classroom with group participation and testing ■ CBT with measures of progress and achievement ■ Certification sessions provided by accreditation bodies, professional societies, HIPAA alliances, and forums

- Classroom with group participation and testing
- Computer-based training (CBT) with measures of progress and achievement
- Intranet or private Internet content
- Educational sessions provided by professional societies, HIPAA alliances, and forums
- Vendor classes and certification
- Self-help.

Table 9-1, a blueprint for an education strategy, depicts which training modality is appropriate for which form of education and audience during each implementation stage.

The Internet and corporate intranets are likely solutions to most large audience awareness and technical training requirements. These online solutions are not, however, appropriate for smaller audiences or tailored departmental manager awareness and orientation sessions. A recent search of the Internet for HIPAA training yielded numerous relevant opportunities, as well as lists of links to additional sites. The types of organizations providing resources differed greatly. HIPAA educational resources were available from the following diverse entities:

- Traditional health care information technology vendors
- Major technical security vendors with service lines deemed responsive to the proposed HIPAA security rule
- Web-based training tool providers with a HIPAA specialty curriculum

- Successful state and regional alliances
- Health care interest groups focusing on HIPAA education
- State governments
- Health industry professional societies
- Health care consultants

Medscout Corporation (http://www.medscout.com/) identifies many of the prominent education and training resources in its online inventory. Look for these specific resources:

- American Health Information Management Association (AHIMA)
- American Medical Association
- American Society for Testing and Materials Technical Standards for Industry Worldwide
- Association for Electronic Health Care Transactions (AFEHCT)
- Computer-based Patient Record Institute (CPRI) (Security Best Practices and Presentation)
- Division of Information Resources Management (IRM)
- Health Care Compliance Association (HCCA)
- Health Data Management
- HIPAA Plus—HCFA
- HIPAAadvisory.com
- HIPAAcomply
- Internet Health Care
- Joint Healthcare Information Technology Alliance (JHITA)
- Maryland Health Care Commission
- Massachusetts Health Data Consortium
- Massachusetts Institute of Technology (MIT)
- MITRE
- Model Laws and Resolutions—*National Conference of Insurance Legislators (NCOIL)*
- National Association of Insurance Commissioners (NAIC)
- National Institute of Standards and Technology (NIST)
- North Carolina Healthcare Information and Communications Alliance (NCHICA)
- Rx2000 Institute!
- Shared Medical Systems' HIPAA Central

No list would be complete without referencing the site maintained by the Workgroup for Electronic Data Interchange (WEDI).

Internet sites such as JAWZ Inc's HIPAA-U.com have chartered themselves to educate the health care community on HIPAA. Sites such as the MIS Training Institute, HCpro's HCprofessor, Easy i Ltd.

(headquartered in England), and http://hipaa-on-line.com/ represent Web-based training sites that deliver some form of online HIPAA curricula.

Clearly, all covered entities and their business associates now have access to multiple competent resources that can satisfy their initial education and training needs. In the future, many of the same sites will likely provide curricula targeted at HIPAA compliance certification.

When selecting a provider of education and training, the organization should consider the following attributes:

- Use of trained and experienced trainers
- Demonstrated competence in CBT curricula, incorporating learning metrics such as progress and proficiency measures
- Availability of multiple training modalities
- Comprehensive suite of HIPAA services covering the complete HIPAA compliance life cycle (Continuity of HIPAA planning assessment and implementation services is key to an efficient implementation.)
- Local training facilities or staff
- Depth and breadth of health care and HIPAA expertise
- Association with existing or proposed HIPAA certification authorities.

Competent HIPAA education and training represents a critical implementation success factor. Although many appropriate resources are available in the public domain, organizations still need to invest heavily in HIPAA curricula that are tailored to their settings. To be effective, organizations must take advantage of different modes of education. To be successful, the HIPAA security and privacy policies and procedures must become a learned and consistently practiced behavior.

chapter 10

Road to Implementation

PROVIDER CHALLENGES

For many health care organizations, the investment in the Health Insurance Portability and Accountability Act of 1996 (HIPAA) offers significant strategic opportunities. Instead of merely complying with the letter of the regulations, they should incorporate all implications of HIPAA into their long-term business planning. For those savvy covered entities that perceive how the underlying goals, principles, and impacts of HIPAA will benefit them strategically, the road to implementation will present challenges worth overcoming.

Provider organizations face significant constraints in undertaking more than the minimal efforts. In particular, they are most often constrained by their application vendors and outside service providers. Regardless of the obvious constraints, they and the payers should take the opportunity to formally work through these key strategic planning processes:

- Agreement on the attributes of their business future state and critical success factors
- Utilization of a formula decision-making model to choose among their various strategic initiatives.

This chapter describes those concepts and explains why a HIPAA implementation can stimulate strategic business opportunities.

Although providers have the best opportunities to realize significant net benefits from their implementations of HIPAA, they also have the greatest challenges. Hospitals, medical centers, and multihospital integrated delivery networks (IDNs) face major threats to their abilities to successfully assess their HIPAA readiness and conduct implementations.

On the one hand, those threats may increase geometrically with the size of the entity. On the other hand, there are economies and advantages that accrue with size. While several industry lobbying groups press for delays and revisions, recent surveys (as noted in the following paragraph) report significant progress toward compliance. This chapter reviews the principal challenges and related issues, key advantages, the likely upshots of facing those challenges, and the strategy that hospital-based covered entities need to adopt.

In an April 2001 survey of more than 600 industry stakeholders, Phoenix Health Systems reported that nearly a third are into their implementations.[1] In February 2001, the Gartner Group's HIPAA Quarterly Panel Study reported mixed improvements.[2] Although there was a significant improvement in the number of HIPAA-covered entities that had at least started the early awareness tasks, only 15% of providers had completed their assessments. In fact, few physicians groups had received funding for or had estimated the total costs of HIPAA compliance. Gartner concluded that the industry would not be HIPAA-compliant by the October 2002 deadline. Most observers, however, sense that payers and clearinghouses can and will meet compliance deadlines.

The challenges are most extreme for the IDNs and affect hospitals and medical centers with large outpatient clinic operations to a lesser degree. Some of the differences among members of an IDN are highlighted below. They also reflect the conditions in smaller hospital systems.

- Local executive teams with differing personalities, leadership styles, vision, embracing of value, strategic plans, and resistance to central direction
  —The different viewpoints range from maintaining the status quo, to exhibiting general optimism, to insisting on the certainty of the value of HIPAA.
  —Some executive team members will reflect the generally prevalent wait-and-see attitude, which, of course, is reinforced by the delaying efforts of prominent professional organizations such as the American Hospital Association, Blue Cross/Blue Shield Association and others.
  —Allina Health System and Providence Health Systems represent two multistate IDNs that have consistently demonstrated a commitment to embrace the best practices inherent in the HIPAA regulations.
- Possible businesses within businesses
  —The enterprise may actually be a "hybrid" HIPAA entity directing, for example, significant provider service lines and a self-funded health plan.
- Financial conditions
  —Some may only see the expense side of the investment in HIPAA administrative simplification and privacy. For instance, government-sponsored health care systems will likely face significant resistance to allocating new funds necessary to benefit from HIPAA from their local government boards. Many local county or district entities provide care to Medicaid and indigent populations regardless of ability to pay. As a result, they may see the proposed benefits as solely

intangible. Leadership in other institutions may be skeptical about their ability to recoup the cost of investing in the "best practice" and value-added HIPAA solutions.

—In March 2001, Moody's Investors Service expressed the view that, in general, most health care hospital entities can meet the necessary HIPAA financial needs.[3]

■ Middle management competencies

■ Configuration of departments within each division (ie, similarly named departments with differing functions)

■ Information technology (IT) competencies

■ Computer systems or use of different versions of the same core health care information system

■ Ancillary and departmental systems and interfaces

—A typical hospital may have implemented as many as 10 different vendor systems.

■ Billing practices, third-party payers, and abilities to perform HIPAA standard electronic data interchange (EDI)

■ Undocumented in-house–developed databases

■ Policies and procedures in varying states of updates, paper forms, and practices

■ Facility environments; different entry points and visitor mix

■ Business associates, as well as numerous complex physician and other provider relationships; different undocumented relationships with patient data exchanges

—A typical Integrated Delivery System (IDS) may have more than 100 IT vendor contracts, many of which are maintained by individual departments.

—A medical center may have as many formal and informal agreements with other patient care service partners.

The many differences will inevitably thwart a comprehensive and timely assessment of compliance requirements as well as agreements on solutions. There are advantages, nonetheless, favoring the IDNs over the single hospital systems, such as the following:

■ Financial strength or funding flexibility

■ Internal competency (With size comes the ability to recruit qualified internal subject matter experts and successful senior managers to lead or guide the institution.)

■ Leverage with vendors

■ Corporate leadership

■ Leveraged benefits (As organizations aim for improved benefits in revenue, cash flow, and lower transaction cost, they can drive improved margins by consolidating and automating their billing, eligibility, referral, and customer service processes).

■ Payer incentives to providers (Payers will undoubtedly target the competent IDNs and the smaller HIPAA-savvy hospital systems to demonstrate the value of EDI. They will likely agree to prompt claim payments, other claims-based incentives, and, hopefully, lower cost benefit plan contracts.)

Specific privacy and security issues that may surface during an assessment for a hospital-based setting would include, but are not limited to, the following:

■ No consistent or formal policy and training on:
  —Sending appointment reminders or requests for billing information
  —Leaving voice mail messages
  —Transmitting faxed material sent to third parties without confirmation of receipt by the intended party
  —Disposing of copies of physician order requisitions and other forms containing protected health care information
■ Inconsistent assigning of personal sign-ons and passwords, particularly at the departmental systems level
■ No consistent formal policy and training for releasing patient information in response to diverse inquiries. Fortunately, most staff are sensitive to maintaining confidentiality, so little personal information is leaked inappropriately. In many hospitals, the medical records department is in control of what data is released; in others, many departments respond to legitimate requests for information but do not log those releases in any formal way.
■ No clear enterprise-wide policy on what information is covered under general consents. Some facilities or departments may assume the general consent applies; others will cautiously insist on a patient's consent for that department or facility.
■ Few facilities use encryption for outbound e-mails containing patient information
■ No formal confidentiality or privacy policy.

The upshots of dealing with the differences and HIPAA deficiencies will likely result in many of the implementation variances outlined below:

■ Different levels of compliance
■ Facility-specific assessments of risks and benefits
■ Possible facility-specific implementations under corporate guidelines or directives
■ Possible further centralization of key HIPAA-related processes, security and privacy, and contracts

- Significant legal counsel involvement to understand and define:
  - —Why and how each facility and service line is covered
  - —Where they are not covered
  - —State versus federal jurisdiction
  - —Employee training and discipline
  - —Risks
  - —Regulatory compliance
  - —Privacy policy
  - —Consents for use of information and authorizations for release of information
  - —Patient amendments of records.
- Possible further commonality and standardization of systems
- Different sources of data for EDI and facility-specific information models
- Tailored security procedures
- Creative solutions to respect differences
- Variances in local facility or department enforcement

As a result of the complexity of the various hospital settings, those covered entities must immediately undertake a thorough enterprise-wide assessment with the following two-pronged strategy:

- Consider early security and privacy business process improvements. Although still debated, the final privacy rule and the proposed security rule reflect a much-needed set of national health care standards. Some technical security solutions can be staged, whereas other technical infrastructure changes should reflect a studied evaluation of the enterprise's needs and ability to afford. Inefficient business processes should be fine-tuned prior to implementation of new or upgraded HIPAA-driven automated solutions.
- Wait until the assessment is complete before objectively analyzing the return on investment (ROI) in business and information systems solutions to the EDI, code set, and identifier requirements. Those solutions should drive at common technologies and consolidations for business processes.

A number of actions can be taken immediately to comply with HIPAA mandates. Those entities committed to meet the best practices embodied in the rules can pace themselves to successfully satisfy the current or slightly delayed deadlines.

PROCURING SOFTWARE SOLUTIONS

To meet the HIPAA deadlines and maximize benefits from implementing HIPAA-compliant solutions, covered entities will need to invest wisely in new or upgraded health care information applications. A comprehensive readiness assessment should determine both the business process and the system's reengineering requirements. New system features and functional requirements will cover a wide gamut of needs and encompass all HIPAA components—transactions, code sets, unique identifiers, security, and privacy.

Note that HIPAA does not require the relevant applications vendors to comply, so software buyers and users must require them to comply. The following discussion reviews key contract and relationship issues, as well as HIPAA-compliant application features.

A wide spectrum of possible vendors offers HIPAA solutions. Because of the likely new requirements for standard EDI and security functions and features, most entities will need to consider adding to the list of vendors they manage. In addition, an organization that has aligned its strategic Internet commerce plans with its HIPAA implementation will have to investigate emerging Web-based vendor solutions.

In general, there are two classes of software vendors: those providing business process solutions and those offering technology infrastructure products. Business system applications fit into three general groups:

- Integrated health care information systems
- Departmental applications
- Niche solutions, such as biomedical devices, diagnostic radiology modalities, and others.

In all areas, there are both long-standing traditional vendors and emerging Web-based vendors. Many Web-based solution vendors have adopted an applications service provider (ASP) model. ASPs reflect a throwback to the application time-sharing or remote communications option. They differ from the previous architecture in their reliance on the universally accessible Internet instead of proprietary and closed networks. ASPs are more attractive now because most organizations no longer wish to develop their own proprietary systems.

HIPAA-related infrastructure services and products include, but are not limited to, the following:

- EDI and interface engines. Clearinghouses perform the same function but often with some value-added services. One advantage to using them is that they are covered by HIPAA.
- Security in all of its diverse forms. Some alternatives include:
  —Niche security solutions
  —Large-scale local and wide area network based packages
  —Single sign-on solutions that permit a secure, perceived integration of diverse patient management and clinical systems common in many provider environments
- Outsourcing, particularly data center operations and hardware.

Many business systems vendors do not yet comply with either the final HIPAA transaction, code sets, and privacy rules or with the proposed security rule and expected future transaction rules. *Healthcare Informatics* published a managed care systems survey in the "Spotlight" section of its March 2001 issue.[4] Eighty-six of 276 vendors responded. Of those responding, 60% indicated they employed some form of EDI or e-Business capability. About half of the EDI respondents' Web sites demonstrated some awareness of HIPAA. Several published a well-developed HIPAA knowledge base. Less than one fourth revealed that they had implemented one of the HIPAA-mandated standard transactions, typically the claims submittal record. Several acknowledged the need to meet the eventual HIPAA security provisions regarding user access audit trails, required access controls, and role-based authorizations to appropriate protected health care information (PHI). Less than a handful stated they were compliant with HIPAA-proposed security provisions.

To meet the soon-to-be published security provisions, most entities exchanging PHI with business associates and those planning to use the Internet will need to seek out new vendors. Internet security needs have spawned a major emerging health care security sector. In addition, HIPAA requirements will compel the covered entities, and possibly their uncovered business associates, to perform a functional upgrade or systems replacement. Thus, regardless of whether an organization's current vendor has previously satisfied the organization's needs, the entity must formally assess their existing vendor's current and planned HIPAA capabilities.

Organizations will need to ask their existing or prospective vendors these questions:

- Will there be an EDI solution? If so, which standard HIPAA transactions will they support? For those transactions required or desired that are not available in the existing practice management or managed care application, the organization will need to require the respective vendor to assist in their implementation.

- How will they accommodate the new transactions and added data requirements? Will they include effective processes and rules to minimize dependence on specialized and general clerical staff? For instance, will their HIPAA solutions include automatic processing of the following or similar processes:
  —Updating member- or patient-specific eligibility data
  —Updating a patient's account based on the payment and explanation of benefits transaction
  —Requesting the status or responding to the status requests of claims, referrals, and eligibility. Acknowledging the response to an eligibility request at the point of service
  —Adjudicating either a claim submission or a referral or authorization request and automatically notifying all respective providers and the patient regarding an approved referral
  —Queuing a claim or referral based on its adjudication status or other criteria

—Reconciling dues payments and patient enrollment transactions

—Attaching required medical information to an electronic claim.

- Will they provide management solutions or tools to efficiently aid in converting to and using the new provider, employer, health plan, and diagnostic and procedure code sets?

- How will they implement the new consent and privacy forms with the concomitant recording of the patient's opting in or out of the disclosed policies?

- How will they implement the necessary audit trails of accesses to computer records?

- How do they plan to comply with the technical security provisions? Business applications vendors will need to address mechanisms such as session time-outs, access controls and authorizations, backups and recovery, reporting of attempted intrusions, data integrity, possible encryption, and, eventually, digital signatures.

- What Web-based HIPAA-related features and functions exist and are planned?

In general, the organizations must pursue the following critical licensing issues:

- An amendment to existing contracts to require HIPAA compliance in all existing and future HIPAA-affected functional areas.

  Some vendor contracts already include general statements that all upgrades and updates are provided as part of their normal software maintenance agreements. In all likelihood, most vendors will offer HIPAA-compliant upgrades at what they deem to be a fair price and not as part of their maintenance agreements.

  Other vendors have agreed in writing that their forms and reports will be kept compliant with state and federal regulations. Computer-generated HIPAA consent and disclosure forms may apply. Unfortunately, implementation of the standard claims transaction records will not likely apply, even though they are meant to replace the standard UB92 and Health Care Financing Administration 1500 billing forms.

- Adherence to HIPAA privacy regulations where the vendors, for whatever reason, must be able to access PHI. Most vendors need to do so when resolving software bugs and testing upgrades and new releases. Failure to comply should involve penalties or reflect a possible breach of contract.

- Meeting HIPAA-prescribed deadlines, with substantial penalties for failure to do so. In all cases, organizations must work with their vendors to gain a binding commitment that the vendors will meet their HIPAA needs before the deadlines.

- Proof of certification in various HIPAA domains as certification authorities are designated by the Department of Health and Human

Services (DHHS). Currently, the Electronic Healthcare Network Accreditation Committee provides standard transaction certification via its Web site for a nominal fee. The group also has been designated to develop a security certification process.

If current vendors are not planning to provide the HIPAA solutions required by the covered entity, the organization should pursue new vendors based on the following attributes:

■ Demonstrated history of active participation with DHHS designated standards maintenance organizations

■ Certification of desired features

■ Willingness to comply with emerging HIPAA contract language, such as the clauses recommended in the May 22, 2000, white paper on model contract language clauses proposed by the Association for Electronic Health Care Transactions

■ Demonstrable internal HIPAA regulatory and compliance team

■ For security needs, additional certifications or accreditations of compliance regarding proposed technical standards

■ For outsourcing relationships, willingness to comply with all HIPAA provisions, including an appropriate business associate and chain-of-trust trading partner agreement. Many such templates are becoming available from industry stakeholders and local alliances.

At health care industry trade shows and professional group conferences, many vendors claim that they are HIPAA-compliant, even though the final security rule has not yet been published. It is incumbent on covered entities to perform rigorous due diligence with their existing and possible new vendors to test those claims. Additionally, once convinced that the vendor's solution is appropriate, they must ensure that the vendor's HIPAA compliance expectations are embodied in its licensing, maintenance, and business associate agreements.

To successfully benefit from the substantial expenditures required for compliance, organizations must carefully protect themselves while developing or maintaining vendor relationships.

FUTURE STATE ATTRIBUTES AND CRITICAL SUCCESS FACTORS

Although efforts by HIPAA advocacy and industry groups may bring about modifications to the privacy rule and perhaps to compliance deadlines, HIPAA-covered entities should not procrastinate over initiating their significant assessment and implementation efforts.

Before undertaking the assessments, covered entities should formally establish their desired future state based on HIPAA requirements and other strategic initiatives. Development of the entity's future state will greatly improve the likelihood of a successful HIPAA compliance implementation.

Confirming the attributes of the future state is an essential part of the planning process. There must be consensus in the defined future state before entities can determine the factors critical to achieving this state. The following discussion reviews the strategic planning components of establishing future state attributes and critical success factors.

Many covered entities, particularly those that have not yet begun their compliance initiatives, are concerned about what appears to be the moving targets of HIPAA rules. These concerns are somewhat legitimate. In a recent meeting, the Workgroup for Electronic Data Interchange (WEDI) confirmed the possibility of changes to both the transaction implementation guides and the level 2 and 3 provisions of the health care procedure coding system. Some WEDI insiders believe changes to the deadlines for some transactions are possible.

Tommy Thompson, secretary of the DHHS, who listened to both sides argue their positions at the annual HIPAA Summit in Washington, D.C., is caught between two strong polar forces: consumer privacy advocates resistant to any relaxation in the rules and the payer and provider professional organizations insistent on further softening of the privacy provisions. In opening the door to comments before the privacy rules became effective on April 14, 2001, the DHHS secretary acknowledged that he intended to "put strong and effective health privacy protections into effect as soon as possible." There is likely to be some tweaking of the existing rules and the other proposed rules in the future, but the need to comply is not seriously in doubt.

In their planning process, covered entities need to establish their strategic goals for implementing both a HIPAA compliance program and their intertwined e-Commerce solutions. These goals would reflect their vision of the future state based on a successful implementation of HIPAA. Entities have the option of committing to a range of future state attributes. They may decide to minimally comply with the provisions or to maximize the ROI in their HIPAA compliance and e-Commerce strategies. Even a minimal compliance strategy merits senior management consensus on the attributes of the associated future state.

Possible Future State Attributes

In a February 2001 presentation to a large, covered governmental health services entity, Dr Alan Dowling, senior vice president of Covansys' Global Health Division, formulated several possible attributes.[5]

- Accomplished compliance on time and within budget.
- Done effectively and efficiently. The assessment and subsequent implementation processes minimized redundant processes, rework efforts, risks, and costs.

- Done right. As a result successfully undertaking and completing their HIPAA implementation, the entity is able to influence and lead other business associates in doing it right.
- Recognized in the community and the industry for their accomplishment and compliance with HIPAA security and privacy rules.
- Reduced the core transaction costs.
- Derived value from the implementation of HIPAA "best practice" solutions such as:
  - —Real-time or same-day processing of referral requests, claims payment and status checking, eligibility and benefits updates, and status requests
  - —Same-day notification of enrollments
  - —Electronic payment of claims and dues
  - —Health plan dues payments by sponsors and synchronized with covered subscribers
  - —Electronic posting of enrollment information into practice management system
  - —Automatically verifying eligibility and collecting a patient's co-payment upon check-in
  - —Collecting member payments for services based on diagnosis and procedure codes upon check-out
  - —Secure Web-based exchanges of clinical information between providers and patients.
- Derived value in related non-HIPAA-mandated processes such as:
  - —Processing third-party liability cases
  - —Automatically adjudicating referrals and claims
  - —Managing patient, provider, employer, and health plan identification across multiple applications.
- Derived value from implementation of related e-Commerce solutions
- Improved quality of clinical data for clinician decision support, research, short- and long-range planning, and contributions to public health studies
- Acquired funds for improvements from industry-granting authorities
- Improved processes for managing compliance with future HIPAA and other regulations
- Others.

Although there may be further examples of future state attributes, the list above demonstrates that there can be many varying and conflicting expectations of outcomes. In addition, by compelling a consensus on future state attributes, an organization is likely to surface opportunities, which might otherwise go ignored.

Possible Critical Success Factors

In truth, the school of critical success factors would insist on the use of only two or three critical factors. Although purists may not deem the factors outlined below as critical, the factors do illustrate conditions necessary to successfully achieve a preferred future state:

- Obtain executive sponsorship and a public statement of their commitment of resources
- Develop a project architecture and project management oversight tailored to the organization's structure
- Develop a plan to ensure transition management and change control
- Develop contingency plans considering:
  —The possible failure of business associates to comply
  —The possible impacts of non-HIPAA-related crises on compliance efforts.
- Participate actively in industry HIPAA alliances, standards bodies, and professional societies able to:
  —Affect current and future HIPAA regulations
  —Share "best practices" and provide tools and models for implementation.
- Develop and implement enforcement policies and procedures
- Ensure certification of standard transactions and security, when and where available.

Most HIPAA compliance efforts will be complex and intensive, particularly in light of the fluid nature of the regulations. To derive the greatest value from an implementation, organizations must understand what they intend to accomplish strategically and what is necessary to be successful prior to initiating their efforts.

MANAGEMENT DECISION-MAKING MODELS

HIPAA effectively mandates significant electronic commerce, security, and privacy business process and system changes. Covered entities have the choice of either minimally or more advantageously complying with the existing final EDI, procedural, and diagnostic code sets and privacy rules, as well as the proposed security rules.

The provisions do not dictate how the entities must implement their solutions. Minimal compliance requires merely meeting the absolute letter of the regulations. To more advantageously comply with HIPAA opens the door to a complex set of challenging options, predicated on a best fit with an entity's strategic business objectives. Deciding on which HIPAA implementation configuration to implement will necessitate a rigorous senior management decision-making process. The following discussion reviews the aspects of a multivalued decision approach for selecting an optimal HIPAA implementation.

Value-oriented decision-making is probably most useful for mid-sized to large covered entities during their strategic planning exercises. In any case, the underlying approach recognizes that effective strategic decisions require a blend of objectives and values and not merely a quantifiable ROI.

For instance, typical health care strategic objectives and their inherent values include:

- Enhancing revenues
- Increasing market penetration
- Improving the quality of care and related health care services
- Establishing or growing a competitive advantage
- Enhancing image in the community
- Containing costs
- Ensuring effective risk management
- Enhancing general employee satisfaction
- Improving the quality of decisions
- Complying with all regulatory and accreditation standards.

At the corporate level, HIPAA represents a regulatory compliance business objective among the many others outlined above. HIPAA solutions can be molded around a balanced combination of strategic objectives. As a result, ROI and, possibly, cost become two of several values that entities must consider when completing their strategic plan.

Many management professionals encourage the use of a formal HIPAA ROI model approach to decision-making. Frequently, they recommend including both quantifiable and nonquantifiable benefits and costs. They often encourage entities to incorporate intangible values such as quality of care, competitive advantage, employee satisfaction, and others in order to make their decisions. They typically do not propose a structured approach to combining those objectives.

Multivalued decision making includes both subjective and objective criteria in accord with an organization's goals. It also requires participation of many internal interests in the process. If executed properly, the results of this decision-making process make it possible to effectively rank alternative solutions. For each strategic alternative, the process results in a single derived value. In this way, entities can rank and prioritize various HIPAA implementation alternatives or rank differing strategic planning objectives, including HIPAA. Organizations should consider taking advantage of formal decision-making models structuring this approach.

HIPAA Strategic Alternatives

Below are examples of strategic planning alternatives that illustrate how organizations can advantageously shape their HIPAA compliance around their long-term objectives. Entities should consider a variety of EDI and health care information security implementations. In the process of deriving a consensus on key business drivers, differentiators, and general objectives, organizations need to address questions such as:

What is our long-term medical information strategy?

Do we need to lay down a foundation for improving quality of care and eliminating error-prone and unsharable paper processes? Do we need to focus on generating significant short-term productivity and cash flow improvements?

- If the answer to the first question is yes, organizations may opt for tempering their investment in the mandated EDI financial transaction standards in order to later invest heavily in the more powerful and versatile health care oriented XML (eXtensible Markup Language) message and document solutions.

    Such minimal EDI solutions which also reflect limited financial resources, would include:

    —Implementing limited solutions to receive and transmit the standard transactions while maintaining and replicating the current paper document processes

    —Utilizing a clearinghouse for sending or receiving the transactions and, possibly, collecting and making the additional data elements required by HIPAA available for later processing.

    Those minimal solutions would likely preclude the immediate need to purchase and implement their current vendor's integrated EDI solutions.

- If the answer to the second question is yes, organizations should maximize the immediate benefits of adopting the EDI standards and insist on effective systems and business process reengineering in order to implement best practices in claims, referral, eligibility, and enrollment processing.

    The maximizing EDI solutions would necessitate some or all of the following:

    —New automated claims and referral adjudication processes

    —Transmission and acceptance of electronic funds transfers, including the electronic posting of payments

    —Integrated eligibility screening, claims processing, and payment posting at point of service

    —For specific managed care health plans, physician management service organizations, and managed care focused medical groups, electronic posting of all enrollment information tied to the receipt of electronic health plan dues payment to enable accurate capitation reconciliation.

- The maximizing EDI solutions will entail significant investments in new or enhanced systems to reengineer current manual processes.

What is our long-term strategy for minimizing risk by securing patient medical records?

Do we need to ensure community recognition that we protect our clients' data? Do we need to greatly improve our relationships with and the health of our covered lives through e-Health programs such as disease management programs (also reducing overall delivery expenses); telemedicine capabilities, including patient–physician information exchanges; wireless provider applications; sharing of diagnostic radiology images; and other customer service management programs that integrate the Internet, traditional telephone services, and the HIPAA-mandated claims, eligibility, and referral status EDI standards?

- If no, then, organizations can minimize their investment in technical security. Some minimal implementations would include, but are definitely not limited to, the following:

    —The most rudimentary data access and authorization mechanisms permitted by the proposed HIPAA security rule

    —An encryption implementation targeted at protecting the EDI transactions and Internet messages

    —Possible outsourcing of network and data center management to ensure adherence to recognized industry security standards

    —Use of system audit trails to address patient disclosures of accesses to medical records.

There are many ways to configure the investment in implementation solutions under the umbrella of the HIPAA provisions. The solutions depend on what organizations consider to be the important attributes of their future state. In addition, investments in HIPAA implementations must be considered alongside investments in other unrelated strategic initiatives. The best HIPAA solution will depend on how well the entities can align HIPAA with their other business objectives, including e-Health. The most successful entities will utilize a structured process to ensure the alignment of HIPAA with other core strategic business values.

REFERENCES

1. Phoenix Health Systems. Quarterly industry survey results—Spring 2001. Available at www.hipaadvisory.com/action/survey/spring01.htm. Accessed Aug 20, 2001.
2. Duncan M. HIPAA panel survey results for 4Q00: early activities. Available at www.gartner.com/3_consulting_services/hipaa_services_g.html. Accessed March 17, 2001.
3. Moody's Investor's Services. Moody reports: HIPAA costs could be readily absorbed with little adverse credit impact on not-for-profit hospitals.

March 26, 2001. Available at www.moodys.com/default.asp. Accessed June 17, 2001.

4. Le Y. Spotlight-Managed Care Systems. *Healthcare Informatics.* March 2001. Available at www.healthcare-informatics.com/issues/2001/03_01/ mcs2001.pdf.

5. Dowling A. In a Covansys Inc marketing presentation to a prospective state department of health services client. Feb 2001.

chapter 11

Into the Future

ELECTRONIC MEDICAL RECORD RULE

During the second half of 2002, the federal government is expected to propose new uniform data standards for patient medical record information. This will allow providers to safely and effectively proceed with implementing electronic medical records. The Department of Health and Human Services has indicated it will release a Notice for Proposed Rule-Making (NPRM) proposing electronic medical record (EMR) standards under a Health Insurance Portability and Accountability Act of 1996 (HIPAA) mandate to "study the issues related to the adoption of uniform data standards for patient medical record information (PMRI) and the electronic exchange of such information."

These EMR standards would undoubtedly go beyond the current HIPAA electronic data interchange (EDI) security and privacy provisions in simplifying clinical processes and exchanges of patient medical information. This chapter reviews the current state of EMRs, the new rule's impacts and benefits, as well as relevant information technology (IT) options and strategies.

The existing final and proposed HIPAA rules reflect the basic administrative and financial patient health care information (PHI) exchange standards. The provisions for HIPAA's EDI transaction standards also call for a master data dictionary to be developed and maintained so that common data definitions are used across current and future standards. To facilitate development of a computer-based patient record (CPR), the HIPAA EMR rule should eventually lead to further electronic data standards regarding health care terminology (ie, code sets, classifications, and nomenclatures), technical security, and, possibly (but not likely), usage of the Internet and wireless technologies.

Although the health care provider industry has supported the concept and vision of the CPR, there is no dominant solution. At this point in its evolution, the CPR still faces many challenges. Significant challenges include:

- Difficulty in demonstrating a return on investment (ROI) for both an enterprise-wide and a longitudinal medical record solution.

- Differences in clinician preferences for clinical classifications, nomenclatures, patient outcomes, and guidelines, often resulting in limited comparability of data exchanged between providers.

  There are approximately 40 different reputable code set, terminology, defined data set, and other descriptive standards prevalent in marketed CPRs. Many are medical discipline specific, while others may overlap in content.

  The American Medical Association (AMA) supports the use of the HIPAA-mandated CPT®-4 and ICD-9 code sets and regards SNOMED (Systematized Nomenclature of Human and Veterinary Medicine) as worthy for standard usage.

- Variances in data quality due to different standards of control, formatting, and editing. Data quality is frequently affected by the difficulty in identifying and linking sets of a patient's records. Since the industry will not likely see a unique patient identifier, its entities will need to take advantage of enterprise-specific solutions.

- Variations in data content. The AMA has also published a recommended core set of EMR data elements and functions required to support medical practice.[1]

- Difficulty integrating the solution into the clinician's work flow.

- Need for physician champion to ensure acceptance and compliance with the system. One active physician opponent to an EMR implementation can cause it to fail.

- Lack of interoperability between various departmental, enterprise-wide, and external systems.

- Inability to either encode all necessary data elements in one structured database or integrate both structured and unstructured records. Note that approximately 95% of a patient's medical record is still on paper forms or other media.

- Variances in state laws regarding the retention and authentication of PMRI.

- Lack of national security, privacy, and confidentiality standards.

- Absence of industry and governmental investment in a national health care information infrastructure.

HIPAA has already addressed and will address several, but clearly not all, of the above challenges. The proposed NPRM on the EMR can deal directly with the issues of data comparability, data content, variances in state laws, and, possibly, new technologies such as mobile health care and XML (eXtensible Markup Language). Lee Barrett, recent past chair of the Workgroup for Electronic Data Interchange and past chair of the ASC X12N Insurance Committee, stated, "The EMR will have a significant positive impact on patient care and will be a critical cornerstone for HIPAA in addressing one of the key HIPAA legislative tenets of portability."[2]

The volatility in the EMR marketplace reflects the impacts of the challenges highlighted above. The May 2000 and 2001 issues of *Healthcare Informatics*, in its Spotlight: CPR Systems, articles, included surveys of CPR vendors.[3,4] Only one third of the vendors responding in each issue survived the full year. Based on the number of companies surveyed in both years, the results suggest that there were about 435 CPR vendors and products active at some time during the period, which was less than 2 years. Many of the survivors are long-standing health care information systems vendors who have developed or acquired functionally rich CPRs.

C. Peter Waegemann, chair of three renowned CPR-related standards groups and executive director of the Medical Records Institute, suggests that, "The Electronic Health Record (EHR) has replaced the outdated CPR and is the basis for e-Health."[5] He points out in a May 2001 *Healthcare Informatics* article[6] that during the 1990s, few CPRs achieved the requirements to be paperless, interoperable, longitudinal, and multidisciplinary. The focus should be on enterprise-specific and components-based solutions justified by a quantifiable ROI. He envisions that the EHR will take advantage of the revolutionary impact of the Internet and emerging wireless technologies and will securely maintain all medical record documentation. To support his position, he points out that more than 10 million people use more than 70 Web sites to store personal health records.

BENEFITS AND IMPACTS OF EMR STANDARDS

On July 6, 2000, the National Committee on Vital Health Statistics (NCVHS) issued a publication titled, "Report to the Secretary of HHS Regarding Uniform Data Standards for Patient Medical Record Information."[7] In that report, the computer-based patient record work group within the NCVHS Subcommittee on Standards and Security, stated that its "recommendations [are] important to the nation because they will facilitate significant improvements in the quality of care, improve productivity and reduce costs." In addition, its recommendations for PMRI standards will be "consistent and compatible with the HIPAA financial and administrative transactions including the upcoming claims attachment standard."

The typical benefits of implementing an EMR include:

- Improved ability to share PMRI
- Improved clinical processes, quality of care, and patient satisfaction
- Facilitated clinical decision-support systems.

The most critical driver for more automation in the medical care delivery process is the need to reduce medical errors.

Benefits and impacts of the new rule would involve:

- Improved medical record information exchange within and across nationwide enterprises

- Less dependency on managing paper-based processes, and among others, a reduction of costly transcription services
- Enhanced ability to attract providers from different disciplines to use automated clinical processes
- Ability to retain current systems and invest primarily in tools for integration and remote accessibility for improved data capture
- New or enhanced EMR applications with greater likelihood of meeting the diverse and complex clinical needs
- More complete electronic patient records, enabling better-quality patient-centric care and more accurate data to support clinical decision support and research.

IT Investments and Strategies

To ensure more successful implementations and clinician acceptance in the future, the covered provider entities should undertake an IT strategy that is based on providing demonstrable ROI and maximizing the values of newer mobile health care and e-Health opportunities. Such investment opportunities would include:

- Computer physician order entry (CPOE). Jane Metzger and Debra Slye in their May 2001, *Medical Informatics* article, "Inpatient Ordering,"[8] point out that as few as 3% of organizations benefit from online physician ordering of patient care services. CPOE can lead to a reduction in medical errors while realizing an ROI.
- Some promising beneficial wireless health care applications interfaced to EMRs include:
  —Remote ordering of inpatient services, medications, and supplies based on the clinician's standard protocols
  —Remote retrieval and review of transcribed reports and the related entry of clinician digital signatures
  —Remote retrieval and follow-up of abnormal diagnostic testing results
  —Remote retrieval and follow-up of critical patient care messages
  —Remote notification and follow-up of a change in a patient's condition or of a patient's emergent condition.
- Prior to publication of the EMR proposed rule, provider entity IT professionals should stay current with the development of XML-based electronic documents. XML may prove to be the means by which all patient documents are exchanged electronically, including via wireless appliances. Health Level 7 (HL7) is developing a powerful data model and processes for generating health care XML-compliant electronic documents. XML documents can deliver useful data for any conceived need when the existing structured database cannot.

- Use of a tool such as the National Library of Medicine's unified medical language system (UMLS) to map, where feasible, currently maintained medical vocabularies and classifications.

IT strategies would include, but are not limited to, the following:

- A studied review of the emerging de facto wireless technology standards not addressed by the EMR proposed rule. In conjunction with the HIPAA standards, the entities must develop or enhance a technical infrastructure strategy.
- New contractual requirements for health care information systems vendors to comply with the standards in order to benefit from further interoperability of systems and reduced dependency on paper and fragmented applications.
- A strategy to assess the current state of systems terminology usage and data content and to adopt the new standards.

To improve the quality of patient care, the industry must improve the exchange of mutually understood, comparable, and complete patient information. In spite of the diverse terminology systems, the likely HIPAA EMR rule will mandate the use of the most appropriate standard terminology and data content. If possible, it should also address the technological changes that have transpired since HIPAA was passed. In the future, the industry should benefit greatly from having electronic data standards covering the full spectrum of administrative, financial, and clinical processes and record keeping.

EXPLOITING THE INTERNET

Organizations covered by HIPAA should consider the use of the Internet to maximize the benefits of compliance and to minimize its costs. Although the standards bodies, federal agencies, and other health care experts that contributed to development of HIPAA provisions did not take into account the likely impacts of the Internet, Internet technologies will bear strongly on how well health care entities realize returns on their investments in HIPAA compliance.

Some of the increasingly apparent benefits of the Internet include:

- A low-cost pipeline between trading partners. Its fixed cost is significantly lower than the costs of conventional private leased lines and dial-up networks.
- Highly scalable volume of transactions transported via the pipeline.
- Almost universal availability to communicate with all health care stakeholders: providers, payers, clearinghouses, employers, pharmacies, suppliers, financial institutions, and individual members and patients. Financial institutions already exchange large volumes of payment transactions using secured e-mail and file transfer protocol.

- Computer and telecommunications device independence. Wireless devices with potential provider applicability in the referral; ordering of services, supplies, and drugs; and results reporting processes will be Web-enabled.
- Maturing shareable, robust, platform-independent, and standards-based security.

The primary benefits will be felt in the efficient and effective implementation of the transactions and their security, integrity, and privacy.

In the provisions for the HIPAA final rule on transactions and code sets, the HIPAA authors addressed the use of the new technology. Early in the rule development process, however, the use of the Internet was deemed not covered by the rule. That initial reaction was quickly overturned. The final rule, published August 17, 2000, now clearly specifies that "the Hypertext Markup Language (HTML) interaction between a server and a browser by which the data elements of a transaction are solicited from a user would not have to use the standards, although the data content must be equal to that required for the standard. Once the data elements are assembled into a transaction by the server, the transmitted transaction would have to comply with the standards." Thus, use of the Internet to enter referral, claims, eligibility, and other HIPAA-mandated transactions does not require conforming to the format of the particular American National Standards Institute (ANSI) X12N transaction standard. In all cases, the online transaction must include the possible entry of all mandated data elements.

The health care industry must successfully deal with significant challenges if it is to quickly and easily take advantage of the new economy technology. Most payer and large provider systems tend to use centralized, proprietary, technological architectures. Many systems still employ character-based user interfaces with PC workstations emulating the mainframe telecommunications protocols. Interfacing to and integrating with these systems is not straightforward. In addition, because of the need to retool staff and systems to tackle the new technologies and the lack of capital to invest in the retooling, most entities will need to slowly adopt the new solutions to meet HIPAA requirements.

The most significant inherent challenge lies in integrating the Web-based opportunities with the processes of the legacy systems. In a typical outpatient registration, the receptionist must break from the flow of the legacy system and use the Internet to establish a managed care patient's eligibility and benefit status. Even if the pertinent information is accessed and retrieved, the legacy system is typically not, at that point, set up to collect the benefits and co-payment information.

Health care entities have, to varying degrees, adopted the Internet. For example, many larger entities have established rich, content-based Web sites. A few have enabled employers and their employees to access health plan benefit information and to enroll in their preferred benefit plan. Large provider groups have developed the ability to enable their patients to communicate with the offices of their primary care providers. Health care suppliers and purchasers participate in opportunities to market pharmaceuticals, durable medical equipment, and other supplies.

The key impacts and opportunities of HIPAA Internet implementations are outlined below.

Impacts and Opportunities of the Internet

In recent surveys[9] of plans for health care information systems investments, HIPAA and e-Commerce easily rank in the top five. The *e-Healthcare Market Reporter* recounted in "e-Healthcare Trends–An Executive Briefing"[10,11] that the emerging e-Health products or services will involve claims, followed by disease management, procurement, the electronic medical record, and then physician–patient communications. HIPAA clearly targets value-added services for streamlining claims processing and several related processes such as eligibility and benefits inquiries and referrals. The convergence of Internet technologies with the health care trends underlying the HIPAA provisions will accelerate the resulting compliance initiatives and the opportunities to realize substantial benefits. These long-term health care trends and, in turn, e-Health drivers include:

- Real-time service authorizations and claims payments
- Empowered consumer-driven health care purchases of benefits and providers
- An even more powerful government role in regulations and rules due to the information revolution and privacy concerns
- Locally and nationally integrated information; medical records becoming the accepted property of the patient
- Provision of care evolves into provision of information
- Online, up-to-date, clinical decision-support systems that use statistically validated data.

All current and proposed HIPAA rules dovetail with the above trends. In the near future, the HIPAA provisions will need to address the impacts of the Internet. The general impacts and opportunities for HIPAA and the covered entities are the following:

- EDI transactions will need to evolve to take advantage of both point-of-service processing efficiencies and the advent of health care XML document and message standards. Within the next 4 to 5 years, providers and payers, in collaboration, will be able to ensure immediate authorization of services and the payments for those services. Physicians will also be able to prescribe and order medications at any point in the delivery process.

- Ubiquitous access to geographically dispersed personal health care records
- Highly securable, personally identifiable information engendering member and patient trust in all parties: payers, providers, and financial institutions. Electronic information will be better secured than any paper-based system. Digital signatures and certificates will significantly reduce fraud and improve both access to and quality of care.
- Improved data integrity, ensuring better-quality clinical decisions.

Although there are major opportunities ahead, health care entities must invest in retooling their technologists and reengineering the affected processes. The future HIPAA rules must also carefully address the Internet impacts and fine-tune the proposed provisions to acknowledge the new paradigm in communications and commerce.

IT Options and Strategies for Internet-driven HIPAA Rules

The Internet's impact is both technological and procedural. Already, most health care organizations have invested in developing a Web site for marketing and consumer affinity purposes. Although new entrants to the health care information systems arena have developed applications to exploit the e-Commerce potential, health care organizations have been reluctant to invest in them. After Y2K, providers, in particular, find themselves with few resources to adopt the new opportunities. Providers and payers need to align HIPAA with their e-Commerce strategies so that they can establish both a solid infrastructure and a high return portfolio of new economy products and services over the next 2 years.

The principal IT investment options and strategies include the following:

- Develop e-Health solutions, either internally using the organization's information systems' staff or with the new e-Health vendors or their legacy system vendors, tied to HIPAA standard transaction, code set, identifier, security, and privacy rules. The solutions should pull from the following opportunities:
  - —Real-time service authorizations, membership enrollments, eligibility and benefits inquiry, and claims status tracking
  - —Real-time point-of-service claims adjudications and payments Payers can work with their provider partners to enable near real-time cash payments.
  - —Real-time drug prescriptions
  - —Digital signatures and certificates to foster the elimination of inefficient paper-driven processes.

- Join the supply-chain communities currently forming on the Internet to ensure fair pricing of equipment and supplies and optimal inventory management
- Stay current with the rapidly changing Internet landscape and the market leaders.

Although future HIPAA rules will continue their stance of technical neutrality, they will strongly influence the direction of both traditional and Internet technologies. The Internet promises to provide cost-effective and high ROIs in HIPAA solutions.

REFERENCES

1. American Medical Association. A recommended core set of EMR data elements and functions required to support medical practice. June 2000. Available at www.ama-assn.org/ama/pub/category/2912.html. Accessed July 20, 2001.
2. Author e-mail communication with Lee Barrett, former executive director of Workgroup for Electronic Data Interchange (WEDI).
3. Le Y. Computer-based patient record system. *Healthcare Informatics.* May 2000:97. Can be accessed at www.healthcare-informatics.com.
4. Le Y. Computer-based patient record system. *Healthcare Informatics.* May 2001:33. Can be accessed at www.healthcare-informatics.com.
5. Waagemann CP. Leading edge—an electronic health record for the real world. *Healthcare Informatics.* May 2001:55–62. Can be accessed at www.healthcare-informatics.com.
6. Waagemann CP. Leading edge—an electronic health record for the real world. *Healthcare Informatics.* May 2001:55–62. Can be accessed at www.healthcare-informatics.com.
7. National Committee on Vital Health Statistics (NCVHS). Report to the secretary HHS regarding uniform data standards for patient medical record information. July 6, 2000. Available at www.ncvhs.hhs.gov. Accessed July 21, 2001.
8. Metzger J, Slyen D. Inpatient e-ordering. *Healthcare Informatics.* May 2001:63
9. Jenkins B, Koste J. e-healthcare trends—an executive briefing. *e-healthcare Market Reporter.* (no date) Available at www.healthresourcesonline. com/edu/ehealth.htm. Accessed May 2001.
10. Jenkins B, Koste J. e-healthcare trends—an executive briefing. *The e-healthcare Market Reporter.* (no date) Available at www. healthresourcesonline.com/edu/ehealth.htm. Accessed May 2001.
11. Healthcare Information and Management Systems Society. 11th annual HIMSS leadership survey, 2000. Available at www.dc.com/hipaa/about.thm. Accessed on Oct 3, 2001.

chapter 12

Conclusion

HIPAA regulations reflect a convergence of many modern health care trends:

- Increasing automation of administrative processes, including billing, eligibility, and referral processing, embodied by the HIPAA subtitle, Administrative Simplification.

- Increasing electronic exchange of medical and billing records via the proposed EDI standards and related advances enabled by the Internet, embodied in the basic tenet of insurance and medical record portability.

- Increasing recognition of patient rights embodied by the final privacy rule and the proposed security rule.

- Increasing focus on the quality of care facilitated by the enhanced accuracy of electronic records and the recognition that privacy fosters confident and complete collection of health care information.

Contrary to many extreme interpretations of the rules, the Department of Health and Human Services and other influential HIPAA authorities have consistently asserted that covered entities should plan to implement practical, reasonable, and scalable processes. In turn, rather than creating new functions, departments, and processes, the solutions should take advantage of existing ones.

The benefits of HIPAA come at a significant financial cost and impact on current operations. In addition, HIPAA may initially inhibit the ability to deploy PHI-driven disease management programs, marketing initiatives, and fund-raising efforts.

In spite of the likely increased burdens due to the many security and privacy provisions, the rules reflect both the basic core confidentiality and privacy values of the health care industry as well as the industry's best practices. By developing a reputation of adhering to those values, providers will be elevated in the eyes of the community and marketplace.

HIPAA is an ongoing rather than a one-time-only regulatory compliance requirement. HIPAA belongs in the covered entities' existing compliance program. To be effective, senior executives and physician office managers should routinely reinforce the appropriate cultural change. The results should be well worth an aggressive investment in compliance.

HIPAA Acronyms

Acronym	Description
ADA	American Dental Association
AHIMA	American Health Information Management Association
AMA	American Medical Association
AMIA	American Medical Informatics Association
ANSI	American National Standards Institute
ASTM	American Society for Testing and Materials
ASC	Accredited Standards Committee
BBA	Balanced Budget Amendment
CDC	Centers for Disease Control and Prevention
CFR	Code of Federal Regulations
CHIM	Center for Healthcare Information Management
CHIME	College of Healthcare Information Management Executives
CIO	Chief Information Officer
CISO or CSO	Chief Information Security Officer/Chief Security Officer
CMS	Centers for Medicare & Medicaid Services (formerly HCFA)
CMSO	Center for Medicaid and State Operations
CPO	Chief Privacy Officer
CPRI	Computer-based Patient Record Institute
DHHS	Department of Health and Human Services
DISA	Data Interchange Standards Association
DMSO	Designated Standards Maintenance Organization
EDI	Electronic Data Interchange
EHNAC	Electronic Healthcare Network Accreditation Commission
EIN	Employer Identification Number
HCFA	Health Care Financing Administration (currently CMS)
HIMSS	Healthcare Information and Management Systems Society
HIPAA	Health Insurance Portability and Accountability Act of 1996
HL7	Health Level 7
NCHS	National Center for Health Statistics
NCPDP	National Council for Prescription Drug Programs
NCQA	National Committee for Quality Assurance

Continued

Continued

Acronym	Description
NCVHS	National Committee on Vital and Health Statistics
NPI	National Provider Identifier
NPRM	Notice of Proposed Rule-Making
NUBC	National Uniform Billing Committee
NUCC	National Uniform Claim Committee
PAYERID	Health Plan Identification Number
SDO	Standards Development Organization
SSN	Social Security Number
UHI	Unique Health Identifier
WC	Workers' Compensation
WEDI	Workgroup for Electronic Data Interchange
X12N	ANSI ASC's EDI Subcommittee on Insurance Standards
Y2K	year 2000 problem
XML	eXtensible Markup Language

HIPAA Web Sites

Organization	Web Site	Type of Information
American Health Information Management Association (AHIMA)	www.ahima.org/hipaa.html	Basic HIPAA information and tips for getting started
Computer-based Patient Records Institute (CPRI)	www.cpri-host.org	Information on confidentiality
Data Interchange Standards Association (DISA)	www.disa.org/x12/x12n	The X12N Insurance Subcommittee develops electronic data interchange standards for all aspects of the insurance industry
Department of Health and Human Services (DHHS)	www.aspe.os.dhhs.gov/admnsimp	Administrative Simplification Web site
DHHS Data Council	www.aspe.os.dhhs.gov/datacncl/	Coordination of health data standards and health information and privacy policy activities
DHHS	www.aspe.os.dhhs.gov/admnsimp/ nprm/seclist.htm	Checklist for confidentiality and security
Electronic Healthcare Network Accreditation Commission (EHNAC)	www.ehnac.org	An independent, not-for-profit, accrediting body
Health Care Financing Administration (HCFA)	www.hcfa.gov/security/ isecplcy.htm	Security policies and frequently asked questions
Health Level 7 (HL7)	www.hl7.org	Claim attachments
National Committee on Vital and Health Statistics (NCVHS)	www.ncvhs.hhs.gov/	Public advisory body to the secretary of the Department of Health and Human Services in the area of health data and statistics; transcripts of all hearings and much written testimony

Continued

Continued

Organization	Web Site	Type of Information
National Council for Prescription Drug Programs (NCPDP)	www.ncpdp.org	Retail pharmacy transaction standards
Washington Publishing Company	www.wpc-edi.com	Electronic data interchange implementation guides
Workgroup for Electronic Data Interchange (WEDI)	www.wedi.org	HIPAA implementation materials and information regarding Notice of Proposed Rule-Makings

Model Trading Partner Agreements

AFEHCT's White Paper on a Model Trading Partner Contract

White Paper
May 22, 2000
Model Contract Language Clauses
Authors
Russell Taylor rwt@gyral.com
Barbara Demster bdemster@healtheon.com

Overview

HIPAA regulations and compliance thereof will require, for many in the health care industry, the development of new intercompany relationships as well as the redefinition of some existing relationships. The purpose of this paper is to identify some of those relationships, define issues inherent in their establishment, and make recommendations for addressing the issues.

Covered Entities Data Exchange

The Health Insurance Association of America estimates that there are close to 1000 health care payers in the US today. The task of each of these payers coming to a contractual agreement with other payers to enable the exchange of Health Care Coordination of Benefit (COB) information could be enormous. The common procedure is as follows.

- Each party sends their contract to the other.
- Each party's legal department either reviews the other's contract or insists that their contract be used as a base for the agreement.
- Responses are exchanged with updates, corrections, and additions, and this step is continued until a mutually acceptable version is developed.
- The contracts are then signed.

Performing each of these steps close to 1000 times would require a significant increase in the legal resources for each entity. The time frame to create these contractual agreements is 24 months from the effective date of the final rule for the privacy regulations as they will need to be in place by the privacy compliance date. The legal negotiation requirements could be lengthy and expensive for all concerned.

Business Partner Data Exchange

Outsourcing parts of health care operations is a normal business practice for health care plans, providers, and clearinghouses (covered entities). HIPAA refers to the companies that provide the outsourced health care treatment, payment or health care operations functions on behalf of the covered entities as "business partners." The HIPAA Privacy provision requires that a contract be signed between covered entities and their business partners with whom they will be exchanging Protected Health Information (PHI). The Privacy provision goes on to state that this contract must include language to essentially extend the covered entity's privacy and confidentiality responsibilities to the business partner.

There are three general data exchange scenarios addressed in the HIPAA regulations.

1) Covered entity-to-covered entity
   a) Payer-to-payer for COB
   b) Payer-to-provider
   c) Payer-to-clearinghouse
   d) Provider-to-clearinghouse
   e) Payer's business partner-to-another covered entity's business partner
2) Covered entity-to-non-covered entity
3) Covered entity-to-its business partner

The major difference among these scenarios is the boundary of responsibility for protected health information (PHI) privacy and confidentiality.

In scenario 1), a covered entity to covered entity PHI exchange, there is a boundary of responsibility for privacy and confidentiality between the sending and receiving parties.

a) The sending covered entity has responsibility for the PHI that it maintains.
b) During the transmission, both entities have responsibility for the security of the connection.
c) Once the PHI has been successfully transferred from one covered entity to another, the confidentiality of the transmitted data becomes the responsibility of the receiver. The sender retains responsibility only for its copy of the PHI.

In scenario 2), a covered entity to non-covered entity PHI exchange, there is a boundary of responsibility for privacy and confidentiality between the sending and receiving parties.

a) The sending covered entity has responsibility for the PHI that it maintains.
b) During the transmission, the sending covered entity has responsibility for the security of the connection.

c) Once the PHI has been successfully transferred from the covered entity to a non-covered entity, the non-covered entity's responsibility for the PHI is ethically rather than legally motivated (because HIPAA rules do not apply). The sender retains responsibility only for its copy of the PHI.

The term "non-covered entities" would apply to certain types of insurance entities that are not covered by HIPAA. The privacy regulations identify the following insurers as examples of non-covered entities, worker's compensation and automobile insurance carriers, other property and casualty insurers, and certain forms of limited benefits coverage, even such arrangements provide coverage for health care services.

In scenario 3), a covered entity to business partner data exchange, the boundary of responsibility is extended to include the business partner's operations and use of the PHI. The business partner is contractually bound to restrict the access and use of the PHI to the extent that is required of the covered entity with which it is doing business or the limits defined in its contract with the covered entity.

a) The sending covered entity has responsibility for the PHI that it maintains.

b) During the transmission, both parties have responsibility for the security of the connection.

c) When the data has been successfully transferred from a covered entity to its business partner, confidentiality of the transmitted data becomes the responsibility of the business partner (receiver). The covered entity (sender) retains responsibility for the copy of the data the sender maintains. In addition, the covered entity retains responsibility for some oversight of the business partner's use of the data.

In this document, we will specifically refer to two of the relationships listed above: 1a) payer-to-payer for COB and 3) covered entity to its business partner. However, all the data exchange relationship scenarios listed should be addressed.

Caveat

The proposal for Payer-to-Payer Coordination of Benefits contracts, Subtopic 1, are based on the final rules for the HIPAA implementation guides for health care claim transactions which are expected to be set as final rules in their current form in June of 2000.

The proposals for HIPAA Covered Entity to Business Partner contract clauses, are based on the Privacy NPRM that is expected to undergo major revision before its designation as a final rule. Thus, some of the requirements and definitions identified in this paper may need to be altered to align with the privacy final rule.

The proposals for Chain of Trust, subtopic 3:, are based on the proposed security regulations which though they are believed to be more stable than the privacy regulations, will need to be reviewed in light of the final security regulations.

The Department of Health and Human Services has promised to consolidate the definitions of business partner and chain of trust in the final rules for security and privacy. So contract clauses relative to these terms should be developed only after the final rules are published.

Subtopic 1: Payer-to-Payer Contracts for Coordination of Benefits

Background

Coordination of Benefits Models

HIPAA regulations, in the NPRM for the 837 transactions, offer two models for EDI-based coordination of benefits (COB). They are
1) Provider-to-Payer-to-Provider and 2) Provider-to-Payer-to-Payer.

COB Model 1: The Provider-to-Payer-to-Provider

Step 1.

In model 1, the provider originates the transaction and sends the claim information to Payer A, the primary payer. See figure 1, *Provider-to-Payer-to-Provider COB Model*. The primary payer, Payer A, adjudicates the claim and sends an electronic remittance advice (RA) transaction (835) back to the provider. The 835 contains the claim adjustment reason code that applies to that specific claim. The claim adjustment reason codes detail what was adjusted and why.

Step 2.

Upon receipt of the 835, the provider sends a second health care claim transaction (837) to Payer B, the secondary payer. Payer B may send a coordination of benefits payment verification request transaction (269) to Payer A to verify Payer A's claim payment amounts that were reported by the provider. Payer A sends a coordination of benefits payment verification response to Payer B. Payer B adjudicates the claim and sends the provider an electronic remittance advice.

Step 3.

If there are additional payers (not shown in figure 1, Provider-to-Payer-to-Provider COB Model), step 2 is repeated.

FIGURE 1

Provider-to-Payer-to-Provider COB Model

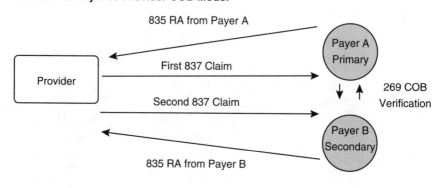

COB Model 2—Provider-to-Payer-to-Payer

Step 1.

In model 2, Provider-to-Payer-to-Payer, the provider originates the transaction and sends claim information (including identifying data for all payers involved in the claim) to Payer A, the primary payer. See figure 2, *Provider-to-Payer-to-Payer COB Model*. The primary payer adjudicates the claim and sends an 835 back to the provider.

Step 2.

Payer A reformats the 837 and sends it to Payer B, the secondary payer.

Step 3.

Payer B receives the claim from Payer A and adjudicates the claim. Payer B sends an 835 to the provider. If there is a tertiary payer, Payer B performs step 2 (not shown in figure 2, Provider-to-Payer-to-Payer COB Model).

In most configurations, the provider has been responsible for claim submission to primary and secondary payers alike. Providers have been required by health care plans, in the role of secondary payer, to submit a copy of the paper Explanation of Provider Payments (EPP) received from the primary payer. This was done to verify what the provider included as the primary payer paid amount.

As a health care payer moves toward electronic transaction exchange the need to send the same information on paper is eliminated. With the use of electronic Remittance Advice, cost savings are not only realized through the elimination of the paper EPPs but also through the elimination of mailing those EPPs. As a result, if the primary payer expects to eliminate paper EPPs, that same payer cannot expect the provider to send a copy of a paper EPP when they are the secondary payer.

F I G U R E 2

Provider-to-Payer-to-Payer COB Model

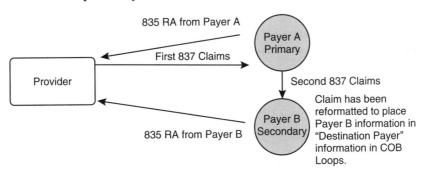

The two models defined above were based on the COB options defined in the proposed HIPAA implementation guides for the 837 Health Care Claim transactions.

In the Provider-to-Payer-to-Provider model the need to verify the accuracy of the amount paid by the primary payer can be satisfied electronically through the use of the Coordination of Benefits Verification (269) transaction. This transaction standard, which has recently been developed and accepted by the X12 standards development committee, is not a HIPAA standard, but is available for public use. The 269 request transaction is sent from the secondary payer to the primary payer providing a claim identifier and the amount the provider included as the primary payer paid amount. The primary payer then responds in the affirmative or the negative if the stated amount equals or does not equal what the primary payer paid on the associated claim.

In the Provider-to-Payer-to-Payer model, there is no need for verification of the amount paid by the primary payer. In this model, the claim is received by the primary payer, adjudicated, updated, with payment information, and then sent to the secondary payer directly.

Each of these models presents an opportunity for health plans to exchange data where they have not done so previously. Traditionally, there has been little or no electronic data exchange between health care payers. Prior to this exchange of data between companies, a contract must be written, agreed upon, and signed by the two payers.

Subtopic 2: HIPAA Covered Entity to Business Partner Contracts

Background

The preamble of the proposed HIPAA Privacy regulations presents a guiding principle of the proposed rules as: "Today's health care system is a complex business involving multiple individuals and organizations engaging in a variety of commercial relationships. An individual's privacy should not be compromised when a covered entity engages in such normal business relationships."

Based on this principle, the proposed privacy rules would "require covered entities to ensure that the business partners with which they share protected health information understand—through contract requirements—"that they are subject to standards regarding use and disclosure of protected health information and agree to abide by such rules. . . ." They go on to assert that "Other than for purposes of treatment consultation or referral, we would *require a contract to exist between the covered entity and the business partner* that would, among other specified provisions, *limit the business partner's uses and disclosures* of protected health information to those permitted by the contract and *would impose certain security, inspection and reporting requirements* on the business partner."

Definition of Business Partner

According to the Proposed Rules, the term b*usiness partner* means "a person to whom a covered entity discloses protected health information so that the *person can carry out, assist with the performance of, or perform on behalf of, a function or activity for the covered entity.*" . . . "and that the business partner receives protected health information from the covered entity as part of providing such activity or function."

Who is a Business Partner?

The privacy regulations define a business partner as a person to whom a covered entity discloses protected health information so that the person can carry out, assist with the performance of, or perform on behalf of, a function or activity for the covered entity.

Under the proposal, billing agents, auditors, third-party administrators, attorneys, private accreditation organizations, clearinghouses, accountants, data warehouses, consultants and many other actors would be considered business partners of a covered entity. Most covered entities will use one or more business partners, to assist with functions such as claims filing, claims administration, utilization review, data storage, or analysis.

Who is Not a Business Partner?

The covered entity may have business relationships with organizations that would not be considered to be business partners because protected health information is not shared or because services are not provided to the covered entity. For example, a covered entity could contract with another organization for facility management or food services; if these organizations do not receive protected health information, they would not be considered business partners.

The term "business partner" would not include a person who is an employee, a volunteer or other person associated with the covered entity on a paid or unpaid basis.

Issues for Consideration in the Development of Business Partner Contracts

Extension of Responsibility for Protected Health Information

A very important parenthetic phrase within this section is the inclusion of business partner-to-business partner transactions. This implies that part of the contract between the covered entity and the principal business partner will be to bind secondary business partners of the principal to the same requirements (ie, limitations on uses and disclosures, security, inspection, and reporting requirements, and binding of tertiary business partners.) This supports the basic concept of the chain-of-trust, where each link in the chain must meet certain minimum standards as the chain is only as strong as its weakest link.

In the same manner that the covered entity is extending the boundary of their health care business operations to their business partners, they are also extending their responsibility for the maintenance of the privacy and confidentiality of PHI to their business partners and their business partners' business partners.

<u>Limitation of Sharing of Protected Health Information</u>
The proposed rules discuss limiting "health care operations to functions and activities performed by a health plan or provider or by a business partner on behalf of a health plan or a provider." Note the exclusion of the clearinghouse in this discussion. The rules go on to state:

"Our definition anticipates that in order for treatment and payment to occur, protected health information would be used within entities, would be shared with business partners, and in some cases would be shared between covered entities (or their business partners). However, a health care operation should not result in protected health information being disclosed to an entity that is not the covered entity (or a business partner of such entity) on whose behalf the operation is being performed."

As long as the contract requirements are met, the proposed HIPAA privacy regulations allow providers and health plans to pass protected health information to a business partner without individual patient authorization if it is for purposes of treatment, payment, or health care operations.

<u>Exceptions</u>
Due to the nature of the clearinghouse business and their removal from direct contact with individuals whose information is protected, the proposed rules provide for exempting clearinghouses from many of the provisions of the rule that would apply to providers and health plans. The rules further state, however, that "We would adopt this position with the caveat that the exemptions would be void for any clearinghouse that had direct contact with individuals in a capacity other than that of a business partner."

<u>Sharing Protected Health Information with Non-covered Entities</u>
The proposed rules discuss real concern regarding disclosures for payments that "may routinely result in disclosures of protected health information to non-covered entities, such as employers, which are not subject to the use and disclosure requirements of this rule." We considered prohibiting disclosures to employers without individual authorization, or alternatively, requiring a contractual relationship, similar to the contracts required for business partners, before such disclosures could occur. We note that the National Committee on Quality Assurance has adopted a standard for the year 2000 that would require health plans to "have policies that prohibit sending identifiable personal health information to fully insured or self-insured employers and provide safeguards against the use of information in any action relating to an individual" (Standard R.R.6, National Committee for Quality Assurance 2000 Standards).

This paragraph seems to be a contradiction to the previous one:
"We note that health care providers would be subject to the provisions of this [privacy] rule with respect to the health care they provide to individuals, even if such providers seek or receive reimbursement from an insurance entity that is not a covered entity under these rules. However, nothing in this rule would be intended to prevent a health care provider from disclosing protected health information to a non-covered insurance entity for the purpose of

obtaining payment for services. Further . . . this rule would permit disclosures by health care providers of protected health information to such insurance entities and to other persons when mandated by applicable law for the purposes of determining eligibility for coverage or benefits under such insurance arrangements. For example, a State workers' compensation law that requires disclosure of protected health information to an insurer or employer for the purposes of determining an individual's eligibility for medical or other benefits, or for the purpose of determining fitness for duty, would not be disturbed by this rule."

Limitations on Uses and Disclosure

Another key principal in the privacy NPRM is the concept of "minimum necessary" where information passed between two parties is the minimum required to accomplish the required activity for which the information was requested. This includes limitations on physical access for "specific employees or business partners, or the types of employees or business partners, who would be qualified to gain access to particular records. . . . Covered entities with advanced technological capabilities should also consider limiting access to appropriate portions of protected health information when it would be practical to do so."

The "minimum necessary" determination would include a determination that the purpose of the use or disclosure could not be reasonably accomplished with information that is not identifiable. Each covered entity would be required to have policies for determining when information must be stripped of identifiers before disclosure. If identifiers are not removed simply because of inconvenience to the covered entity, the "minimum necessary" rule would be violated.

List of Contract Requirements

The proposed HIPAA Privacy regulations state that the written contract between a covered entity and a business partner would be required to contain the following specifically listed elements:

- Prohibit the business partner from further using or disclosing the protected health information for any purpose other than the purpose stated in the contract.

- Prohibit the business partner from further using or disclosing the protected health information in a manner that would violate the requirements of this proposed rule if it were done by the covered entity. The covered entity could not permit the business partner to make uses or disclosures that the covered entity could not make.

- Require the business partner to maintain safeguards as necessary to ensure that the protected health information is not used or disclosed except as provided by the contract. The details can be negotiated to meet the particular needs of each arrangement.

- Require the business partner to report to the covered entity any use or disclosure of the protected health information of which the business partner becomes aware that is not provided for in the contract.

■ Require the business partner to ensure that any subcontractors or agents to whom it provides protected health information received from the covered entity will agree to the same restrictions and conditions that apply to the business partner with respect to such information.

■ Establish how the covered entity would provide access to protected health information to the subject of that information, as would be required under §164.514, when the business partner has made any material alteration in the information. The covered entity and the business partner would determine in advance how the covered entity would know or could readily ascertain, when a particular individual's protected health information has been materially altered by the business partner, and how the covered entity could provide access to such information.

■ Require the business partner to make available its internal practices, books and records relating to the use and disclosure of protected health information received from the covered entity to HHS or its agents for the purposes of enforcing the provisions of this rule.

■ Establish how the covered entity would provide access to protected health information to the subject of that information, as would be required under §164.514, in circumstances where the business partner will hold the protected health information and the covered entity will not.

■ Require the business partner to incorporate any amendments or corrections to protected health information when notified by the covered entity that the information is inaccurate or incomplete.

■ At termination of the contract, require the business partner to return or destroy all protected health information received from the covered entity that the business partner still maintains in any form to the covered entity and prohibit the business partner from retaining such protected health information in any form.

■ State that individuals who are the subject of the protected health information disclosed are intended to be third-party beneficiaries of the contract.

■ Authorize the covered entity to terminate the contract, if the covered entity determines that the business partner has repeatedly violated a term of the contract required by this paragraph.

Other areas mentioned in the proposed regulations are:

■ Address provisions for minimum necessary use & disclosure

■ Physical access by classes of employees or types of data

■ Minimum security requirements (reference chain of trust agreement)

■ Requirement to bind subsequent business partners to the same standards

■ Assignment of responsibilities when a covered entity acts as a business partner of another covered entity.

■ Statement that the Business Partner is bound by the terms of the notice of practices of the covered entity from which it obtains protected health information.

Subtopic 3: Chain of Trust

Background

Chain of Trust Partner Agreement—

The Chain of Trust partner agreement is a contract entered into by two business entities in which they agree to electronically exchange data and protect the integrity and confidentiality of the data exchanged. This chain of trust concept would apply to all the general data exchange scenarios mentioned in the Overview of this document.

Chain of Trust is referenced as a requirement in the Security Proposed Rules. The Chain of Trust terminology is not used in the Privacy Proposed Rules, although the concept is certainly present. The WEDI Security Summit developed in their implementation guide an outline for the components of a Chain of Trust agreement. The Privacy Proposed Rules require that the covered entity impose security requirements on the business partner. We believe that this Chain of Trust agreement is actually a subset of the total Business Partner agreement as defined in the Privacy Proposed Rules and propose that the WEDI requirements would suffice for this requirement in the Business Partner agreement.

Note: We have gotten word that HHS intends to blend the concepts of business partner agreements and chain of trust agreements in the forthcoming final rules.

Chain of Trust Partner Agreements should:

- **Be a signed contract**: any organization that exchanges confidential electronic data with external organizations must have a signed contract or agreement with the external organization that includes data handling and confidentiality. This agreement may be a free standing contract, a part of a larger contract, or an addendum to an existing contract;

- **Define the Terms and Conditions**: Each contract must contain language that defines confidential information, conditions for disclosure, data rights of each trading partner, and required security levels of responsibility and accountability for each partner;

Contain, at a minimum, the following elements:

- Signatures of agreeing parties;
- Contract start date, expiration date and/or Review/Renew dates;
- Definition of Terms and Conditions to include confidential information conditions or disclosure, data rights of each trading partner, and minimum levels of security to be maintained;
- Procedures for Reporting Breaches;
- Penalties for non-compliance with agreement (intentional versus unintentional);
- Retention and Destruction Schedules;

TABLE 1

Component	COB	Business Partner	Chain of Trust
Use of Clearinghouses or Third Party Service Providers	X	X	X
Systems Operations—Each party will, at its own expense, provide and maintain the equipment, software, services, and testing necessary to effectively and reliably transmit and receive transactions.	X	X	X
Security Procedures—per HIPAA standards	X	X	X
Transaction Source Authentication	X	X	X
Proper Receipt Acknowledgment	X	X	X
Garbled Transmissions	X	X	X
Terms and Conditions	X	X	X
Confidentiality—per HIPAA standards	X	X	
Validity: Enforceability	X	X	X
Termination of Agreement	X	X	X
Severability	X	X	X
Entire Agreement—This agreement and the appendix constitute the complete agreement of the parties relating to the matters specified in this agreement . . .	X	?	?
Force Majeure—No party shall be liable for any failure to perform its obligation with any Transaction or any Document where such failure results from any act of God or other cause beyond such party's reasonable control which prevent such party from transmitting or receiving any documents.	X	?	?
Limitation of Damages	X	X	X
Arbitration	X	X	X
Limitations on Uses and Disclosures of PHI		X	
Inspection Provisions		X	X
Reporting Provisions		X	X
Binding on Subsequent BP		X	X
Renewal Provisions		X	X

- Be reviewed and/or renewed at the following intervals and evidence of such a review (i.e., regular certification audit) must be documented and attached to the contract or agreement:
    - —Upon contract renewal;
    - —Concurrent with full security review/certification review;
    - —Upon regulatory changes requiring revision; or
    - —Upon breach of agreement trigger.
- Each party in the agreement must keep an incident log of any breaches to the agreement. The party who breaches the agreement must notify the other of any breaches within an agreed upon period of time or provide the incident log for periodic inspection and upon demand.

Business Drivers

The reasons for writing this White Paper are:

- To provide the health care industry with an outline of issues required to address the contract language requirements of the proposed rules
- To identify the need to define the boundaries of liabilities for covered entities and their business partners
- To suggest the need for model contract language to reduce conflicting interpretations and increase understanding of the rules
- To provide a structure of consistency across the industry to reduce administrative costs of creating and negotiating individual contracts

Recommendation/Solution

Our recommendation is for the health care community to support a workgroup to create a set of model contract clauses that could be used across the industry. The focus of the model contract language will be in development of two agreements for electronic exchange of the data.

They are, as identified in the Overview above, 1a) *payer-to-payer for COB* and 3) *covered entity to its business partner*. Please note that this is not an exhaustive itemization of issues but merely a preliminary attempt to illustrate the type of research required to fully meet this requirement across the industry.

Payer-to-Payer for COB Contract

For the Payer-to-Payer contract, it is expected that a complete contract model could be developed since the requirements for COB data exchange will not vary significantly from health plan to health plan.

Much of the work for creation of this model has been done. The American Bar Association's Electronic Messaging Services Task Force under the auspices of the Subcommittee on Electronic Commercial Practices of the Uniform Commercial Code

Committee, Section of Business Law has created the *Model Electronic Data Interchange Trading Partner Agreement and Commentary*. Using this as a base, the industry could develop the model by adding language that would address any HIPAA regulatory requirements.

Covered Entity to Its Business Partner Contract Clauses

For the Covered Entity to Its Business Partner contract, it is expected that a set of model clauses that address each of the issues identified in the HIPAA regulations be developed. Given the varied nature and functions possible in a covered entity's agreements with its business partners, the most value would be added by a workgroup that delivered a set of model contract clauses rather than attempting to create a full contract model. These clauses could then be added to existing contracts and to contracts that are to be written with the assurance that, if included, the contract sufficiently addresses HIPAA concepts and contract requirements.

If included in the language of contracts for the identified interfaces and adhered to, we would like to recommend these models be used as a definition of a legal "safe harbor" (i.e., if a covered entity does this minimum, they will be considered in compliance with the regulation).

Value Proposition

■ Define the scope of contracts

■ Reduce legal costs in creation of unique agreement for each business partner

■ Reduce variation between business partner agreements

■ Increase thoroughness or completeness of requirements in agreements

The benefits of this recommendation are the reduction of the time and resources required to establish data exchange contracts between HIPAA covered entities and between HIPAA covered entities and their business partners. Each covered entity that agrees to present and accept these models should experience a reduction in the intercourse required between respective legal departments in the establishment of the general PHI data exchange relationships mentioned in the overview. Over the course of development of hundreds of new data exchange relationships with other covered entities or the updating of contract with business partners, this time and resource savings will be significant.

Source: Used with permission from Barbara Demester and Russell Taylor.

PrivacySecurityNetwork™s
Model Business Associate Contract

MODEL BUSINESS ASSOCIATE CONTRACT

THIS CONTRACT is entered into on this _____ day of _____, 2001, between Provider/Plan/Clearinghouse (ie, COVERED ENTITY) and Vendor/Person(s) (BUSINESS ASSOCIATE).

WITNESSETH:

WHEREAS, COVERED ENTITY will make available and/or transfer to BUSINESS ASSOCIATE certain Information, in conjunction with goods or services that are being provided by BUSINESS ASSOCIATE to COVERED ENTITY, that is confidential and must be afforded special treatment and protection.

WHEREAS, BUSINESS ASSOCIATE will have access to and/or receive from COVERED ENTITY certain Information that can be used or disclosed only in accordance with this Contract and the HHS Privacy Regulations.

NOW, THEREFORE, COVERED ENTITY and BUSINESS ASSOCIATE agree as follows:

1. **Definitions**. The following terms shall have the meaning ascribed to them in this Section. Other capitalized terms shall have the meaning ascribed to them in the context in which they first appear.

2. Contract shall refer to this document.

3. BUSINESS ASSOCIATE shall mean [name of organization receiving the Information]

4. COVERED ENTITY shall mean [name of organization providing/ making available the Information]

5. HHS Privacy Regulations shall mean the Code of Federal Regulations (C.F.R.) at Title 45, Sections 160 and 164.

6. Individual shall mean the person who is the subject of the Information, and has the same meaning as the term individual is defined by 45 C.F.R. 164.501.

7. Information shall mean any "health information" provided and/or made available by COVERED ENTITY to BUSINESS ASSOCIATE, and has the same meaning as the term "health information" is defined by 45 C.F.R. 160.102.

8. Parties shall mean BUSINESS ASSOCIATE and COVERED ENTITY.

9. Secretary shall mean the Secretary of the Department of Health and Human Services (HHS) and any other officer or employee of HHS to whom the authority involved has been delegated.

10. **Term**. The term of this Contract shall commence as of _____ (the "Effective Date"), and shall expire when all of the Information provided by COVERED ENTITY to BUSINESS ASSOCIATE is destroyed or returned to COVERED ENTITY pursuant to Clause 6.9.

11. **Limits on Use and Disclosure Established by Terms of Contract**. BUSINESS ASSOCIATE hereby agrees that it shall be prohibited from using or disclosing the Information provided or made available by COVERED ENTITY for any purpose other than as expressly permitted or required by this Contract. (Ref.164.504 (e)(2)(i).)

12. **Stated Purposes for Which BUSINESS ASSOCIATE May Use or Disclose Information**. The Parties hereby agree that BUSINESS ASSOCIATE shall be permitted to use and/or disclose Information provided or made available from COVERED ENTITY for the following stated purposes:
[Include a general statement describing the stated purposes that BUSINESS ASSOCIATE may use or disclose the Information. These uses and disclosures must be within the scope of the BUSINESS ASSOCIATE's representation of the COVERED ENTITY.] (Ref. 164.504(e)(2)(i); 65 Fed. Reg. 82505.)

13. **Additional Purposes for Which BUSINESS ASSOCIATE May Use or Disclose Information**. In addition to the Stated Purposes for which BUSINESS ASSOCIATE may use or disclose Information described in clause 4, BUSINESS ASSOCIATE may use or disclose Information provided or made available from COVERED ENTITY for the following additional purpose(s):

14. **Use of Information for Management, Administration and Legal Responsibilities**. BUSINESS ASSOCIATE is permitted to use Information if necessary for the proper management and administration of BUSINESS ASSOCIATE or to carry out legal responsibilities of BUSINESS ASSOCIATE. (Ref. 164.504(e)(4)(i)(A-B).)

15. **Disclosure of Information for Management, Administration and Legal Responsibilities**. BUSINESS ASSOCIATE is permitted to disclose Information received from COVERED ENTITY for the proper management and administration of BUSINESS ASSOCIATE or to carry out legal responsibilities of BUSINESS ASSOCIATE, provided:

16. The disclosure is required by law; or

17. The BUSINESS ASSOCIATE obtains reasonable assurances from the person to whom the information is disclosed that it will be held confidentially and used or further disclosed only as required by law or for the purposes for which it was disclosed to the person, the person will use appropriate safeguards to prevent use or disclosure of the information, and the person immediately notifies the BUSINESS ASSOCIATE of any instance of which it is aware in which the confidentiality of the information has been breached. (Ref. 164.504 (e)(4)(ii).)

18. **Data Aggregation Services**. BUSINESS ASSOCIATE is also permitted to use or disclose Information to provide data aggregation services, as that term is defined by 45 C.F.R. 164.501, relating to the health care operations of COVERED ENTITY. (optional)(Ref. 164.504(e)(2)(i)(B).)

19. **BUSINESS ASSOCIATE OBLIGATIONS:**

20. **Limits on Use and Further Disclosure Established by Contract and Law**. BUSINESS ASSOCIATE hereby agrees that the Information provided or made available by COVERED ENTITY shall not be further used or disclosed other

than as permitted or required by the Contract or as required by law. (Ref. 45 C.F.R. 164.504(e)(2) (ii)(A).)

21. **Appropriate Safeguards**. BUSINESS ASSOCIATE will establish and maintain appropriate safeguards to prevent any use or disclosure of the Information, other than as provided for by this Contract. (Ref. 164.504(e)(2)(ii)(B).)

22. **Reports of Improper Use or Disclosure**. BUSINESS ASSOCIATE hereby agrees that it shall report to COVERED ENTITY within two (2) days of discovery any use or disclosure of Information not provided for or allowed by this Contract. (Ref. 164.504(e)(2)(ii)(C).)

23. **Subcontractors and Agents**. BUSINESS ASSOCIATE hereby agrees that any time Information is provided or made available to any subcontractors or agents, BUSINESS ASSOCIATE must enter into a subcontract with the subcontractor or agent that contains the same terms, conditions, and restrictions on the use and disclosure of Information as contained in this Contract. (Ref. 164.504(e)(2)(ii)(D).)

24. **Right of Access to Information**. BUSINESS ASSOCIATE hereby agrees to make available and provide a right of access to Information by an Individual. This right of access shall conform with and meet all of the requirements of 45 C.F.R. 164.524, including substitution of the words "Covered Entity" with BUSINESS ASSOCIATE where appropriate. (Ref. 164.504(e)(2)(ii)(E).)

25. **Amendment and Incorporation of Amendments**. BUSINESS ASSOCIATE agrees to make Information available for amendment and to incorporate any amendments to Information in accordance with 45 C.F.R. 164.526, including substitution of the words "Covered Entity" with BUSINESS ASSOCIATE where appropriate. (Ref. 164.504(e)(2)(ii)(F).)

26. **Provide Accounting**. BUSINESS ASSOCIATE agrees to make Information available as required to provide an accounting of disclosures in accordance with 45 C.F.R. 164.528, including substitution of the words "Covered Entity" with BUSINESS ASSOCIATE where appropriate. (Ref. 164.504(e)(2)(ii)(G).)

27. **Access to Books and Records**. BUSINESS ASSOCIATE hereby agrees to make its internal practices, books, and records relating to the use or disclosure of Information received from, or created or received by BUSINESS ASSOCIATE on behalf of the COVERED ENTITY, available to the Secretary or the Secretary's designee for purposes of determining compliance with the HHS Privacy Regulations. (Ref. 164.504(e)(2)(ii)(H).)

28. **Return or Destruction of Information.** At termination of this Contract, BUSINESS ASSOCIATE hereby agrees to return or destroy all Information received from, or created or received by BUSINESS ASSOCIATE on behalf of COVERED ENTITY. BUSINESS ASSOCIATE agrees not to retain any copies of the Information after termination of this Contract. If return or destruction of the Information is not feasible, BUSINESS ASSOCIATE agrees to extend the protections of this Contract for as long as necessary to protect the Information and to limit any further use or disclosure. If

BUSINESS ASSOCIATE elects to destroy the Information, it shall certify to COVERED ENTITY that the Information has been destroyed. (Ref. 164.504(e)(2)(ii)(I).)

29. **Mitigation Procedures**. BUSINESS ASSOCIATE agrees to have procedures in place for mitigating, to the maximum extent practicable, any deleterious effect from the use or disclosure of Information in a manner contrary to this Contract or the HHS Privacy Regulations. (Ref. 164.530(f).)

30. **Sanction Procedures**. BUSINESS ASSOCIATE agrees and understands that it must develop and implement a system of sanctions for any employee, subcontractor, or agent who violates this Agreement or the HHS Privacy Regulations. (optional, see 164.530(e)(1).)

31. **Property Rights**. The Information shall be and remain the property of COVERED ENTITY. BUSINESS ASSOCIATE agrees that it acquires no title or rights to the Information, including any de-identified information, as a result of this Contract. (optional)

32. **Termination of Contract**. BUSINESS ASSOCIATE agrees that COVERED ENTITY has the right to immediately terminate this Contract and seek relief under the Disputes Article if COVERED ENTITY determines that BUSINESS ASSOCIATE has violated a material term of this Contract. (Ref. 164.506(e)(2)(iii).)

33. **Grounds for Breach**. Any non-compliance by BUSINESS ASSOCIATE with this Contract or the HHS Privacy Regulations will automatically be considered to be a Grounds.

    For Breach, if BUSINESS ASSOCIATE knew or reasonably should have known of such non-compliance and failed to immediately take reasonable steps to cure the non-compliance. (optional)

34. **Choice of Law**. This Contract shall be governed by the law of the State of _____. [The Parties also agree that for purposes of privacy rights, the HHS Privacy Regulations shall supersede all applicable state laws.] (optional)

35. **Disputes**. Any controversy or claim arising out of or relating to the Contract will be finally settled by compulsory arbitration in accordance with the Commercial Arbitration Rules of the American Arbitration Association (AAA), except for injunctive relief as described below in article [or in court of competent jurisdiction]. (optional)

36. **Injunctive Relief**. Notwithstanding any rights or remedies provided for in this Contract, COVERED ENTITY retains all rights to seek injunctive relief to prevent or stop the unauthorized use or disclosure of Information by BUSINESS ASSOCIATE or any agent, contractor, or third party that received Information from BUSINESS ASSOCIATE. (optional)

37. **Miscellaneous.**

38. **Binding Nature and Assignment**. This Contract shall be binding on the Parties hereto and their successors and assigns, but neither Party may assign this

Agreement without the prior written consent of the other, which consent shall not be unreasonably withheld. (optional)

39. **Notices**. Whenever under this Contract one party is required to give notice to the other, such notice shall be deemed given if mailed by First Class United States mail, postage prepaid, and addressed as follows: (optional)

COVERED ENTITY

[Name/Address]

BUSINESS ASSOCIATE

[Name/Address]

Either Party may at any time change its address for notification purposes by mailing a notice stating the change and setting forth the new address.

40. **Good Faith**. The Parties agree to exercise good faith in the performance of this Contract. (optional)

41. **Article Headings**. The article headings used are for reference and convenience only, and shall not enter into the interpretation of this Contract. (optional)

42. **Force Majeure**. BUSINESS ASSOCIATE shall be excused from performance under this Contract for any period BUSINESS ASSOCIATE is prevented from performing any services pursuant hereto, in whole or in part, as a result of an Act of God, war, civil disturbance, court order, labor dispute, or other cause beyond its reasonable control, and such nonperformance shall not be grounds for termination. (optional)

43. **Attorney's Fees**. Except as otherwise specified in this Contract, if any legal action or other proceeding is brought for the enforcement of this Contract, or because of an alleged dispute, breach, default, misrepresentation, or injunctive action, in connection with any of the provisions of this Contract, each party shall bear their own legal expenses and the other cost incurred in that action or proceeding. (optional)

44. **Entire Agreement**. This Contract consists of this document, and constitutes the entire agreement between the Parties. There are no understandings or agreements relating to this Agreement which are not fully expressed in this Contract and no change, waiver, or discharge of obligations arising under this Contract shall be valid unless in writing and executed by the Party against whom such change, waiver, or discharge is sought to be enforced. (optional)

45. **Limitation of Liability.** (optional)

46. **Insurance.** (optional)

47. **Indemnification.** (optional)

48. **Payment.** (optional)

49. **New Statutory and Legislative Requirements.** (optional)

IN WITNESS WHEREOF, BUSINESS ASSOCIATE and COVERED ENTITY have caused this Contract to be signed and delivered by their duly authorized representatives, as of the date set forth above.

BUSINESS ASSOCIATE   COVERED ENTITY

By: _____   By: _____

Print Name: _____   Print Name: _____

Title:_____   Title:_____

Note: This material is used with permission. Alexander J. Brittin, Esq., of the Brittin Law Group, P.L.L.C., 1990 K Street, N.W., Washington, DC 20006, prepared this Contract. He can be reached at alex@brittinlaw.com. The Contract also appears in the "HIPAA Handbook, What Your Organization Needs To Know About The Privacy Regulations," published by URAC. This Agreement does not constitute nor substitute the need for legal advice. For further information about HIPAA see www.privacysecuritynetwork.com/ healthcare.

Model Business Associate Agreements

Davis Wright Tremaine's Model Business Associate Contract Addendum

This form agreement is offered for informational purposes only and does not constitute legal advice or a comprehensive guide to issues to be considered in entering into a business associate agreement.

[Note: This form applies to the relationship between a HIPAA-covered entity and i ts business associate. A different form should be used for a relationship between two covered entities exchanging PHI and having reciprocal business associate obligations.]

HIPAA BUSINESS ASSOCIATE ADDENDUM

This HIPAA Business Associate Addendum ("Addendum") supplements and is made a part of the agreement ("Agreement") by and between Covered Entity ("CE") and Business Associate ("Associate"), and is effective as of _____ (the "Addendum Effective Date").

RECITALS

A.   CE wishes to disclose certain information ("Information") to Associate pursuant to the terms of the Agreement, some of which may constitute Protected Health Information ("PHI").

B.   CE and Associate intend to protect the privacy and provide for the security of PHI disclosed to Associate pursuant to the Agreement in compliance with the Health Insurance Portability and Accountability Act of 1996, Public Law 104-191 ("HIPAA") and regulations promulgated thereunder by the U.S. Department of Health and Human Services (the "HIPAA Regulations") and other applicable laws.

C.   The purpose of this Addendum is to satisfy certain standards and requirements of HIPAA and the HIPAA Regulations, including, but not limited to, Title 45, Section 164.504(e) of the Code of Federal Regulations ("CFR"), as the same may be amended from time to time.

In consideration of the mutual promises below and the exchange of information pursuant to this Addendum, the parties agree as follows:

1.   **Definitions.**

   a.   *"Business Associate"* shall have the meaning given to such term under the HIPAA Regulations, including, but not limited to, 45 CFR Section 160.103.

   b.   *"Covered Entity"* shall have the meaning given to such term under HIPAA and the HIPAA Regulations, including, but not limited to, 45 CFR Section 160.103.

   c.   *"Protected Health Information" or "PHI"* means any information, whether oral or recorded in any form or medium: (i) that relates to the past, present, or future physical or mental condition of an individual; the provision of health care to an individual; or the past, present, or future payment for the provision of health care to an individual, and (ii) that identifies the individual or with respect to which there is a reasonable basis to believe the information can be used to identify the individual, and shall have the meaning given to such term under HIPAA and the HIPAA Regulations, including, but not limited to, 45 CFR Section 164.501. *[45 CFR § 160.103; 45 CFR § 501]*

2.   **Obligations of Associate.**

   a.   *Permitted Uses and Disclosures.* Associate may use and/or disclose PHI received by Associate pursuant to this Agreement ("CE's PHI") solely in accordance with the specifications set forth in *Exhibit A*, which is incorporated herein by reference. In the event of any conflict between this Agreement and *Exhibit A*, this Agreement shall control. *[45 CFR § 164.504(e)(2)(i)]*

   b.   *Nondisclosure.* Associate shall not use or further disclose CE's PHI otherwise than as permitted or required by this Agreement or as required by law. *[45 CFR § 164.504(e)(2)(ii)(A)]*

   c.   *Safeguards.* Associate shall use appropriate safeguards to prevent use or disclosure of CE's PHI otherwise than as provided for by this Agreement. *[45 CFR § 164.504(e)(2)(ii)(B)]* Associate shall maintain a comprehensive written information privacy and security program that includes administrative, technical, and physical safeguards appropriate to the size and complexity of the Associate's operations and the nature and scope of its activities.

d. *Reporting of Disclosures.* Associate shall report to CE any use or disclosure of CE's PHI otherwise than as provided for by this Agreement of which Associate becomes aware. *[45 CFR § 164.504(e)(2)(ii)(C)]*

e. *Associate's Agents.* Associate shall ensure that any agents, including subcontractors, to whom it provides PHI received from (or created or received by Associate on behalf of) CE agree to the same restrictions and conditions that apply to Associate with respect to such PHI. *[45 CFR § 164.504(e)(2)(D)]*

f. *Availability of Information to CE.* Associate shall make available to CE such information as CE may require to fulfill CE's obligations to provide access to, provide a copy of, and account for disclosures with respect to PHI pursuant to HIPAA and the HIPAA Regulations, including, but not limited to, 45 CFR Sections 164.524 and 164.528. *[45 CFR § 164.504(e)(2)(E) and (G)]*

g. *Amendment of PHI.* Associate shall make CE's PHI available to CE as CE may require to fulfill CE's obligations to amend PHI pursuant to HIPAA and the HIPAA Regulations, including, but not limited to, 45 CFR Section 164.526 and Associate shall, as directed by CE, incorporate any amendments to CE's PHI into copies of such PHI maintained by Associate. *[45 CFR § 164.504(e)(2)(F)]*

h. *Internal Practices.* Associate shall make its internal practices, books, and records relating to the use and disclosure of PHI received from CE (or created or received by Associate on behalf of CE) available to the Secretary of the U.S. Department of Health and Human Services for purposes of determining Associate's compliance with HIPAA and the HIPAA Regulations. *[45 CFR § 164.504(e)(2)(H)]*

i. *Associate's Insurance. [This provision should be negotiated.]*

j. *Notification of Breach.* During the term of this Agreement, Associate shall notify CE within twenty-four (24) hours of any suspected or actual breach of security, intrusion, or unauthorized use or disclosure of PHI and/or any actual or suspected use or disclosure of data in violation of any applicable federal or state laws or regulations. Associate shall take (i) prompt corrective action to cure any such deficiencies and (ii) any action pertaining to such unauthorized disclosure required by applicable federal and state laws and regulations. *[This provision should be negotiated.]*

3. **Obligations of CE.** CE shall be responsible for using appropriate safeguards to maintain and ensure the confidentiality, privacy, and security of PHI transmitted to Associate pursuant to this Agreement, in accordance with the standards and requirements of HIPAA and the HIPAA Regulations, until such PHI is received by Associate. Any specifications defining the point of receipt of CE's PHI by Associate shall be set forth in *Exhibit A*.

4. **Audits, Inspection, and Enforcement.** From time to time upon reasonable notice, upon a reasonable determination by CE that Associate has breached this Agreement, CE may inspect the facilities, systems, books, and records of Associate to monitor compliance with this Addendum. Associate shall promptly remedy any violation of any

term of this Addendum and shall certify the same to CE in writing. The fact that CE inspects, or fails to inspect, or has the right to inspect, Associate's facilities, systems, and procedures does not relieve Associate of its responsibility to comply with this Addendum, nor does CE's (i) failure to detect or (ii) detection, but failure to notify Associate or require Associate's remediation of any unsatisfactory practices constitute acceptance of such practice or a waiver of CE's enforcement rights under this Agreement. *[This provision should be negotiated.]*

5. **Termination.**

    a. *Material Breach.* A breach by Associate of any provision of this Addendum, as determined by CE, shall constitute a material breach of the Agreement and shall provide grounds for immediate termination of the Agreement by CE pursuant to Section *[termination for breach section]* of the Agreement. *[45 CFR § 164.504(e)(2)(iii)]*

    b. *Reasonable Steps to Cure Breach.* If CE knows of a pattern of activity or practice of Associate that constitutes a material breach or violation of the Associate's obligations under the provisions of this Addendum or another arrangement and does not terminate this Agreement pursuant to Section 4(a), then CE shall take reasonable steps to cure such breach or end such violation, as applicable. If CE's efforts to cure such breach or end such violation are unsuccessful, CE shall either (i) terminate this Agreement, if feasible, or (ii) if termination of this Agreement is not feasible, CE shall report Associate's breach or violation to the Secretary of the Department of Health and Human Services. *[45 CFR § 164.504(e)(1)(ii)]*

    c. *Judicial or Administrative Proceedings.* Either party may terminate this Agreement, effective immediately, if (i) the other party is named as a defendant in a criminal proceeding for a violation of HIPAA or (ii) a finding or stipulation that the other party has violated any standard or requirement of HIPAA or other security or privacy laws is made in any administrative or civil proceeding in which the party has been joined.

    d. *Effect of Termination.* Upon termination of this Agreement for any reason, Associate shall return and destroy all PHI received from CE (or created or received by Associate on behalf of CE) that Associate still maintains in any form, and shall retain no copies of such PHI or, if return or destruction is not feasible, it shall continue to extend the protections of this Agreement to such information, and limit further use of such PHI to those purposes that make the return or destruction of such PHI infeasible. *[45 CFR § 164.504(e)(2)(I)]*

6. **Indemnification.** Each party will indemnify, hold harmless, and defend the other party to this Agreement from and against any and all claims, losses, liabilities, costs, and other expenses incurred as a result of, or arising directly or indirectly out of, or in connection with: (i) any misrepresentation, breach of warranty, or non-fulfillment of any

undertaking on the part of the party under this Agreement; and (ii) any claims, demands, awards, judgments, actions, and proceedings made by any person or organization arising out of or in any way connected with the party's performance under this Agreement. *[This provision should be negotiated.]*

7. **Limitation of Liability.** *[A covered entity may wish to seek an exception to any limitation of liability provision for the benefit of the business associate with regard to damages related to a breach of the business associate's privacy or security obligations under the Agreement.]*

8. **Disclaimer.** CE makes no warranty or representation that compliance by Associate with this Addendum, HIPAA, or the HIPAA Regulations will be adequate or satisfactory for Associate's own purposes or that any information in Associate's possession or control, or transmitted or received by Associate, is or will be secure from unauthorized use or disclosure. Associate is solely responsible for all decisions made by Associate regarding the safeguarding of PHI.

9. **Certification.** To the extent that CE determines that such examination is necessary to comply with CE's legal obligations pursuant to HIPAA relating to certification of its security practices, CE or its authorized agents or contractors, may, at CE's expense, examine Associate's facilities, systems, procedures, and records as may be necessary for such agents or contractors to certify to CE the extent to which Associate's security safeguards comply with HIPAA, the HIPAA Regulations, or this Addendum.

10. **Amendment.**

    a. *Amendment to Comply with Law.* The parties acknowledge that state and federal laws relating to electronic data security and privacy are rapidly evolving and that amendment of this Agreement may be required to provide for procedures to ensure compliance with such developments. The parties specifically agree to take such action as is necessary to implement the standards and requirements of HIPAA, the HIPAA Regulations, and other applicable laws relating to the security or confidentiality of PHI. The parties understand and agree that CE must receive satisfactory written assurance from Associate that Associate will adequately safeguard all PHI that it receives or creates pursuant to this Agreement. Upon CE's request, Associate agrees to promptly enter into negotiations with CE concerning the terms of an amendment to this Agreement embodying written assurances consistent with the standards and requirements of HIPAA, the HIPAA Regulations, or other applicable laws. CE may terminate this Agreement upon [*30*] days written notice in the event (i) Associate does not promptly enter into negotiations to amend this Agreement when requested by CE pursuant to this Section or (ii) Associate does not enter into an amendment to this Agreement providing assurances regarding the safeguarding of PHI that CE, in its sole discretion, deems sufficient to satisfy the standards and requirements of HIPAA and the HIPAA Regulations.

b. *Amendment of Exhibit A. Exhibit A* may be modified or amended by mutual agreement of the parties at any time without amendment of this Agreement.

11. **Assistance in Litigation or Administrative Proceedings.** Associate shall make itself, and any subcontractors, employees, or agents assisting Associate in the performance of its obligations under this Agreement, available to CE, at no cost to CE, to testify as witnesses, or otherwise, in the event of litigation or administrative proceedings being commenced against CE, its directors, officers, or employees based upon claimed violation of HIPAA, the HIPAA Regulations, or other laws relating to security and privacy, except where Associate or its subcontractor, employee, or agent is a named adverse party.

12. **No Third Party Beneficiaries.** Nothing express or implied in this Agreement is intended to confer, nor shall anything herein confer, upon any person other than CE, Associate, and their respective successors or assigns, any rights, remedies, obligations, or liabilities whatsoever.

13. **Effect on Agreement.** Except as specifically required to implement the purposes of this Addendum, or to the extent inconsistent with this Addendum, all other terms of the Agreement shall remain in force and effect.

14. **Interpretation.** This Addendum and the Agreement shall be interpreted as broadly as necessary to implement and comply with HIPAA, HIPAA Regulations, and applicable state laws.

The parties agree that any ambiguity in this Addendum shall be resolved in favor of a meaning that complies and is consistent with HIPAA and the HIPAA Regulations.

IN WITNESS WHEREOF, the parties hereto have duly executed this Addendum as of the Addendum Effective Date.

CE	*ASSOCIATE*
_____	_____
By: _____	By: _____
Print Name: _____	Print Name: _____
Title: _____	Title: _____
Date: _____	Date: _____

EXHIBIT A

PERMITTED USES AND DISCLOSURES

This Exhibit sets forth the permitted uses and disclosures of Information by Associate pursuant to Section 2 of the Addendum to the [FULL NAME OF AGREEMENT] ("Agreement") by and between CE and Associate, dated _____, and is effective as of _____ (the "Exhibit Effective Date"). This Exhibit may be amended from time to time as provided in Section 5(b) of the Addendum.

1. *Purpose(s) of Disclosure.* The purpose(s) for which CE shall disclose Information to Associate are as follows: _____
_____
_____
_____
_____

2. *Information to be Disclosed.* CE shall disclose the following Information to Associate in accordance with the terms of the Agreement: _____
_____
_____
_____
_____

3. *Permitted Uses and Disclosures of Information.* Associate shall be limited to the following uses and/or disclosures of CE's PHI: _____
_____
_____
_____
_____

4. *Subcontractor(s).* If Associate intends to utilize any subcontractor(s) in performing Associate's obligations under the Agreement, such subcontractor(s) shall be identified as follows:_____
_____
_____
_____
_____

[5. *Use for Management and Administration.* Associate may use PHI received by Associate in its capacity as a Business Associate of CE for the proper management and administration of Associate, if such disclosure is necessary (i) for the proper management and administration of Associate or (ii) to carry out the legal responsibilities of Associate.] *[Optional; 45 CFR § 164.504(e)(4)(i)]*

[6.   *Disclosure for Management and Administration.* Associate may disclose PHI received by Associate in its capacity as a Business Associate of CE for the proper management and administration of Associate if (i) the disclosure is required by law or (ii) Associate (a) obtains reasonable assurances from the person to whom the PHI is disclosed that it will be held confidentially and used or further disclosed only as required by law or for the purpose for which it was disclosed to the person and (b) the person notifies Associate of any instances of which it becomes aware in which the confidentiality of the PHI has been breached.] *[Optional; 45 CFR § 164.504(e)(4)(ii)]*

[7.   *Data Aggregation Services.* For purposes of this Section, "Data Aggregation" means, with respect to CE's PHI, the combining of such PHI by Associate with the PHI received by Associate in its capacity as a Business Associate of another Covered Entity to permit data analyses that relate to the health care operations of the respective Covered Entities. Associate shall provide the following Data Aggregation services relating to the health care operations of CE:] *[Optional; 45 CFR § 164.504(e)(2)(i)(B); 45 CFR § 164.501]*

_____

_____

_____

_____

[8.   *Receipt.* Associate's receipt of CE's PHI pursuant to the transactions contemplated by this Agreement shall be deemed to occur as follows, and Associate's obligations under this Addendum shall commence with respect to such PHI upon such receipt:]

_____

_____

_____

_____

[9.   *Additional Restrictions on Use of Data.* CE is a Business Associate of certain other Covered Entities and, pursuant to such obligations of CE, Associate shall comply with the following restrictions on the use and disclosure of PHI:] _____

_____

_____

_____

_____

10.   *Additional Terms. [This section may include specifications for disclosure format, method of transmission, use of an intermediary, use of digital signatures or PKI, disaster*

recovery planning, authentication, additional security or privacy specifications, de-identification of data, and other additional terms.]

_____

_____

_____

_____

_____

_____

_____

_____

_____

_____

_____

_____

CE	*ASSOCIATE*
_____	_____
By: _____	By: _____
Print Name: _____	Print Name: _____
Title: _____	Title: _____
Date: _____	Date: _____

Davis Wright Tremaine's HIPAA Business Associate "Placeholder Provisions"

HIPAA COMPLIANCE

During the term of this Agreement, Business Associate ("Associate") may receive from Covered Entity ("CE"), or may receive or create on behalf of CE, certain confidential health or medical information ("Protected Health Information" or "PHI," as further defined below). This PHI is subject to protection under state and/or federal law, including the Health Insurance Portability and Accountability Act of 1996, Public Law 104-191 ("HIPAA") and regulations promulgated thereunder by the U.S. Department of Health and Human Services ("HIPAA Regulations"). Associate represents that it has in place policies and procedures that will adequately safeguard any PHI it receives or creates, and Associate specifically agrees, on behalf of itself, its subcontractors and agents, to safeguard and protect the confidentiality of Protected Health Information consistent with applicable law, including currently effective provisions of HIPAA and the HIPAA Regulations.

The parties acknowledge that state and federal laws relating to electronic data security and privacy are rapidly evolving and that amendment of this Agreement may be required to provide for procedures to ensure compliance with such developments. The parties specifically agree to take such action as is necessary to implement the requirements of HIPAA, the HIPAA Regulations, and other applicable laws relating to the security or confidentiality of PHI. The parties understand and agree that CE must receive satisfactory written assurance from Associate that Associate will adequately safeguard all Protected Health Information that it receives or creates. Upon CE's request, Associate agrees promptly to enter into negotiations with CE concerning the terms of an amendment to this Agreement embodying written assurances consistent with the requirements of HIPAA and the HIPAA Regulations.

Notwithstanding any other provision of this Agreement, CE may terminate this Agreement upon thirty (30) days' notice in the event: (a) Associate does not promptly enter into negotiations to amend this Agreement when requested by CE, or (b) Associate does not execute and deliver to CE an amendment to this Agreement providing assurances regarding the safeguarding of PHI that CE, in its sole judgment, deems sufficient to meet requirements and standards of HIPAA and the HIPAA Regulations.

Notwithstanding any other provision of this Agreement, CE may immediately terminate this Agreement in the event: (a) Associate or any of its subcontractors or agents discloses PHI in a manner that is not authorized by CE or by applicable law; (b) Associate breaches any of the provisions of this section; or (c) Associate or any of its subcontractors or agents engages in any other act or omission that is contrary to the obligations of a "business associate" under any currently effective provisions of HIPAA or the HIPAA Regulations, or that otherwise prevents either party from meeting the requirements of HIPAA, the HIPAA Regulations, or other applicable law concerning the security or confidentiality of PHI.

Upon termination of this Agreement for any reason, Associate shall return or destroy all PHI received from CE (or created or received by Associate on behalf of CE) that Associate still maintains in any form and shall retain no copies of such PHI. If return or destruction is not feasible, Associate shall notify CE, continue to extend the protections of this Agreement to such information, and limit further use of such PHI to those purposes that make the return or destruction of PHI infeasible.

For purposes of this section, "Protected Health Information" means any information, whether oral or recorded in any form or medium: (a) that relates to the past, present, or future physical or mental health or condition of an individual; the provision of health care to an individual; or the past, present, or future payment for the provision of health care to an individual; and (b) that identifies the individual or with respect to which there is a reasonable basis to believe the information can be used to identify the individual.

This section shall be interpreted in a manner consistent with HIPAA, the HIPAA Regulations, and other state or federal laws applicable to PHI.

© Davis Wright Tremaine LLP 2001.

Source: This material is used with permission. The author is W. Reece Hirsch, Davis Wright Tremaine LLP, (reecehirsch@dwt.com). These forms are supplied by Davis Wright Tremaine, LLP, as samples and are not substitutes for legal advice pertinent to any specific circumstances. You should consult legal counsel before utilizing any sample forms, including this one. For more information about Davis Wright Tremaine, LLP, please consult the Web site www.dwt.com. HIPAA-focused material can also be found at www.ehealthlaw.com.

Model Requests for Assessment

PrivacySecurityNetwork™'s Sample Request for Proposal to Conduct HIPAA Assessment

1. Request for Proposal Specifications

    1.1. Purpose

    1.2. Key Dates

    1.3. Questions and Answers

    1.4. Copies of Proposal

    1.5. Negotiation of Contract

2. Request for Proposal Information

    2.1. Statement of Need

    2.2. Objectives and Goals of Assessment

    2.3. Vendor Responsibilities

        2.3.1. Scope of Work

            2.3.1.1. HIPAA Education and Training

                2.3.1.1.1. Education for Managers and Staff Involved

                2.3.1.1.2. Education for HIPAA Core Team

            2.3.1.2. Baseline Privacy and Security Assessment

            2.3.1.3. E-Business Assessment and Strategic Approach for HIPAA

            2.3.1.4. Development of a Strategic Approach for HIPAA

            2.3.1.5. Development of Detailed Implementation Plans and Budget

        2.3.2. Deliverables

    2.4. [YOUR COMPANY™S] Environment

        2.4.1. Overview of [YOUR COMPANY]

        2.4.2. Overview of Current Technical Environment

        2.4.3. Overview of Current Applications Environment

3. Response Guidelines

    3.1. Response Guidelines

        3.1.1. Preparation Costs Borne By Vendor

        3.1.2. Rights of Non-Response

    3.2. Contents of the Response

        3.2.1. Section I: Introduction

        3.2.2. Section II: Vendor Qualifications

            3.2.2.1. Qualifications and Experience of the Company

            3.2.2.2. Management Capability

            3.2.2.3. References

            3.2.2.4. Subcontractors

        3.2.3. Section III: Understanding of Requirements, Scope of Work, and Deliverables

        3.2.4. Section IV: Provide Work Plan and Schedule

        3.2.5. Section V: Proposed Costs

4. Evaluation of Proposal

5. Appendix: [YOUR COMPANY™S] Organization Chart

6. Appendix: [YOUR COMPANY™S] Core Application Inventory and Schematic

7. Appendix: [YOUR COMPANY™S] Current Privacy and Security Policies

Used with permission by Alexander J. Brittin, Esq., of the Brittin Law Group, P.L.L.C., 1900 K Street, N.W., Washington, DC 20006. He can be reached at alex@brittinlaw.com. For further information about HIPAA see www.privacysecuritynetwork.com/healthcare.

Southern California HIPAA Forum
Assessment Template

Request for Proposal Template

Consulting Services to Assist the Purchaser Comply with Health Insurance Portability and Accountability Act of 1996. This proposal template was created solely for the purpose of sharing. It was made available on www.HIPAAUSA.com/social/workgroups.html

OBJECTIVE

To obtain the services of a consulting firm(s) (Vendor), to provide a qualified team of individuals to assist XXX Purchaser to comply with HR 3103, the Health Insurance Portability and Accountability Act of 1996 (HIPAA), assess the current environment, provide recommendations for achieving HIPAA compliance within the required time frames, and, at the option of XXX, to provide remediation and training. Vendor will also be required to provide a principal person to assist the XXX Project Manager in the coordination of various activities, participate in the presentations to the XXX executive team and committees.

INTRODUCTION

The health care industry has been awaiting the promulgation of HIPAA rules. The rules fall into five major categories:

- EDI transaction standards, including code sets
- Coordination of benefits processing
- Unique identifiers (including allowed uses) for individuals, employers, health plans, and health care providers
- Security, confidentiality, and electronic signatures
- Privacy for individually identifiable health information

Final rules for the EDI transaction standards (with the exception of the 275 Claims Attachment standard) including code sets have been issued. Final rules for the remaining parts of the legislation are expected to be issued before the November 2000 election, with the exception of rules pertaining to unique identifiers and electronic signatures.

Health care providers and payers have a 26-month window of time within which to implement these rules. Given this, XXX is beginning its HIPAA compliance effort with the establishment of an enterprise-wide HIPAA compliance function and with the engagement of a consulting firm or firms to assess our current environment, to provide recommendations for achieving HIPAA compliance within the required time frames, and at the option of XXX, to provide project oversight, remediation, and training.

This assessment engagement will initially focus on the transaction standards and code sets but will ultimately include all portions of the legislation, even those portions where final rules have not yet been issued. While update information received through various sources indicates that the principles expressed in those rules not yet promulgated may change to require a greater level of attention to security, privacy, data accessibility, there is also an indication that the first issuance of the final rules will not deviate substantially from the proposed rules currently available to us.

The optional remediation effort will be to make all necessary changes to all systems, data, procedures, and policies to be in HIPAA compliance. The other optional area of this Work Order is to develop curricula and provide the training to XXX trainers and employees.

BACKGROUND

[Size of organization and potential scope of project.]

Instructions on Completion of Objectives

The successful completion of each objective below will require the development of a comprehensive written report and the development of illustrative materials and the presentation of each product. The comprehensive report will be submitted to the XXX Project Manager. Upon approval of the comprehensive report, the presentation materials will be prepared and presented at both an Executive Summary level for top management and at a detailed level for mid-managers, first line supervisors, and key personnel as identified by XXX. The goal of these presentations is to ensure enterprise-wide understanding of the environment, the impact of the legislation, and the effort and commitment required in attaining compliance. Presentations to the XXX Board and other senior managers may also be required from time to time.

Project tracking of the objectives will include regular status reports and status meetings where progress on objectives as defined in the work plan is measured. Specific reasons for delay of any objective must be provided in status reports and at status meetings.

Completion of the objectives outlined in this document will understandably require the assistance of XXX personnel. To that end, XXX fully intends to provide to the Vendor the following, but not limited to, types of information:

- Organization charts
- Contact personnel for each entity within XXX
- Descriptions of service provided by XXX with available statistics
- Inventory of all known published and draft policies and procedures
- Inventory of all known standardized hard copy and automated forms used within the organization
- Inventory of all known information systems used within the organization

- Inventory of all known commercial software used on all computers (desktop, mid-range, and mainframe)
- Inventory of all known partnerships with XXX
- Inventory of all contracts with a brief description of service provided by vendor

In the event the above kinds of information or documents have not been received from the various XXX organizations or managers by a reasonable due date, the XXX Project Manager shall be notified immediately. The Vendor shall also report to XXX Project Manager any concerns about either the numbers or abilities of the XXX team members provided. Any delays or inability to complete affected deliverables by such problems shall be discussed for a mutually agreed upon resolution.

XXX understands that changes between proposed rules used for this assessment and final rules may occur and result in the need for modification of deliverables. Vendor will be expected to make whatever modifications may be required to completed or in-process work products. Modifications may be made either through update or issuance of addendum depending on the current state of the work product. This requires Vendor to continually maintain current knowledge of proposed legislation and use that knowledge to update or amend work products. Vendor will also be required to include this new knowledge in regularly produced status reports.

Completion of deliverables shall be only upon written acceptance by XXX Project Manager of the deliverable.

ASSESSMENT OBJECTIVES

Objective 1: Develop a Project Plan for the Engagement

Vendor shall prepare a complete Project Plan, which enumerates and defines all tasks to be completed, identifies milestones, identifies resources required to complete each task, and estimates the elapsed time for the task to be completed. The Project Plan should clearly identify those tasks that require XXX personnel participation or which are the responsibility of XXX. The Project Plan shall define the roles of Vendor Project Manager, project team that will include Vendor and XXX personnel, as well as key contact personnel with whom the Vendor will require frequent and timely contact. The Project Plan shall define the authority of the Vendor Project Manager, each Vendor project team member, and the required authority of each XXX team member, in order to enable XXX to establish appropriate internal authority structures. The Project Plan shall also include a method of problem escalation and resolution as well as define the escalation tree for both Vendor and XXX.

Deliverable 1: Project Plan

Vendor shall submit a comprehensive report as directed in Section IV (Instructions on Completion of Objectives) above that includes, but is not limited to:

- Assessment Project Work Plan with milestones, specific tasks, resources required, and task duration.
- Description of project team, including skills, responsibilities, and authority.
- Problem resolution approach and escalation tree.

Objective 2: Provide an Executive Project Director to Assist XXX Project Manager

Vendor shall provide an Executive Project Director who shall assist the XXX Project Manager in the following, but not limited to:

- Meet with the XXX Project Manager not less than once per week.
- Coordinate all necessary activities between Vendor Project Manager, other Vendor staff, and the managers of the various XXX facilities.
- Maintain status reports.
- Document critical decisions made and actions taken.
- Process and maintain all necessary records.
- Disseminate all pertinent project information and materials to the appropriate parties.
- Assist the XXX Project Manager prepare for presentations to executive-level staff and other government officials.
- Participate in the presentations to executive-level staff and other government officials.

Deliverable 2: Executive Project Director

Vendor shall submit a comprehensive report as directed in Section IV (Instructions on Completion of Objectives) above that includes, but is not limited to, written status reports in the format and at a frequency mutually agreed upon and written summaries of meetings and presentations after each event.

Objective 3: Perform a HIPAA Requirements Assessment and Translation

In order for XXX to comply with the administrative simplification rules promulgated under HIPAA, it is necessary to understand the requirements defined by the rules. While HIPAA rules set parameters for compliance with HIPAA legislation, in most cases the rules are of a general nature and do not give specifics as to the steps that might be taken to comply with the specific rule.

Therefore, Vendor shall provide, for *ALL* HIPAA rules (whether proposed or finalized), an orientation document and at least one orientation session where the rules are translated into terms that clearly indicate to the readers and audience (selected by XXX Project Manager) the kinds of steps that must be taken to achieve compliance.

Deliverable 3: HIPAA Requirements Assessment and Translation

Vendor shall submit a comprehensive report as directed in Section IV (Instructions on Completion of Objectives) above that includes, but is not limited to:

- Description of the intent of all HIPAA rules, proposed or finalized, and a description of the problems the rule is attempting to address.
- Outline of the requirements set forth in the rule.
- Identification of those organizations that must comply with the rule (eg, provider, payer, etc.).
- Identification of which parts of the organization must assume responsibility for compliance (eg, Finance, Clinical staff, Information Technology, etc.).
- Identification of the types of transactions or processes to which the rule applies.
- Examples of methods of compliance with the rule.
- Any additional information necessary to understand the implications of the rule.
- Bibliography of all sources used in preparation of document.

Objective 4: Perform and Document a Complete Assessment of XXX's Current State That Identifies All Processes and Data Sources, Both Automated and Manual, That Involve Patient, Provider, or Payer Data That Will Be Impacted by HIPAA Regulations

In order to identify the steps required for XXX to comply with HIPAA rules, Vendor shall review the current state of XXX's technical, business, and data storage environment, including security, confidentiality, and privacy for individually identifiable health information concerns, and compare it to HIPAA regulations in order to determine the impact of HIPAA regulations on XXX's environment.

Vendor shall conduct the assessment through the use of all documentation provided as well as through personal interviews with whatever level of personnel Vendor feels is necessary to obtain the required information.

For each entry in the completed assessment, Vendor shall provide a description of how the data/process is impacted by the HIPAA compliance requirements. Impact statement at minimum should include:

- A description of the specific rules that create an impact.
- An assessment of the legal liabilities and/or monetary sanctions that could be imposed for failure to comply with the associated rules.

Deliverable 4: Assessment of XXX's Current State

Vendor shall submit a comprehensive report, as directed in Section IV (Instructions on Completion of Objectives) above a final assessment document, which must include, but not be limited to, an inventory of the *current* XXX business and technical environment that will be *impacted by HIPAA regulations.* The assessment process and final document should include results of assessing the following as well as any other areas Vendor deems appropriate:

- Business operations and processes where patient data is created, modified, reviewed, transferred, or exchanged.
- Existing documentation of patient information flow, whether automated or manual.
- Sources and repositories of patient information, whether automated (eg, databases, data warehouses, data marts, disk files, diskette files, tape files) or manual (eg, hard-copy films, clinicians' notes, lab orders and results, appointment data, documents with patient signature, or other documents normally found in a patient record).
- Electronic transaction formats, identifiers, data element values, and code sets related to patient data and their associated source(s) and destination(s).
- Local HCPCS codes, types, and uses.
- Manual forms with associated data element values and code sets related to patient data and their associated source(s) and destination(s).
- Policies and procedures related to the processing of patient information, addressing both automated and manual processes.
- Policies and procedures related to security, confidentiality, and privacy of patient data that address both automated and manual data.
- Business partner relationships and associated memorandums of understanding, contracts, and agreements for relationships where transfer of patient data may occur (eg, subcontracted or partner providers, subcontracted benefit managers, clearinghouse arrangements, delegated medical management, contracted medical record review, transcription services, contracted benefit managers, third-party administrators, primary and secondary payers, etc).
- Information technology, systems, one-way interfaces, automated data exchange, and e-Commerce applications that use, create, or modify patient data.
- Automated security features and mechanisms (eg, network and systems architectures, firewalls, DMZs, user authentication features, public key and certificate features, electronic signature implementation, and back-up storage and retrieval processes).
- Network transmission data defining current traffic related to patient identifiable information in any format, including file transfers, batch processes, online real-time transactions, e-mail and e-mail attachments, Web uploads or downloads, and Web-site inquiries.
- Automated and manual data recovery processes and storage locations.

- Sources and repositories of provider information, including provider number, whether automated (eg, databases, data warehouses, data marts, disk files, diskette files, tape files) or manual documents; forms; and reports containing provider information.

- Current portfolio of IT and business initiatives in process of implementation that affect the handling of either patient or provider information.

Objective 5: Perform a Gap Analysis That Identifies and Prioritizes Those Areas in the Current Environment Where Non-compliance Exists

Vendor shall prepare a document that identifies each business process or data source that is non-compliant with HIPAA regulations. Additionally, Vendor shall indicate areas that may currently be compliant but may not be compliant with future versions of rules (eg, ICD-9 is currently compliant but ICD-10 will be required by 2003). Analysis should define the risks involved in continuing to be non-compliant and should prioritize the non-compliance issues that must be addressed. Prioritization of non-compliance should be based on scheduled compliance time frames vs. work required to achieve compliance and on sanctions attached to compliance.

Deliverable 5: Gap Analysis

Vendor shall submit a comprehensive report as directed in Section IV (Instructions on Completion of Objectives) above that includes, but is not limited to:

- Itemization of each process or data sources that are not currently HIPAA compliant.

- Description of reason for non-compliance for each identified area of non-compliance.

- Prioritized list of areas of non-compliance in order of importance.

- Explanation of the reason for the priority given.

- Identification of those positions/units within XXX whose effort is required to effect compliance.

- Identification of areas currently in compliance but may be affected by proposed or pending rule changes.

Objective 6: Recommend an Approach and Strategies for HIPAA Compliance for All Areas of Non-compliance Identified

Compliance with any regulation can usually be achieved in more than one manner. It can be achieved minimally, where the "letter of the law" is fulfilled, but where improvement of the current operation is not addressed, or it can be achieved in a manner that benefits from the need to change and incorporates related operational improvements as well.

Vendor shall prepare recommendations for achieving compliance that include at least two proposed solutions: one a "minimalist" approach that requires the least expenditure of resources to reach compliance and the other an "optimum" approach (where available) that would, in addition to achieving compliance, also improve the current operation in some manner. Minimalist approaches should require the least amount of time to compliance but may not be the most economical method of compliance on an ongoing basis. The optimum approaches should be the "best practice" approach to completion.

Recommendations for achieving compliance should address both the technical and operational aspects of the issue. For data element and code set non-compliance issues, the analysis should include a determination of all the modifications required in existing information systems to achieve compliance. Particular attention should be paid, while formulating recommendations, on ways to minimize the amount of impact to the current operation. For example, perhaps the easiest and quickest way to transition to new code sets or values is to develop data mapping programs and processes rather than modifying a multitude of existing processes and computer systems. However, the quickest way may result in staff inability to proficiently interact with external health care providers, as they will not have a working knowledge of the new code sets. This in turn could result in substantial additional "soft costs" to the organization.

Each recommendation should include an estimate of the resources required (based on best available information) for each option presented. Each recommendation should also include advantages and disadvantages as well as risks associated with each option. For each area of non-compliance, recommendations should be made as to any "short-term" or preliminary actions that could be taken to progress toward compliance, even before completion of the assessment.

Deliverable 6: Recommendations and Strategies

Vendor shall submit a comprehensive report as directed in Section IV (Instructions on Completion of Objectives) above in a clear and easily understandable format that includes, but is not limited to:

- Recommendations for achieving compliance—"minimalist" and "optimum" with recommended approach for compliance.
- Estimations of resources required for each recommendation.
- Pros and cons of each proposed recommendation that clearly outline the risks for minimalist or non-compliance.

Objective 7: Develop a Remediation Project Plan and Cost Estimate for Achieving Compliance

Working with XXX, Vendor shall identify, for each area of non-compliance, the approach to be pursued by XXX. Upon identification of the approach to compliance for each area of non-compliance, Vendor shall develop a comprehensive remediation project plan, which identifies and prioritizes the tasks to be completed and identifies numbers and levels of resources required for each task. Additionally, develop a cost and benefit estimate for the implementation of each recommendation. Where synergies exist between multiple recommendations, note cost accordingly.

During this phase, selected vendor is responsible for ensuring that XXX project team members and senior and mid-level management have complete understanding of the recommendations, the tasks within the project plans, the reasons for the sequencing of tasks, the reasons for the resources requested, and the basis for the cost estimates.

Deliverable 7: Remediation Project Plan and Cost Estimate

Vendor shall submit a comprehensive report as directed in Section IV (Instructions on Completion of Objectives) above that includes, but is not limited to:

- Document outlining the remediation solution selected by the XXX Project Manager, based on Deliverable 6: Recommendations and Strategies, for each area of non-compliance.
- Comprehensive remediation project plan.
    - i)   Cost and benefit estimates for the implementation of each recommended solution.
    - ii) Communication of the recommendations to the project team.

Objective 8: Updates or Addendums to Deliverables Due to Changes in the HIPAA Regulations

Vendor shall keep abreast of any changes or modifications to any interim HIPAA regulations and the final regulations. Vendor shall advise the XXX Project Manager of such changes and their effects on any objective of this Work Order and prepare an update or addendum to the affected deliverable(s).

Deliverable 8: Updates or Addendums to Deliverables Due to Changes in the HIPAA Regulations

For any deliverable, already approved in writing by XXX Project Manager, affected by any changes or modifications of the HIPAA regulations, Vendor shall submit a comprehensive report as directed in Section IV (Instructions on Completion of Objectives) above that includes, but is not limited to:

- A comparison of the old and new regulation.
- A detailed summary of how the change affects the deliverable(s).
- The corrected deliverable(s) in whole or only the parts affected in a mutually agreed upon format.

Objective 9: Implementation of Remediation Project Plan

At the option of XXX, Vendor shall implement a remediation project plan. The final remediation effort may be whole or selected parts or modified combination of minimalist and optimum approaches as accepted in Deliverables 6 and 7 above.

Remediation may include, but not be limited to, modifications to:

- In-house IT and business systems where patient data is created, modified, reviewed, transferred, or exchanged.
- Sources, repositories, and recovery process of patient information (manual and electronic).
- Electronic transaction formats, identifiers, data element values, and code sets related to patient data.
- Policies and procedures related to the processing of patient information, addressing both automated and manual processes.
- Policies and procedures related to security, confidentiality, and privacy of patient data that address both automated and manual data.
- Information technology, systems, one-way interfaces, automated data exchange, and e-Commerce applications that use, create, or modify patient data.
- Automated security features and mechanisms.
- Network data transmissions and transactions.
- Sources, repositories, and recovery process of provider information (manual and electronic).

Deliverable 9: Remediation

Vendor shall submit a comprehensive report as directed in Section IV (Instructions on Completion of Objectives) above that includes, but is not limited to:

- Certification of completion of the implementation process and compliance with all HIPAA regulations.
- A status report of systems and software maintained or supported by outside vendors affected by HIPAA regulations.
- Provide electronic and hard-copy lists and related documentation of all changes and modifications as mutually defined.

Objective 10: Provide Training

At the option of XXX, Vendor shall develop two training curriculums and any necessary materials and documents, one for XXX trainers and one for XXX employees, to be identified by XXX Project Manager, in the use and maintenance of the systems, software, coding, automated and manual procedures, and policies to ensure continued compliance with HIPAA regulations.

At the option of XXX, Vendor shall provide the training to the trainers and employees.

Deliverable 10: Training

Vendor shall submit a comprehensive report as directed in Section IV (Instructions on Completion of Objectives) above that includes, but is not limited to:

- The curriculum and any other documentation relating to the training in the different affected areas as it relates to HIPAA regulations.
- A summary of the training sessions.

MINIMUM BID REQUIREMENTS

To effectively respond, a bidder must present the following minimum information:

- A current résumé for individual(s) assigned to this project.
- Corporate/individual qualifications.
- Each individual team member must meet at least one of the following requirements. The team as a whole shall meet all of the following requirements. Representative(s) of the corporation and individual team members, particularly individuals submitted for Executive Project Director, may be interviewed prior to final selection.

Project Management

- Has demonstrated knowledge of HIPAA regulations.
- Has provided HIPAA overview, project planning, and general regulation and impact summary reports to large health care organization.
- Has developed a health care assessment and strategy analysis programs, or management and assessment tool, or operational software that (relating to requirements similar to HIPAA):
  - —Facilitates standardization
  - —Facilitates requirements and policy compliance
  - —Includes structured cost–benefit model
  - —Includes EDI standard tables and reports
  - —Includes core assessment checklist and summaries
  - —Includes other collaborative methodology products
  - —Will aid in the rapid execution of the required planning and operational document functions.

- Has interacted with, and made presentations to, senior-level executives, senior-level managers, and high-level government officials.
- Has experience in managing integration, implementation, or development projects for large government agencies.

Assessment

- Has demonstrated knowledge of HIPAA regulations.
- Has used a management and assessment tool or operational software (relating to requirements similar to HIPAA).
- Has developed policy and procedure design and implementation, risk analysis, disaster recovery management reports.
- Has implemented HIPAA transaction sets, code sets, and identifiers.
- Has knowledge and understanding of HCPCS, ICD, DRG, and other health care regulations and standards (ie, JCAHO, NCQA).
- Has participated in projects that required an assessment of XXX's internal structure.
- Has 10 years experience in health insurance systems.

Security

- Has performed HIPAA security compliance surveys and made recommendations.
- Has developed comprehensive security software management programs that apply the requirements contained in the HIPAA to:
  —satisfy IT security requirements
  —assure privacy protection
  —make systems secure from intrusions
  —secure database software.
- Has used a comprehensive security software management program that applies the requirements contained in HIPAA.
- Has developed information security policies, audit procedures and reports, and job-level security matrix.
- Has experience with information system security (network and telecommunications) management in organizations similar to XXX.

Data Storage

- Has at least 5 years EDI experience in a major health system.
- Has knowledge of data interchange mapping such as HL7, EDIFACT, and X.12.
- Has provided EDI readiness assessments for major health care insurer or provider.
- Has EDI claims technical and business expertise.
- Has been an active participant in WEDI, EHNAC, and ANSI ASC X.12N.

References

References shall include company name, contact person, telephone number, and an overview of the consulting services provided by the individual or the firm. These references may be called for their assessment of Vendor's or proposed team member's work performed and to verify experience claimed to meet the above requirements.

HIPAA Assessment Agreement

Vendor shall propose a form of agreement pursuant to which Vendor's services would be performed, based on the model contract attached as Exhibit A. Vendor shall supply, as part of its response, a version of such an Agreement, which Vendor is prepared to execute in the event Vendor is the successful proponent, as well as a version of the Agreement comparing it to the form provided with this request, with an explanation of deviations in the proposed Agreement from the form.

PERIOD OF PERFORMANCE

The period of performance shall commence upon execution of the Work Order and continue for 24 months or until each deliverable is completed and approved in writing by XXX's Project Manager.

INVOICES AND PAYMENT

Vendor shall submit an invoice upon completion of each deliverable. Deliverables shall be considered complete only upon written acceptance by XXX Project Manager. XXX reserves the right to withhold 25% of the cost of Deliverables 4, 6, and 7, until all deliverables have been accepted in writing by XXX Project Director. Each invoice shall include, at minimum, detail of objective(s) and deliverable(s) completed and the fixed price.

PRICING SCHEDULE

All cost associated with the completion of work under this Work Order should be fully factored into the fixed prices submitted by the vendor. No out-of-pocket expenses shall be billable by vendor or team members.

	Fixed Price
Deliverable 1: Project Plan	$_____
Deliverable 2: Executive Project Director	$_____
Deliverable 3: HIPAA Requirements Assessment and Translation	$_____
Deliverable 4: Assessment of XXX's Current State	$_____
Deliverable 5: Gap Analysis	$_____
Deliverable 6: Recommendations and Strategies	$_____
Deliverable 7: Remediation Project Plan and Cost Estimate	$_____
Deliverable 8: Updates or Addendums to Deliverable(s) Due to Changes in the HIPAA Regulations	$_____

OPTIONAL DELIVERABLES

The following deliverables are at the sole option of XXX. Best-guess estimates are requested, based on:

i)   XXX patient load, existing XXX facilities, and systems as indicated in Section III, Background, above;

ii) Information requested in Deliverables 1 through 8 above; and

iii) Vendor's past experience.

   Upon acceptance of Deliverables 1 through 8, at XXX's sole discretion, the fixed prices for Deliverables 9 and/or 10 may be renegotiated or released for new bids. Failure to bid on Deliverables 9 and 10 will disqualify Vendor from consideration if deliverables are released for new bids.

Deliverable 9: Remediation

Minimalist approach $_____
Optimum approach $_____
50/50 (Minimalist/Optimum) approach $_____

Deliverable 10: Training

Training of 25 trainers (@ $_____ per 25 if more than 25) $_____
Training of 100 employees (@ $_____ per 100 if more than 100) $_____
TOTAL $_____

Source: This proposal template was created solely for the purpose of sharing and can be accessed at www.HIPAAUSA.com/social/ workgroups.html. It was created by Cecilia Bull of LA County Department of Health Services and Gerry Hinkley of Davis Wright Tremaine, LLP.

The Healthcare Privacy Project's HIPAA Myths and Facts

MYTHS AND FACTS ABOUT THE FEDERAL MEDICAL PRIVACY REGULATION

Myth 1: The regulation will "jeopardize the quality and timeliness of patient care" and "drive a wedge between individuals and their care providers."

Sources: "Wedge" comment—"HIPAA's Privacy Standards: Driving a Wedge Between Patients and the Health Field," by Marilou M. King, attorney representing the American Hospital Association (page 1).

"Quality of Care" comment: Testimony of Blue Cross and Blue Shield Association before the Senate Committee on Health, Education, Labor, and Pensions, presented February 8, 2001 (page 11)("This standard . . . could jeopardize the quality and timeliness of patient care . . .")

Fact: The regulation will improve the quality of care and the patient–provider relationship. Concerns about lack of privacy now drive a wedge between patients and their providers and impede the provision of quality care because patients withhold information, avoid asking certain questions, or fail to seek care altogether. Among other benefits, the regulation creates the opportunity for patients and their health care providers to engage in a dialogue about how their information will be used and gives patients more control over uses and disclosures. This regulation will go a long way toward promoting confidence in the privacy of medical information and in the health care system.

Myth 2: "If a patient is sharing a room with another patient, which is often the case, physicians may be constrained to discuss openly vital care and treatment issues for fear of running afoul of HIPAA's many prohibitions." A similar charge being made is that "new soundproof walls and offices may need to be built in health care facilities."

Sources: "Oral communications and single rooms" comment: Testimony of the American Hospital Association before the Senate Committee on Health, Education, Labor, and Pensions, presented February 8, 2001 (page 10).

"Sound-proof" comment: Testimony of Blue Cross and Blue Shield Association before the Senate Committee on Health, Education, Labor, and Pensions, presented February 8, 2001 (page 7).

Fact: Health care professionals, and the hospitals in which they work, should take reasonable steps to make sure that conversations about one patient are not overheard by others. The regulation merely requires covered entities to "reasonably safeguard protected health information from any intentional or unintentional use or disclosure that is in violation of the standards." Screens or curtains often separate patients from one another in hospital rooms to protect the privacy of patients. Health care professionals can and should modulate their voices so that private conversations can take place. This is true whether the conversation takes place in the patient's room or in the hallways, corridors, or elevators.

Myth 3: Family members and friends will no longer be able to pick up prescriptions for others at the pharmacy.

Source: "'As Craig Fuller has told me, the way it's set up right now, if you are married and you're too sick to go to the drug store, you can't send your spouse down to pick up your medicine,' [HHS Secretary] Thompson said during a National Chamber Foundation meeting March 1 in Washington, D.C." F-D-C Reports' Research Services, "Consulting NACDS," The Pink Sheet, March 5, 2001 (page 5).

Fact: The regulation explicitly provides that this common practice can continue. The regulation states that covered entities can use their professional judgment and experience with such practices so that family members, friends, and others may pick up items like filled prescriptions, medical supplies, or X-rays.

Myth 4: The "minimum necessary" standard will disrupt communications between providers involved in treating a patient. Some charge that providers treating patients will not be able to examine the patient's entire medical record.

Sources: "The minimum necessary rules may still place artificial limits on the ability of doctors to use and disclose health information for critical treatment situations—threatening the overall quality of care." Testimony of Blue Cross and Blue Shield Association before the Senate Committee on Health, Education, Labor, and Pensions, presented February 8, 2001 (page 11).

"The regulation includes a strong discouragement regarding the release of entire medical records of patients. The complete exchange of medical information is absolutely critical to assuring a patient receives the right treatment at the right time." Testimony of Blue Cross and Blue Shield Association before the Senate Committee on Health, Education, Labor, and Pensions, presented February 8, 2001 (page 11).

"Limiting the ability of teams of health professionals, and health profession trainees, in a hospital setting to use a patient's complete medical chart or freely discuss and communicate among themselves in the course of treating patients could be disruptive and potentially dangerous." Testimony of the Healthcare Leadership Council before the Senate Committee on Health, Education, Labor, and Pensions, submitted February 8, 2001 (page 5).

Fact: The regulation explicitly exempts from the "minimum necessary" standard all disclosures to providers for treatment purposes. It also exempts all requests by health care providers for information to be used for treatment purposes. As a result, information will flow freely between and among providers involved in treatment. Provisions in the regulation that require special justification for disclosing the entire medical record **do not apply** to treatment-related disclosures because they are not subject to the minimum necessary standard in the first place. With respect to **uses** of health care information for treatment purposes, the regulation allows the use of the entire medical record when it is specifically justified as the amount that is "reasonably necessary" to accomplish the purpose of the use. A provider is only required to have a policy as to the amount of health information that is to be used: a case-by-case determination is not required or anticipated. In fact, HHS states in the preamble to the regulation that "HHS expect[s] that covered entities will implement policies that allow persons involved in treatment to have access to the entire record, as needed." 65 Fed. Reg. 2544.

Myth 5: Providers that disclose medical information for treatment purposes must meet the minimum necessary standard.

Source: "This exemption [from the minimum necessary standard] does not cover . . . 'disclosures **by**' providers." (Emphasis added) Testimony of Blue Cross and Blue Shield Association before the Senate Committee on Health, Education, Labor, and Pensions, presented February 8, 2001 (page 11).

Fact: This assertion takes the minimum necessary exemption out of context. The general rule imposes the minimum necessary standard on covered entities, including providers, when they are "disclosing protected health information." The provision goes on to state: "This requirement does not apply to: . . . Disclosures to . . . a health care provider for treatment." When read as a whole, it is clear that the exemption applies to disclosures **by** health care providers.

Myth 6: The regulation will impede the training of medical students, in part, because the regulation will not allow medical students to see a patient's entire medical record.

Source: The Association of American Medical Colleges has "grave concerns" about "the effects of the rule on medical and health education." "The AAMC supports the proposition that medical residents and medical and nursing students, as well as other health professions students, as necessary, should have unrestricted access to medical information of their patients . . . —a proposition that the rule seems to recognize, peculiarly, only with respect to psychotherapy notes." Testimony of the Association of American Medical Colleges before the Senate Committee on Health, Education, Labor, and Pensions, presented on February 8, 2001 (pages 2, 4).

Fact: The regulation respects the important role that covered entities play in the training of medical students. It includes the following within the definition of "health care operations": "conducting training programs in which students, trainees, or practitioners in areas of health care learn under supervision to practice or improve their skills as health care providers." Therefore, once a provider obtains a consent, an individual's health information can be used not only for treating the patient but also for training medical students. Disclosures, for treatment purposes, to medical students providing health care services to patients would not be subject to the minimum necessary standard because such medical students would be considered "health care providers." Medical students— even those not actually considered "health care providers" because they do not furnish care—would be able to review a patient's entire medical record when the covered entity makes a policy determination that the entire medical record is "reasonably necessary to achieve the purpose" of training medical students.

Myth 7: Stakeholders have not had an opportunity to comment on the provisions requiring that health care providers obtain patient consent for treatment, payment, and health care operations purposes because such a provision was not in the proposed rule.

Source: "Our concern about this consent process is that it was not subject to meaningful notice and comment. Neither the AHA, nor other affected providers, had an opportunity to comment on how this potentially confusing and burdensome procedure would affect patient care or hospital operations. Therefore, it is only prudent to re-open the rule so that the pros and cons of HHS' imposed consent scheme can be fully considered." Testimony of the American Hospital Association before the Senate Committee on Health, Education, Labor, and Pensions, presented February 8, 2001 (pages 9–10).

Fact: It is true that HHS did not propose such an approach, but HHS made it clear in the proposed rule that it was interested in receiving comments on its approach to consent and on other approaches. Specifically, the proposed rule states: "We recognize . . . that other approaches could be of interest. We invite comments on whether other approaches to protecting individuals' health information would be more effective." (*See* 64 Fed. Reg. at 59941.) Since everything in the proposed rule was just that—a proposal—and since the question of actual consent or "statutory" consent was a key threshold issue, many stakeholders did submit comments on the proposed approach to individual consent. The failure of some organizations to take advantage of this opportunity is no reason to delay or reopen the regulation for additional comment. AHA's argument would lead to a never-ending cycle of comments, since every change adopted to a proposed regulation would necessitate yet another round of comments.

Myth 8: The regulation is so complex it is 1,500 pages long.

Source: *U.S. News & World Report* (January 29, 2001, p. 47) refers to the regulation as "the 1,500-page doorstopper."

Fact: The text of the actual regulation only covers 32 pages in the Federal Register. The preamble that precedes the regulation covers 337 pages in the Federal Register. Over half of the preamble is devoted to summarizing and responding to the more than 50,000 comments received by HHS.

Myth 9: "Health care providers would have to keep track of everyone who received medical information from them. Patients could demand an accounting of all of these disclosures."

Source: Amitai Etzioni, New Medical Privacy Rules Need Editing, *USA Today* at 13A (February 22, 2001).

Fact: This is simply not true. Providers are *not* required by this regulation to keep an accounting of anyone within their own organization who has received (or had access to) medical information. This is because the accounting provision only covers "disclosures," which are defined as the sharing of health information with someone *outside* of an organization. Furthermore, the regulation specifically states that a provider does not have to keep account of information disclosed (ie, shared with someone outside of the organization) for treatment, payment, or health care operations. For example, a hospital would not have to keep track of health information sent to outside doctors providing follow-up care to patients. The result of these exclusions is that providers are required to account for only a narrow category of disclosures that primarily are *not related to health care*, such as those made to law enforcement personnel or pursuant to a request for documents in a lawsuit.

Myth 10: The regulation allows patients to demand that doctors correct their medical records.

Source: "We all would be the beneficiaries if the regulations as currently constituted were not allowed to go into effect until they are subject to an expeditious and thorough trimming and simplification. . . . And while patients should be allowed to see their medical records and attach their comments, they should not be allowed to demand that doctors 'correct' the records." Amitai Etzioni "New Medical Privacy Rules Need Editing, *USA Today* at 13A (February 22, 2001).

Fact: There is no provision allowing patients to demand that doctors "correct" their records. An individual may request that a provider (or other covered entity) *amend* his or her records and append or otherwise provide a link to the location of the amendment. There are several grounds under which a provider may deny such a request.

Myth 11: The final regulation requires disclosures of protected health information to a variety of federal government departments and agencies.

Source: "What has not been widely reported are the rule's new mandates requiring doctors, hospitals, and other health care providers to share patients' personal medical records with the federal government, sometimes without notice or advance warning. (See, for example, Federal Register, Vol. 65, No. 250, December 28, 2000, p. 82802, Sec. 160.310.) . . . Handing sensitive medical records to federal departments and agencies that are ill-equipped to protect that information is not a solution; it is inviting abuse, errors, scandal, and tragedy." Letter from Dick Armey, House Majority Leader, to Secretary Thompson (dated March 5, 2001).

Fact: The regulation **requires** covered entities to make only two types of disclosures: (1) disclosures to the individual who is the subject of the protected health information and (2) disclosures to HHS for the purpose of enforcing the regulation. The regulatory section cited by Majority Leader Armey in his letter only requires disclosures to HHS for compliance purposes. It restricts such disclosures to that information that is "pertinent to ascertaining compliance with [the Privacy Rule]." Without this provision, HHS would have no way of determining whether a covered entity had complied with the regulation, making enforcement of the law impossible. Moreover, HHS is limited in what it can do with health information obtained in this fashion. The regulation prohibits HHS from disclosing such information except where necessary to ascertain or enforce compliance with the regulation or as required by other law. Under an executive order issued contemporaneously with the Privacy Rule, HHS is also prohibited from using protected health information concerning an individual discovered during the course of health oversight activities for unrelated civil, administrative, or criminal investigations.

The regulation does not require disclosures to any other person or entity, including to other federal agencies or departments. The regulation **permits** disclosures to government agencies only where the agency requesting or receiving the information has authority to request or receive the information through some other law.

Myth 12: The regulation will be too costly to implement.

Source: "An AHA-commissioned study, looking at hospital costs alone, found that the cost of only three key provisions of the proposed rule . . . could be as much as $22.5 billion over five years." Testimony of the American Hospital Association before the Senate Committee on Health, Education, Labor, and Pensions, presented February 8, 2001 (page 6).

Fact: HHS estimates that the cost associated with implementing the privacy regulation (approximately $17 billion over 10 years) will be greatly offset by the cost savings associated with implementing HIPAA's transactions standards (approximately $29 billion **saved** over 10 years).If implemented together, as contemplated by Congress, consumers will benefit, health care organizations will benefit, and the health of our communities will benefit. Delay could actually be more costly for industry because it would need to redesign and retool systems a second time if privacy protections are not put in place along with the transactions standards.

Myth 13: Delay of the effective date and/or the compliance date is essential to give covered entities time to comply with the regulation.

Source: "The overwhelming financial impact of the final privacy rule is exacerbated by its overly aggressive implementation schedule." Testimony of the American Hospital Association before the Senate Committee on Health, Education, Labor, and Pensions, presented February 8, 2001 (p. 3).

Fact: Covered entities are devoting substantial, precious resources to stopping the regulation from ever taking effect, rather than on a good-faith effort to begin the process of complying. There is no reason to delay the effective date. If HHS finds that there are any real and serious implementation problems with certain aspects of the regulation, HHS can remedy the situation without delaying the effective date. HHS has authority under HIPAA to modify the regulation **after it takes effect** to make changes that are "necessary in order to permit compliance."

Delay of the effective date will jeopardize the confidentiality of patients' medical information. Every day there are new advances in transmitting and storing health information in an electronic format. The HIPAA transactions standards encourage this movement. Fostering these technical advancements without adequate security and privacy protections in place is irresponsible.

Should any serious implementation problems develop in the future due to the 2-year compliance time frame established by Congress in HIPAA, the industry can ask Congress to delay the compliance date.

Source: Used with permission by the Institute for Health Care Research and Policy, Georgetown University, 2233 Wisconsin Avenue, NW Suite 525, Washington, DC 20007, Phone 202.687.0880, fax 202.784.1265; www.healthprivacy.org. Last updated: April 4, 2001.

HIPAA Definition of Terms

ASC X12

The Accredited Standards Committee chartered by the American National Standards Institute to design national electronic standards for a wide range of business applications.

ASC X12N

The ASC X12 subcommittee chartered to develop electronic standards specific to the insurance industry.

CODE SET

Any set of codes used for encoding data elements, such as tables of terms, medical concepts, medical diagnosis codes, or medical procedure codes. [Section 1171(1)]

MEDICAL CARE

Used in the definition of health plan. The diagnosis, cure, mitigation, treatment, or prevention of disease, or amounts paid for the purpose of affecting any body structure or function of the body; amounts paid for transportation primarily for and essential to these items; and amounts paid for insurance covering the items and the transportation specified in this definition. [Section 2791 of the Public Health Service Act]

PARTICIPANT

Any employee or former employee of an employer, or any member or former member of an employee organization, who is or may become eligible to receive a benefit of any type from an employee benefit plan that covers employees of such an employer or members of such organizations, or whose beneficiaries may be eligible to receive any such benefits.

TRANSACTION STANDARD

Any such data element or transaction that meets each of the standards and implementation specifications adopted or established by the Secretary with respect to the data element or transaction under sections 1172 through 1174 of the Act. Under our definition, a standard would be a set of rules for a set of codes, data elements, transactions, or identifiers promulgated either by an organization accredited by ANSI or the HHS for the electronic transmission of health information. [Section 1171]

TRANSACTION

The exchange of information between two parties to carry out financial and administrative activities related to health care. A transaction would be: (a) any of the transactions listed in section 1173(a)(2) of the act, and (b) any determined appropriate by the Secretary in accordance with section 1173(a)(1)(B) of the act. In the order of the regulations text, a transaction would mean any of the following:

Health Claims or Equivalent Encounter Information

This transaction may be used to submit health care claim billing information, encounter information, or both, from health care providers to health plans, either directly or via intermediary billers or claims clearinghouses.

Health Care Payment and Remittance Advice

This transaction may be used by a health plan to make a payment to a financial institution for a health care provider (sending payment only), to send an explanation of benefits or remittance advice directly to a health care provider (sending data only), or to make payment and send an explanation of benefits or remittance advice to a health care provider via a financial institution (sending both payment and data).

Coordination of Benefits

This transaction can be used to transmit health care claims and billing payment information between health plans with different payment responsibilities where coordination of benefits is required or between health plans and regulatory agencies to monitor the rendering, billing, and/or payment of health care services within a specific health care/insurance industry segment. Congress, when writing this provision, intended for these standards to apply to the electronic form for coordination of benefits and sequential processing of claims.

Health Claim Status

This transaction may be used by health care providers and recipients of health care products or services (or their authorized agents) to request the status of a health care claim or encounter from a health plan.

Enrollment and Disenrollment in a Health Plan

This transaction may be used to establish communication between the sponsor of a health benefit and the health plan. It provides enrollment data, such as subscriber and dependents, employer information, and health care provider information. The sponsor is the backer of the coverage, benefit, or product. A sponsor can be an employer, union, government agency, association, or insurance company. The health plan refers to an entity that pays claims, administers the insurance product or benefit, or both.

Eligibility for a Health Plan

This transaction may be used to inquire about the eligibility, coverage, or benefits associated with a benefit plan, employer, plan sponsor, subscriber, or a policy. It also can be used to communicate information about or changes to eligibility, coverage, or benefits from information sources (such as insurers, sponsors, and health plans) to information receivers (such as physicians, hospitals, third-party administrators, and government agencies).

Health Plan Premium Payments

This transaction may be used by, for example, employers, employees, unions, and associations to make and keep track of payments of health plan premiums to their health insurers.

Referral Certification and Authorization

This transaction may be used to transmit health care service referral information between health care providers, health care providers furnishing services, and health plans. It can also be used to obtain authorization for certain health care services from a health plan.

First Report of Injury

This transaction may be used to report information pertaining to an injury, illness, or incident to entities interested in the information for statistical, legal, claims, and risk management processing requirements. Although they are proposing a definition for this transaction, they are not proposing a standard for it in this published rule.

Health Claims Attachments

This transaction may be used to transmit health care service information, such as subscriber, patient, demographic, diagnosis, or treatment data for the purpose of a request for review, certification, notification, or reporting the outcome of a health care services review. Although they are proposing a definition for this transaction, they are not proposing a standard for it in this *rule* because the legislation gave the Secretary an additional year to designate this standard.

ANSI

This stands for the American National Standards Institute.

BUSINESS ASSOCIATE

(1) Except as provided in paragraph (2) of this definition, *business associate* means, with respect to a covered entity, a person who:

    (i) On behalf of such covered entity or of an organized health care arrangement (as defined in §164.501 of this subchapter) in which the covered entity participates, but other than in the capacity of a member of the workforce of such covered entity or arrangement, performs, or assists in the performance of:

        (A) A function or activity involving the use or disclosure of individually identifiable health information, including claims processing or administration, data analysis, processing or administration, utilization review, quality assurance, billing, benefit management, practice management, and repricing; or

        (B) Any other function or activity regulated by this subchapter; or

    (ii) Provides, other than in the capacity of a member of the workforce of such covered entity, legal, actuarial, accounting, consulting, data aggregation (as defined in §164.501 of this subchapter), management, administrative, accreditation, or financial services to or for such covered entity, or to or for an organized health care arrangement in which the covered entity participates, where the provision of the service involves the disclosure of individually identifiable health information from such covered entity or arrangement, or from another business associate of such covered entity or arrangement, to the person.

(2) A covered entity participating in an organized health care arrangement that performs a function or activity as described by paragraph (1)(i) of this definition for or on behalf of such organized health care arrangement, or that provides a service as described in paragraph (1)(ii) of this definition to or for such organized health care arrangement, does not, simply through the performance of such function or activity or the provision of such service, become a business associate of other covered entities participating in such organized health care arrangement.

(3) A covered entity may be a business associate of another covered entity.

COMPLIANCE DATE

This term refers to the date by which a covered entity must comply with a standard, implementation specification, requirement, or modification adopted under this subchapter.

COVERED ENTITY

Means:

(1) A health plan

(2) A health care clearinghouse

(3) A health care provider who transmits any health information in electronic form in connection with a transaction covered by this subchapter.

GROUP HEALTH PLAN

Group health plan (also see definition of *health plan* in this section) means an employee welfare benefit plan (as defined in section 3(1) of the Employee Retirement Income and Security Act of 1974 (ERISA), 29 U.S.C. 1002(1)), including insured and self-insured plans, to the extent that the plan provides medical care (as defined in section 2791(a)(2) of the Public Health Service Act (PHS Act), 42 U.S.C. 300gg-91(a)(2)), including items and services paid for as medical care, to employees or their dependents directly or through insurance, reimbursement, or otherwise, that:

(1) Has 50 or more participants (as defined in section 3(7) of ERISA, 29 U.S.C. 1002(7)); or

(2) Is administered by an entity other than the employer that established and maintains the plan.

HCFA

This is the acronym for Health Care Financing Administration within the Department of Health and Human Services.

HHS

This is the acronym for the Department of Health and Human Services.

HEALTH CARE

This term refers to care, services, or supplies related to the health of an individual. *Health care* includes, but is not limited to, the following:

(1)   Preventive, diagnostic, therapeutic, rehabilitative, maintenance, or palliative care, and counseling, service, assessment, or procedure with respect to the physical or mental condition, or functional status, of an individual or that affects the structure or function of the body; and

(2)   Sale or dispensing of a drug, device, equipment, or other item in accordance with a prescription.

HEALTH CARE CLEARINGHOUSE

This refers to a public or private entity, including a billing service, repricing company, community health management information system, or community health information system, and "value-added" networks and switches, that does either of the following functions:

(1)   Processes or facilitates the processing of health information received from another entity in a nonstandard format or containing nonstandard data content into standard data elements or a standard transaction.

(2)   Receives a standard transaction from another entity and processes or facilitates the processing of health information into nonstandard format or nonstandard data content for the receiving entity.

HEALTH CARE PROVIDER

This means a provider of services (as defined in section 1861(u) of the act, 42 U.S.C. 1395x(u)), a provider of medical or health services (as defined in section 1861(s) of the act, 42 U.S.C. 1395x(s)), and any other person or organization who furnishes, bills, or is paid for health care in the normal course of business.

HEALTH INFORMATION

This means any information, whether oral or recorded in any form or medium, that:

(1)   Is created or received by a health care provider, health plan, public health authority, employer, life insurer, school or university, or health care clearinghouse; and

(2)   Relates to the past, present, or future physical or mental health or condition of an individual; the provision of health care to an individual; or the past, present, or future payment for the provision of health care to an individual.

HEALTH INSURANCE ISSUER

Health insurance issue (defined in section 2791(b)(2) of the PHS Act, 42 U.S.C. 300gg-91(b)(2) and used in the definition of *health plan* in this section) means an insurance company, insurance service, or insurance organization (including an HMO) that is licensed to engage in the business of insurance in a state and is subject to state law that regulates insurance. Such term does not include a group health plan.

HEALTH MAINTENANCE ORGANIZATION (HMO)

Health maintenance organization (defined in section 2791(b)(3) of the PHS Act, 42 U.S.C. 300gg-91(b)(3) and used in the definition of *health plan* in this section) means a federally qualified HMO, an organization recognized as an HMO under state law, or a similar organization regulated for solvency under state law in the same manner and to the same extent as such an HMO.

HEALTH PLAN

This means an individual or group plan that provides, or pays the cost of, medical care (as defined in section 2791(a)(2) of the PHS Act, 42 U.S.C. 300gg-91(a)(2)).

(1)   *Health plan* includes the following, singly or in combination:
  (i)   A group health plan, as defined in this section
  (ii)   A health insurance issuer, as defined in this section
  (iii) An HMO, as defined in this section
  (iv)   Part A or Part B of the Medicare program under title XVIII of the act
  (v)   The Medicaid program under title XIX of the act, 42 U.S.C. 1396, et seq
  (vi)   An issuer of a Medicare supplemental policy (as defined in section 1882(g)(1) of the act, 42 U.S.C. 1395ss(g)(1))
  (vii) An issuer of a long-term care policy, excluding a nursing home fixed-indemnity policy
  (viii) An employee welfare benefit plan or any other arrangement that is established or maintained for the purpose of offering or providing health benefits to the employees of two or more employers

    (ix)   The health care program for active military personnel under title 10 of the United States Code

    (x)   The veterans health care program under 38 U.S.C. chapter 17.

    (xi)   The Civilian Health and Medical Program of the Uniformed Services (CHAMPUS) (as defined in 10 U.S.C. 1072(4))

    (xii)   The Indian Health Service program under the Indian Health Care Improvement Act, 25 U.S.C. 1601, et seq.

    (xiii)   The Federal Employees Health Benefits Program under 5 U.S.C. 8902, et seq.

    (xiv)   An approved state child health plan under title XXI of the act, providing benefits for child health assistance that meet the requirements of section 2103 of the act, 42 U.S.C. 1397, et seq.

    (xv)   The Medicare + Choice program under Part C of title XVIII of the Act, 42 U.S.C. 1395w-21 through 1395w-28.

    (xvi)   A high-risk pool that is a mechanism established under state law to provide health insurance coverage or comparable coverage to eligible individuals.

    (xvii)   Any other individual or group plan, or combination of individual or group plans, that provides or pays for the cost of medical care (as defined in section 2791(a)(2) of the PHS Act, 42 U.S.C. 300gg-91(a)(2)).

(2)   *Health plan* excludes:

    (i)   Any policy, plan, or program to the extent that it provides, or pays for the cost of, excepted benefits that are listed in section 2791(c)(1) of the PHS Act, 42 U.S.C. 300gg-91(c)(1); and

    (ii)   A government-funded program (other than one listed in paragraph (1)(i)-(xvi) of this definition):

        (A)   Whose principal purpose is other than providing, or paying the cost of, health care; or

        (B)   Whose principal activity is:

            (1)   The direct provision of health care to persons; or

            (2)   The making of grants to fund the direct provision of health care to persons.

IMPLEMENTATION SPECIFICATION

This means specific requirements or instructions for implementing a standard.

MODIFY OR MODIFICATION

This refers to a change adopted by the Secretary, through regulation, to a standard or an implementation specification.

SECRETARY

This means the Secretary of the Department of Health and Human Services or any other officer or employee of HHS to whom the authority involved has been delegated.

SMALL HEALTH PLAN

This means a health plan with annual receipts of $5 million or less.

STANDARD

This means a rule, condition, or requirement:

(1) Describing the following information for products, systems, services, or practices:
   (i) Classification of components;
   (ii) Specification of materials, performance, or operations; or
   (iii) Delineation of procedures; or
(2) With respect to the privacy of individually identifiable health information.

STANDARD SETTING ORGANIZATION (SSO)

This means an organization accredited by the American National Standards Institute that develops and maintains standards for information transactions or data elements, or any other standard that is necessary for, or will facilitate the implementation of, this part.

STATE

This refers to one of the following:

(1) For a health plan established or regulated by federal law, *state* has the meaning set forth in the applicable section of the United States Code for such health plan.
(2) For all other purposes, *state* means any of the several states, the District of Columbia, the Commonwealth of Puerto Rico, the Virgin Islands, and Guam.

TRADING PARTNER AGREEMENT

This means an agreement related to the exchange of information in electronic transactions, whether the agreement is distinct or part of a larger agreement, between each party to the agreement. (For example, a trading partner agreement may specify, among other things, the duties and responsibilities of each party to the agreement in conducting a standard transaction.)

WORKFORCE

This refers to employees, volunteers, trainees, and other persons whose conduct, in the performance of work for a covered entity, is under the direct control of such entity, whether or not they are paid by the covered entity.

PREEMPTION OF STATE LAW

§ 160.202 Definitions.
For purposes of this subpart, the following terms have the following meanings:

Contrary when used to compare a provision of state law to a standard, requirement, or implementation specification adopted under this subchapter, means:

(1)   A covered entity would find it impossible to comply with both the state and federal requirements; or

(2)   The provision of state law stands as an obstacle to the accomplishment and execution of the full purposes and objectives of part C of title XI of the act or section 264 of Pub. L. 104-191, as applicable.

More stringent means, in the context of a comparison of a provision of state law and a standard, requirement, or implementation specification adopted under subpart E of part 164 of this subchapter, a state law that meets one or more of the following criteria:

(1)   With respect to a use or disclosure, the law prohibits or restricts a use or disclosure in circumstances under which such use or disclosure otherwise would be permitted under this subchapter, except if the disclosure is:

   (i)   Required by the Secretary in connection with determining whether a covered entity is in compliance with this subchapter; or

   (ii)   To the individual who is the subject of the individually identifiable health information.

(2)   With respect to the rights of an individual who is the subject of the individually identifiable health information of access to or amendment of individually identifiable health information, permits greater rights of access or amendment, as applicable; provided that, nothing in this subchapter may be construed to preempt any state law to the extent that it authorizes or prohibits disclosure of protected health information about a minor to a parent, guardian, or person acting *in loco parentis* of such minor.

(3)   With respect to information to be provided to an individual who is the subject of the individually identifiable health information about

a use, a disclosure, rights, and remedies, provides the greater amount of information.

(4)   With respect to the form or substance of an authorization or consent for use or disclosure of individually identifiable health information, provides requirements that narrow the scope or duration, increase the privacy protections afforded (such as by expanding the criteria for), or reduce the coercive effect of the circumstances surrounding the authorization or consent, as applicable.

(5)   With respect to record keeping or requirements relating to accounting of disclosures, provides for the retention or reporting of more detailed information or for a longer duration.

(6)   With respect to any other matter, provides greater privacy protection for the individual who is the subject of the individually identifiable health information.

Relates to the privacy of individually identifiable health information, with respect to a state law, this means that the state law has the specific purpose of protecting the privacy of health information or affects the privacy of health information in a direct, clear, and substantial way.

State law means a constitution, statute, regulation, rule, common law, or other state action having the force and effect of law.

PRIVACY OF INDIVIDUALLY IDENTIFIABLE HEALTH INFORMATION

§ 164.501 Definitions.
As used in this subpart, the following terms have the following meanings:

Correctional institution means any penal or correctional facility, jail, reformatory, detention center, work farm, halfway house, or residential community program center operated by, or under contract to, the United States, a state, a territory, a political subdivision of a state or territory, or an Indian tribe, for the confinement or rehabilitation of persons charged with or convicted of a criminal offense or other persons held in lawful custody. *Other persons held in lawful custody* includes juvenile offenders adjudicated delinquent, aliens detained awaiting deportation, persons committed to mental institutions through the criminal justice system, witnesses, or others awaiting charges or trial.

Covered functions means those functions of a covered entity the performance of which makes the entity a health plan, health care provider, or health care clearinghouse.

Data aggregation means, with respect to protected health information created or received by a business associate in its capacity as the business associate of a covered entity, the combining of such protected health information by the business associate with the protected health information received by the business associate in its capacity as a business associate of another covered entity, to permit data analyses that relate to the health care operations of the respective covered entities.

Designated record set

(1) A group of records maintained by or for a covered entity that is:
- (i)   The medical records and billing records about individuals maintained by or for a covered health care provider;
- (ii) The enrollment, payment, claims adjudication, and case or medical management record systems maintained by or for a health plan; or
- (iii) Used, in whole or in part, by or for the covered entity to make decisions about individuals.

(2) For purposes of this paragraph, the term *record* means any item, collection, or grouping of information that includes protected health information and is maintained, collected, used, or disseminated by or for a covered entity.

Direct treatment relationship means a treatment relationship between an individual and a health care provider that is not an indirect treatment relationship.

Disclosure means the release, transfer, provision of access to, or divulging in any other manner of information outside the entity holding the information.

Health care operations means any of the following activities of the covered entity to the extent that the activities are related to covered functions, and any of the following activities of an organized health care arrangement in which the covered entity participates:

(1) Conducting quality assessment and improvement activities, including outcomes evaluation and development of clinical guidelines, provided that the obtaining of generalized knowledge is not the primary purpose of any studies resulting from such activities; population-based activities relating to improving health or reducing health care costs, protocol development, case management and care coordination, contacting of health care providers and patients with information about treatment alternatives; and related functions that do not include treatment;

(2) Reviewing the competence or qualifications of health care professionals; evaluating practitioner and provider performance and health plan performance; conducting training programs in which students, trainees, or practitioners in areas of health care learn under supervision to practice or improve their skills as health care providers; training of non-health care professionals; accreditation; certification; licensing; or credentialing activities;

(3) Underwriting, premium rating, and other activities relating to the creation, renewal, or replacement of a contract of health insurance

or health benefits, and ceding, securing, or placing a contract for reinsurance of risk relating to claims for health care (including stop-loss insurance and excess of loss insurance), provided that the requirements of § 164.514(g) are met, if applicable;

(4) Conducting or arranging for medical review, legal services, and auditing functions, including fraud and abuse detection and compliance programs;

(5) Business planning and development, such as conducting cost-management and planning-related analyses related to managing and operating the entity, including formulary development and administration, development or improvement of methods of payment or coverage policies; and

(6) Business management and general administrative activities of the entity, including, but not limited to:

(i) Management activities relating to implementation of and compliance with the requirements of this subchapter;

(ii) Customer service, including the provision of data analyses for policy holders, plan sponsors, or other customers, provided that protected health information is not disclosed to such policy holder, plan sponsor, or customer.

(iii) Resolution of internal grievances;

(iv) Due diligence in connection with the sale or transfer of assets to a potential successor in interest, if the potential successor in interest is a covered entity or, following completion of the sale or transfer, will become a covered entity; and

(v) Consistent with the applicable requirements of §164.514, creating de-identified health information, fund-raising for the benefit of the covered entity, and marketing for which an individual authorization is not required as described in §164.514(e)(2).

Health oversight agency means an agency or authority of the United States, a state, a territory, a political subdivision of a state or territory, or an Indian tribe, or a person or entity acting under a grant of authority from or contract with such public agency, including the employees or agents of such public agency or its contractors or persons or entities to whom it has granted authority, that is authorized by law to oversee the health care system (whether public or private) or government programs in which health information is necessary to determine eligibility or compliance, or to enforce civil rights laws for which health information is relevant.

Indirect treatment relationship means a relationship between an individual and a health care provider in which:

(1) The health care provider delivers health care to the individual based on the orders of another health care provider; and

(2)   The health care provider typically provides services or products, or reports the diagnosis or results associated with the health care, directly to another health care provider, who provides the services or products or reports to the individual.

Individual means the person who is the subject of protected health information.

   Individually identifiable health information refers to information that is a subset of health information, including demographic information collected from an individual, and:

(1)   Is created or received by a health care provider, health plan, employer, or health care clearinghouse; and

(2)   Relates to the past, present, or future physical or mental health or condition of an individual; the provision of health care to an individual; or the past, present, or future payment for the provision of health care to an individual; and

   (i)   That identifies the individual; or

   (ii)   With respect to which there is a reasonable basis to believe the information can be used to identify the individual.

   Inmate means a person incarcerated in or otherwise confined to a correctional institution.

   Law enforcement official means an officer or employee of any agency or authority of the United States, a state, a territory, a political subdivision of a state or territory, or an Indian tribe, who is empowered by law to:

(1)   Investigate or conduct an official inquiry into a potential violation of law; or

(2)   Prosecute or otherwise conduct a criminal, civil, or administrative proceeding arising from an alleged violation of law.

Marketing means to make a communication about a product or service a purpose of which is to encourage recipients of the communication to purchase or use the product or service.

(1)   *Marketing* does not include communications that meet the requirements of paragraph 2 of this definition and that are made by a covered entity:

   (i)   For the purpose of describing the entities participating in a health care provider network or health plan network, or for the purpose of describing if and the extent to which a product or service (or payment for such product or service) is provided by a covered entity or included in a plan of benefits; or

   (ii)   That are tailored to the circumstances of a particular individual and the communications are:

      (A)   Made by a health care provider to an individual as part of the treatment of the individual, and for the purpose of furthering the treatment of that individual; or

(B)   Made by a health care provider or health plan to an individual in the course of managing the treatment of that individual, or for the purpose of directing or recommending to that individual alternative treatments, therapies, health care providers, or settings of care.

(2)   A communication described in paragraph (1) of this definition is not included in marketing if:

(i)   The communication is made orally; or

(ii)   The communication is in writing and the covered entity does not receive direct or indirect remuneration from a third party for making the communication.

Organized health care arrangement

(1)   A clinically integrated care setting in which individuals typically receive health care from more than one health care provider.

(2)   An organized system of health care in which more than one covered entity participates, and in which the participating covered entities:

(i)   Hold themselves out to the public as participating in a joint arrangement; and

(ii)   Participate in joint activities that include at least one of the following:

(A)   Utilization review, in which health care decisions by participating covered entities are reviewed by other participating covered entities or by a third party on their behalf;

(B)   Quality assessment and improvement activities, in which treatment provided by participating covered entities is assessed by other participating covered entities or by a third party on their behalf; or

(C)   Payment activities, if the financial risk for delivering health care is shared, in part or in whole, by participating covered entities through the joint arrangement and if protected health information created or received by a covered entity is reviewed by other participating covered entities or by a third party on their behalf for the purpose of administering the sharing of financial risk.

(3)   A group health plan and a health insurance issuer or HMO with respect to such group health plan, but only with respect to protected health information created or received by such health insurance issuer or HMO that relates to individuals who are or who have been participants or beneficiaries in such group health plan;

(4)   A group health plan and one or more other group health plans each of which are maintained by the same plan sponsor; or

(5)   The group health plans described in paragraph (4) of this definition and health insurance issuers or HMOs with respect to such group

health plans, but only with respect to protected health information created or received by such health insurance issuers or HMOs that relates to individuals who are or have been participants or beneficiaries in any of such group health plans.

Payment

(1)   The activities undertaken by:
   (i)   A health plan to obtain premiums or to determine or fulfill its responsibility for coverage and provision of benefits under the health plan; or
   (ii)   A covered health care provider or health plan to obtain or provide reimbursement for the provision of health care; and

(2)   The activities in paragraph (1) of this definition relate to the individual to whom health care is provided and include, but are not limited to:

   (i)   Determinations of eligibility or coverage (including coordination of benefits or the determination of cost sharing amounts), and adjudication or subrogation of health benefit claims

   (ii)   Risk adjusting amounts due based on enrollee health status and demographic characteristics

   (iii)   Billing, claims management, collection activities, obtaining payment under a contract for reinsurance (including stop-loss insurance and excess of loss insurance), and related health care data processing

   (iv)   Review of health care services with respect to medical necessity, coverage under a health plan, appropriateness of care, or justification of charges

   (v)   Utilization review activities, including pre-certification and pre-authorization of services, concurrent and retrospective review of services; and

   (vi)   Disclosure to consumer reporting agencies of any of the following protected health information relating to collection of premiums or reimbursement:
      (A)   Name and address
      (B)   Date of birth
      (C)   Social security number
      (D)   Payment history
      (E)   Account number; and
      (F)   Name and address of the health care provider and/or health plan.

Plan sponsor
As defined at section 3(16)(B) of ERISA, 29 U.S.C. 1002(16)(B).

Protected health information
This means individually identifiable health information:

(1) Except as provided in paragraph (2) of this definition, that is:
  (i) Transmitted by electronic media;
  (ii) Maintained in any medium described in the definition of
    electronic media at §162.103 of this subchapter; or
  (iii) Transmitted or maintained in any other form or medium.
(2) *Protected health information* excludes individually identifiable health
    information in:
  (i) Education records covered by the Family Educational Right
    and Privacy Act, as amended, 20 U.S.C. 1232g; and
  (ii) Records described at 20 U.S.C. 1232g(a)(4)(B)(iv).

Psychotherapy notes refers to notes recorded (in any medium) by a
health care provider who is a mental health professional documenting or
analyzing the contents of conversation during a private counseling
session or a group, joint, or family counseling session and that are
separated from the rest of the individual's medical record. *Psychotherapy
notes* excludes medication prescription and monitoring, counseling
session start and stop times, the modalities and frequencies of treatment
furnished, results of clinical tests, and any summary of the following
items: diagnosis, functional status, the treatment plan, symptoms,
prognosis, and progress to date.

Public health authority means an agency or authority of the United
States, a state, a territory, a political subdivision of a state or territory, or
an Indian tribe, or a person or entity acting under a grant of authority
from or contract with such public agency, including the employees or
agents of such public agency or its contractors or persons or entities to
whom it has granted authority, that is responsible for public health
matters as part of its official mandate.

Required by law means a mandate contained in law that compels a
covered entity to make a use or disclosure of protected health
information and that is enforceable in a court of law. *Required by law*
includes, but is not limited to, court orders and court-ordered warrants;
subpoenas or summons issued by a court, grand jury, a governmental or
tribal inspector general, or an administrative body authorized to require
the production of information; a civil or an authorized investigative
demand; Medicare conditions of participation with respect to health care
providers participating in the program; and statutes or regulations that
require the production of information, including statutes or regulations
that require such information if payment is sought under a government
program providing public benefits.

Research means a systematic investigation, including research development, testing, and evaluation, designed to develop or contribute to generalized knowledge.

Treatment means the provision, coordination, or management of health care and related services by one or more health care providers, including the coordination or management of health care by a health care provider with a third party; consultation between health care providers relating to a patient; or the referral of a patient for health care from one health care provider to another.

Use means, with respect to individually identifiable health information, the sharing, employment, application, utilization, examination, or analysis of such information within an entity that maintains such information.

§164.504 Uses and disclosures: Organizational requirements.
    (a)   *Definitions.* As used in this section:

Common control exists if an entity has the power, directly or indirectly, to significantly influence or direct the actions or policies of another entity.

Common ownership exists if an entity or entities possess an ownership or equity interest of 5% or more in another entity.

Health care component
(1)   Components of a covered entity that perform covered functions are part of the health care component.
(2)   Another component of the covered entity is part of the entity's health care component to the extent that:
    (i)   It performs, with respect to a component that performs covered functions, activities that would make such other component a business associate of the component that performs covered functions if the two components were separate legal entities; and
    (ii)   The activities involve the use or disclosure of protected health information that such other component creates or receives from or on behalf of the component that performs covered functions.

Hybrid entity means a single legal entity that is a covered entity and whose covered functions are not its primary functions.

Plan administration functions means administration functions performed by the plan sponsor of a group health plan on behalf of the group health plan and excludes functions performed by the plan sponsor in connection with any other benefit or benefit plan of the plan sponsor.

Summary health information means information, that may be individually identifiable health information, and:

(1)   That summarizes the claims history, claims expenses, or type of claims experienced by individuals for whom a plan sponsor has provided health benefits under a group health plan; and

(2)   From which the information described at §164.514(b)(2)(i) has been deleted, except that the geographic information described in §164.514(b)(2)(i)(B) need only be aggregated to the level of a five-digit zip code.